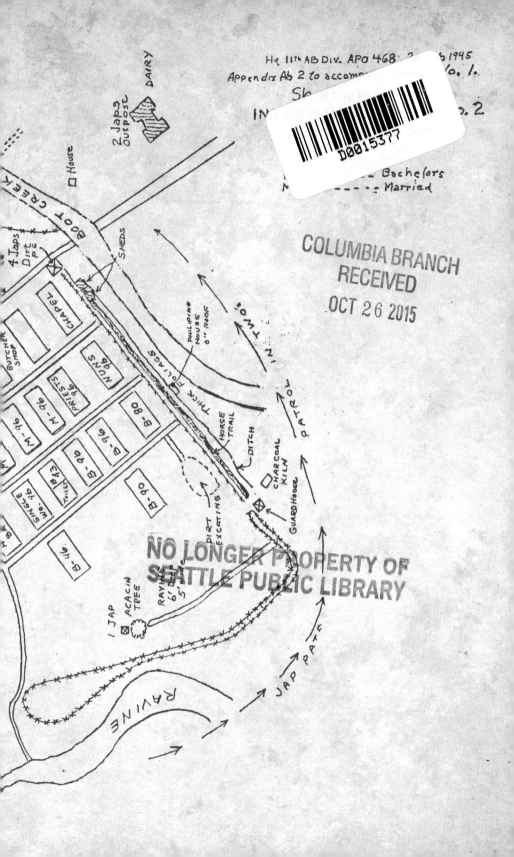

Hq. 11th AB Div. APO 468 · 2 · ? 5 1945
Appendix Ab 2 to accom?... ... No. 1.
Sb

IN... ... ... ... 2

————— Bachelors
—————— Married

DAIRY

2 Japs
Outpost

☐ House

4 Japs
Dirt
PE

BOOT CREEK

SHEDS

CHAPEL

BUTCHER SHOP

PRIESTS 96

NUNS 96

B-80

B-90

B-96

M-96

M-96

SINGLE WO. 96

TRIPLE 96 343

B-96

W....

B-46

PHILIPINE HOUSE
0" ROOF

THICK FOLIAGE

HORSE TRAIL

DITCH

CHARCOAL KILN ☐

GUARD HOUSE

PATROL

IN TWO'S

DIRT EXCAVTING

RAVINE
6' DEEP
5' WIDE

1 JAP

ACACIN
TREE

RAVINE

JAP PATH

# RESCUE AT LOS BAÑOS

## Also by Bruce Henderson

*Hero Found: The Greatest POW Escape of the Vietnam War*

*Down to the Sea: An Epic Story of Naval Disaster
and Heroism in World War II*

*And the Sea Will Tell* (with Vincent Bugliosi)

*Fatal North: Adventure and Survival on the First North Pole Expedition*

*Trace Evidence: The Hunt for the I-5 Serial Killer*

*True North: Peary, Cook, and the Race to the Pole*

*Ring of Deceit: Inside the Biggest Sports and Banking Scandal in History*

Find Bruce Henderson on the web at:
www.BruceHendersonBooks.com

# RESCUE AT LOS BAÑOS

## THE MOST DARING PRISON CAMP RAID OF WORLD WAR II

## BRUCE HENDERSON

WM
WILLIAM MORROW
An Imprint of HarperCollins*Publishers*

HarperCollins books may be purchased for educational, business, or sales promotional use. For information please e-mail the Special Markets Department at SPsales@harpercollins.com.

FIRST EDITION

*Designed by Diahann Sturge*

Map of Los Baños Raid by Nick Springer, copyright © 2014 Springer Cartographics LLC

Library of Congress Cataloging-in-Publication Data has been applied for.

ISBN 978-0-06-232506-8 (hardcover)
ISBN 978-0-06-240329-2 (international edition)

15 16 17 18 19 OV/RRD 10 9 8 7 6 5 4 3 2 1

For Laura Jason—friend, lover, muse

# CONTENTS

I doubt that any airborne unit in the world will ever be able to rival the Los Baños prison raid. It is the text-book airborne operation for all ages and all armies.

GENERAL COLIN POWELL, U.S. ARMY
CHAIRMAN, JOINT CHIEFS OF STAFF
FEBRUARY 25, 1993

# RESCUE AT LOS BAÑOS

# ONE

# The Fall of Manila

Benjamin Franklin Edwards, a mechanic with Pan American Airways for less than a year, arrived in Manila aboard the airline's famed "China Clipper" on October 2, 1941. The big Martin M-130 flying boat was known by Pan Am employees as "Sweet Sixteen" (NR 14716) and had been the first seaplane delivered to the airline and the first to fly scheduled air service across the Pacific. It touched down on Manila Bay and taxied to the ramp at Pan Am's Cavite base eight miles southwest of the Philippine capital known worldwide as the Pearl of the Orient for its picturesque seaside location, tropical beauty, and golden sunsets from the shoreline of its enchanting bay.

For Edwards, soon to turn twenty-three, single as a jaybird and with a good-paying job in an industry that offered international travel and adventure, the flight from Honolulu, where he had worked on seaplanes for six months after training at Treasure Island in San Francisco Bay, for his new assignment had been a wide-eyed thrill the entire way. The crossing had taken four days, with overnight stops at Midway, Wake, and Guam, island outposts few Americans had heard of, but names that would soon appear in newspaper headlines in the coming months.

While assisting the cabin steward on the flight, Edwards had met a number of well-to-do Manila residents who encouraged him to look them up. He occasionally spelled the flight engineer, keeping a watchful eye on the array of gauges for the flight systems. He even got to sit in the cockpit when one of the pilots went to stretch his legs. This was heady stuff for a Midwestern farm boy who had come of age during the Depression, dropped out of high school and left home to escape an abusive stepfather, and lived with various relatives, sometimes arriving at their door with only a paper bag filled with his worldly possessions. Growing up, the boy, who was named after American patriot and founding father Benjamin Franklin, learned how to fight and survive, but along the way he picked up a zest for life rather than a chip on his shoulder.

Edwards was a trim, handsome man just shy of six feet, with a shock of dark hair, a swarthy complexion, chiseled jaw, and neatly trimmed mustache. He reminded people of dashing leading man Errol Flynn, which didn't hurt when it came to his being invited into the social circle of expatriate Americans living and working in Manila. For two glorious months, he spent weekdays working on the big seaplanes as they came and went on their long transpacific flights, and most nights and weekends being wined and dined and meeting young women. "Really, I'm having a swell time," he wrote to his sister in California. Then one early December day, things changed forever for Ben and the rest of the world.

Edwards came to work as usual on Monday morning, December 8. The international dateline in the middle of the Pacific Ocean put the Philippines a day ahead of Hawaii and the continental United States, where it was Sunday, December 7, 1941.

The guard at the Pan Am gate, an older American and a veteran of World War I, hollered to Edwards: "Have you heard?"

"Heard what?"

"We're at war with Japan!"

Edwards joked that the guard shouldn't drink on the job, but the unsmiling man countered with enough details about the surprise attack on Pearl Harbor to be convincing. Rushing inside, Edwards heard the latest radio bulletins, none of which were good. Pearl Harbor was ablaze with burning and sinking U.S. warships.

Edwards had heard a lot of talk in Hawaii about a possible war with Japan, although he never believed it would happen. But there had been a very realistic air-raid drill at Pearl shortly before he left that made him wonder if rumors of war weren't so farfetched after all. Still, he had not been overly worried about coming to the Philippines, which by treaty was under U.S. protection. Everyone believed Japan was a paper tiger and had no chance against America's military might. If war came, conventional wisdom was that the United States would win quickly.

Ben Edwards in California, 1945.
*Courtesy Ann (Edwards) MacDonnell.*

The next two days were a blur for Edwards. The Pan Am facilities were sandwiched between the Cavite Navy Yard and Sangley Point Naval Base, both prime military targets. The last scheduled Pan Am seaplane had passed through days earlier, headed for Hong Kong, where it had been destroyed in the bay by Japanese planes only hours after the Pearl Harbor attack. Pan Am had urgently recalled all its aircraft to the United States. None would be stopping at Manila, so orders came to dispose of the large supply of fifty-five-gallon drums of aviation gasoline by rolling them into the bay during an outgoing tide. Alarmingly, the incoming tide brought them back, but they were quickly salvaged by Filipinos who anticipated a shortage of fuel for their fishing boats.

The Pan Am employees were now standing round-the-clock watches for Japanese aircraft at the facility, so the company decided they should be armed. Ben, who like many farm boys knew his way around guns from hunting jackrabbits, was handed an old Enfield rifle like the one Sergeant York, another experienced jackrabbit hunter, had used to sharp-shoot his way to the Medal of Honor in the First World War.

On December 10, Edwards was on duty in the office around noontime when the teletype started clacking. It was an urgent message from San Fernando, 140 miles north of Manila. More than fifty twin-engine Japanese bombers were headed down the coast. Ben called the commanding officer at Sangley Point and asked: "Do you think they're coming for us?" It didn't take long before they had their answer.

Ben was standing on an outside deck looking skyward when he heard the planes and saw the first bombs fall into the waters off Sangley Point. He ran for the makeshift shelter they had built with sandbags beneath a grove of coconut palms several days earlier. Several other airline employees were there already. They didn't have a roof, which meant they had a front-row view of the silver planes with red-meatball insignias crisscrossing the sky unmolested. Anti-aircraft fire boomed in the distance, but it was ineffective, exploding nowhere near the attacking aircraft. For an hour, bombs fell and secondary explosions lit off.

When the attack stopped, Edwards left the shelter. Stunned, he watched a long procession of the wounded and dying being ferried past the front gate to the nearby naval hospital.

Before long, the street was red with blood.


DOROTHY STILL NEVER PLANNED TO BECOME A NURSE. THE LOS Angeles native grew up wanting to be a dress designer and dreamed of working at Warner Bros. or one of the other Hollywood studios. But in 1932, with the country in the Depression, her mother, who considered nursing a noble profession for young women, took Dorothy, then eighteen, to L.A. County General Hospital to sign her up for the nursing program. After graduating, Dorothy worked at local hospitals before joining the Navy Nursing Corps in 1937. Her first assignment was at San Diego's Balboa Naval Hospital, and in 1939, she transferred to Manila.

Now thirty years old, the freckled blonde with a dimpled, girl-next-door smile had grown fond of Manila. She liked her work at the hospital, and the concentration of military bases in the area created lots of social opportunities for young nurses. They joined bridge clubs, played golf, went sightseeing around Luzon, and were frequent guests at military dinners and dances where the men wore dress uniforms and the women attired themselves in formal gowns. At their quarters, the nurses had Filipina servants who did the cooking, cleaning, and washing, giving the nurses more free time. Life in Manila before the war was exotic, rewarding, and fun. But now it was time for her to go home. Dorothy's orders had come through a couple of weeks earlier for her to leave the Philippines in January 1942.

U.S. Navy nurse Dorothy Still. *Courtesy U.S. Navy Bureau of Medicine and Surgery.*

On December 10, 1941, before the Japanese attack began, Dorothy was having lunch with several other nurses at their two-story quarters with wraparound screened verandas. The 150-bed Cañacao Naval Hospital, where they all worked, was only a few blocks away. With the war barely forty-eight hours old, they were discussing radio reports that had little new information to offer. The nurses had been speculating about how swiftly the U.S. fleet would avenge Pearl Harbor. Then suddenly, when the air-raid sirens went off, they hurried outside and ducked underneath the building where a section of its exposed foundation was enclosed by sandbags.

The nurses huddled in the dark with hands cupped over their ears as wave after wave of Japanese planes released their bombs. Every bit as frightening as the explosions were the staccato bursts of machine-gun fire from low-flying aircraft. When the all clear sounded, the nurses rushed to the hospital, where they were immediately ordered to discharge ambulatory patients to make room for what they knew would be an onslaught of casualties.

Dorothy was shocked by what she saw on Ward C. She'd been through numerous triage drills, but nothing had prepared her for the horrific casualties that poured in, servicemen as well as civilians of all ages. They were putting two or three patients to each bed, and when they ran out, the injured were placed on chairs between beds and even on the floor in rooms and crowded corridors.

The stench of burned flesh and the sight of mangled bodies were nauseating. Arms and legs were broken at odd angles, some dangling by a shred of ligament; others with jagged stumps and exposed bones. The burn victims were shivering and glassy-eyed from shock; they would not have recognized their faces in a mirror. Some were barely breathing as their wounds oozed serum. Many patients were so overwrought they were hyperventilating, while others looked to be frozen in a mile-long stare. Some of the wounded men were yelling out to each other.

"Our shells just weren't reaching those sons of bitches!"

"My buddy was there one minute, then he just wasn't."

Surrounded by shrieks, moans, and cries, Dorothy and the rest of the staff worked feverishly to identify and treat the most seriously injured first. Tourniquets were applied, tetanus shots given, and morphine injected. Injuries had to be assessed in an effort to save those who could be saved. The nurses' uniforms were soon blood-spattered as they went from one patient to the next, pressed into giving care and making decisions customarily restricted to physicians. They worked long into the night.

The operating rooms were so backed up that surgeries were being hastily done in corridors and on steps with no time to worry about unsterile conditions. The telephone and power lines were down, and the elevators were out. The auxiliary unit could only supply electricity to the emergency room and surgical suites on the ground floor. Through the night, other spaces were illuminated by flashlights and battle lanterns.

One patient on a metal gurney told Dorothy he was dying.

"I heard the doctor say there was no use operating," he bemoaned.

The young sailor had no visible injuries. Dorothy was sure he was confused by shock or pain medications. She reassured him he had likely overhead a doctor talking about someone else.

"You'll be fine, sailor," she said.

"It's true—doc said no use trying to sew up my stomach."

Dorothy raised the edge of the blanket covering him. The man's abdomen was split wide open; his stomach and intestines, awash in bloody excrement, were visible, with the tissues that normally covered the internal organs missing. *How could he still be alive?*

She had been trained not to tell patients they were dying. Nurses were supposed to give hope even when hope was nonexistent. She again told him he would be okay, this time while having to hide what she knew was the truth. Returning to her rounds, Dorothy kept thinking of the young man. She felt bad about being dishonest with him and wondered what she could have said or done differently. Maybe he needed a shot of morphine? Or a drink of water? She had run away so fast she hadn't even asked if there *was* anything she could do for him.

After a while, she found the courage to go back. When she did, the gurney was empty, and a corpsman was hurriedly wiping it down.

The young man had died and his body had been hauled off to the morgue in the basement. Dorothy started shaking, turned away, and burst into tears. She made it to the back door of the hospital without anyone taking notice. She was surprised to find that it was already nightfall, although the fires all around made the sky red with flames. The shipyard was burning, and so was Manila. After a long cry, she returned to her duties.

In the days that followed, with the Cavite shipyard in ruins but the Sangley airfield operational and a prime target for more attacks, the patients at Cañacao were transferred to civilian hospitals a few miles away in Manila.

U.S. Army General Douglas MacArthur's air forces had been largely destroyed on the ground at Clark Field, forty miles northwest of Manila, in the hours after Pearl Harbor. To save the Far East fleet, the Navy ordered its ships to Java and Australia, 1,500 miles away. With no naval or air defenses, MacArthur directed all remaining Army ground units to withdraw to the Bataan peninsula, a tongue of land on the northwestern shore of Manila Bay. The day after Christmas, he declared Manila an open city, which under international laws meant that it would not put up any resistance to an invading army. This was done to avoid unnecessary harm to noncombatants and property. The last U.S. and Philippine military forces left the city the next day for Bataan. While MacArthur did this to spare Manila's destruction, it didn't stop the Japanese from continuing to bomb and shell the besieged Philippine capital and its residents.

Within a week, the streets of Manila looked like they belonged in a ghost town, as many of the locals had left for Bataan or other parts of Luzon. Although rising fears of war had caused many military wives and dependents in the Philippines to return to the United States by mid-1941, the American and British expatriates in Manila now had no place to go. Their wait for the Japanese occupation was agonizing. Everyone had heard about the Nanking massacre in 1937 when the Imperial Japanese Army captured the Chinese city and murdered tens of thousands of civilians. Now the citizens of the Philippines feared the same raping, looting, and wanton killing. Women stayed off the streets, choosing to remain behind doors in hotels or homes, many of them with their children. Men gathered in quiet groups to discuss recent war news and rumors, but they never went far from their families and kept a watchful eye on the empty streets for the enemy.

Dorothy and ten other Navy nurses ended up at Manila's Santa Scholastica College, where the Army had set up a temporary hospital after the bombings. All the Army patients were evacuated by ship to Australia, and the Army nurses soon after left for Bataan, where eventually they would make their way to the tip of the peninsula and across the bay to Corregidor. Originally, there had been a dozen Navy nurses at Cañacao, several of whom had come over together from the States on the same ship two years earlier. One of them,

Ann Bernatitus, a surgical nurse, had been assigned to an Army surgical unit that left for Bataan with the Army nurses.

At night, the eleven Navy nurses still in Manila—they had no patients or other duties and were mystified that their orders to evacuate hadn't come through—would meet in a third-floor tower at the front of Santa Scholastica. From there, they watched as the skies across the bay over Bataan lit up from artillery fire. Their world was changing, and they all knew it. *Where would they end up and how would they end up there?*

Only last week, Dorothy and some other nurses had met several officers from the newly commissioned submarine USS *Sealion* (SS-195) at the Sangley Officers Club and accepted their invitation to dinner. Now *Sealion*, one of the Navy's most modern subs, which had been tied to a wharf at Cavite, was at the bottom of the bay after taking two direct hits (killing four sailors) during the December 10 bombing and being scuttled to keep it from falling into enemy hands.

The nurses were at their perch on the night of January 2, 1942, when, shortly before dusk, elements of the Imperial Japanese Army entered Manila. It was a triumphal march for a ragtag force, complete with a bemedaled general in an open car with Rising Sun flags flying from the bumpers.

The initial wave of troops rode bicycles, followed by the cavalry, with large horses carrying small soldiers in sloppy-looking khaki uniforms. They were trailed by ranks of infantry with long bayonets attached to rifles, artillery batteries, and rumbling tanks. The sounds of rolling military stock and marching soldiers were mixed with chilling, high-pitched chants.

"Bonzai! Bonzai! Bonzai!"

Gerald Sams, a former U.S. Marine and Coast Guardsman and now a civilian Navy employee working as a senior radio engineer, had been in his office at Cavite Navy Yard when the first wave of Japanese bombers arrived overhead at noon on December 10. Rushing outside, he was repeatedly knocked down by blasts as nearby ships and buildings took direct hits. Red-orange flames licked skyward, and huge plumes of black smoke rolled across the shipyard. The entire facility was soon on fire. All the base's water pumps were electric, and with the power knocked out, there was no way to fight the inferno.

The shipyard, built on a small island in the bay, was connected to the shoreline by a narrow causeway. With flames, explosions, and thick smoke blocking the only exit, Sams turned toward the bay and ran for the water. He had never been much of a swimmer; in fact, he had never swum more than a hundred yards in his life. Nevertheless, he dove in, completely clothed, only briefly thinking of sharks in the warm bay. But during the grueling two-mile swim to the mainland, he didn't spot a single fin. The sharks were either killed by bombs exploding in the water or scared away by all the noise.

Sams had been a radio operator in the Marines from 1930 to 1931 and with the Coast Guard from 1932 to 1935. He had since undergone training in radar, an acronym coined by the U.S. Navy in 1940 for Radio Detection And Ranging. Even the word itself was classified, and Sams was among a handful of experts with high-security clearances sent by the Navy to the Philippines to set up a half-dozen early-warning radar sites so that the new object-detecting system that used radio waves would be in place in the event of war.

Sams, a thirty-year-old Chicago native, was blue-eyed, and stood a solid five foot nine. He had a studious disposition, which had helped him exceed his high school education by studying enough mathematics and electronics that he was now making a respectable $3,800 a year. He had arrived in Manila in early September 1941, and while he had an important job and worked long hours during the week, on weekends he had done a fair amount of solo exploring around Luzon, both on foot and by car. Invariably he would get lost following some roundabout road or footpath, but this never fazed him. He always seemed to find some youngsters playing in a creek or an old fisherman and somehow got the directions he needed. Jerry Sams was like that: curious, adventurous, and capable.

When Manila was declared an open city, Sams and the other members of his radar team moved to the town of Mariveles on the tip of the Bataan peninsula. Soon realizing they needed some equipment they'd left behind, Sams drove back to Manila to retrieve it. But on the trip back, he discovered that several bridges had been blown up by retreating U.S. forces to stop the advancing Japanese, and there was no way for him to return to Bataan.

Back in Manila, Sams sought the assistance of a friend at the Nicaraguan consulate. He suggested Jerry come directly over to the consulate and pose as one of the consular staff, all of whom were certain—with their diplomatic immunity—to be repatriated to Nicaragua. Sams knew he could easily get from Central America back to the United States.

The roundup of Americans and other foreigners began within days of the Japanese arrival in Manila. The orders were delivered by armed squads sent into neighborhoods. Japanese with bullhorns kept repeating in English: "Food and clothing for three days." People were told they had thirty minutes to line up in front of their homes.

On January 4, 1942, the Japanese arrived at the Nicaraguan consulate in a fashionable part of Manila. They took one look at the very Anglo-looking Jerry Sams and ordered him out of the building.

Jerry had already decided that if he were taken prisoner of war, he would not spill a word about his top secret work for the Navy, even under the most severe interrogation. The Japanese did not have radar, and he knew they would be desperate to get it. He had also decided he would do everything they did *not* want him to do. Short of losing his life, Jerry planned to resist his captors any way he could.

He and the other foreigners were picked up in and around Manila, loaded into canvas-topped troop transports, and delivered to the main campus of Santo Tomás, an old university in the center of the city surrounded by high walls with gates guarded by Japanese soldiers. For thousands of Americans and other foreigners, those "three days" for which they had packed would turn into more than three years of wartime captivity.

MARGARET SHERK CLIMBED DOWN FROM A JAPANESE MILITARY truck at Santo Tomás on January 8, 1942, carrying her three-year-old son, David, in one arm and a suitcase with all their worldly possessions in the other. With only twenty dollars' worth of pesos and feeling very alone, she was worried sick about how she could properly care for her child in a prison camp.

Born in Oklahoma, she had spent her childhood in Beaumont, a sleepy Southern California town on Route 66. Growing up, she envied people who were traveling through on their way to new places. She was determined that one day she would be one of them. Her dream came true in 1936, when, after two years at Riverside Junior College, she journeyed to Manila to marry her hometown boyfriend, Bob Sherk, a mining engineer.

Like many Americans during the Depression, Bob had been attracted to work in the Philippines by the pay and perks, as well as his own desire for travel and adventure. He and Margaret had been dating since high school, and when he left Beaumont, he said he would get settled, and even though they weren't yet married, he would send for her. He wrote wonderful letters to her filled with descriptions of exotic people and locales. After several months, he announced that his future was secure enough for her to join him. For Margaret, not yet twenty, a blue-eyed, curly-haired brunette with graceful lines and delicate features, the move was mostly about growing up and gaining independence.

Bob was tall, with dark hair and a nice smile. In high school and college he had been a good student and star football player. Their romance had never been sizzling, but it was solid and comfortable. They had known each other most of their lives and shared similar dreams and ambitions. Soon after she arrived, they were married in Manila. Margaret had expected they would live in Baguio, a picturesque city in northern Luzon known as the summer capital of the Philippines. But Bob was offered a supervisory position in an isolated mining camp some fifty miles into the mountains above Baguio, where he oversaw local Filipinos in blasting, digging, and hauling ore to the surface. He and Margaret were provided with a furnished house with electricity and water, and they were able to send most of Bob's earnings home to start building a nest egg. Margaret settled in and made the best of life in the boondocks. In 1938, after a difficult pregnancy, she gave birth to David.

Now she was being directed by a platoon of armed Japanese soldiers who were herding her and her son, along with about one hundred other prisoners, into one of Santo Tomás's sixty-two classrooms, where more than three thousand civilian internees would be housed in a walled-off rectangular section of downtown approximately ten blocks long and eight blocks wide. Once in the room, now stripped of chairs, desks, and other furnishings, Margaret plopped down on the cement floor like everyone else. Only later did she realize that she should have been quicker and staked out a corner, because this was where she and David would sleep in the crowded classroom: smack in front of an open doorway.

Margaret was exhausted and disgusted in equal measure. In November, after most of the U.S. military wives and families had already returned to the States, she and David had boarded a plane in Baguio for Manila, where she went to the U.S. high commissioner's office to ask if she and her son should go home. She was told, "Stay, by all means. Manila is the safest place in the Orient." Listening to this advice and returning to the mountains instead of taking her son to the States was the biggest mistake of her life.

After Pearl Harbor, it was too late to leave, and Bob and Margaret could only wait like everyone else. They stayed in the mountains until just before Christmas when they were awakened one day at 6 A.M. and told the U.S. Army had ordered an evacuation because the Japanese were headed their way on the only road, which the Army intended to blow up. Given an hour to get ready, they were soon on their way to Manila with other fleeing refugees, including other foreigners and Filipinos.

Once in Manila, Bob heard the Army was looking for engineers on Bataan, where MacArthur's forces would make a stand against the Japanese. Bob wanted to do his part, and Margaret understood. She told him she would have done the same thing in his position. He was sworn into the U.S. Army on the spot and left for Bataan on New Year's Day with other American expatriates who had joined up.

Margaret's brave front began to crumble almost immediately; without a husband, with little money, and no friends in a war-torn city about to be occupied by a cruel enemy, how were she and David going to survive? She thought about her very average, ordinary, and yet safe small-town life back in Beaumont. It seemed so far away.

That first night at Santo Tomás, she huddled with her little boy on the bare, dirty floor, without a blanket or mosquito net. She tried to fan the mosquitoes off him to no avail. David cried the whole night.

Margaret took some measure of hope from a story making the rounds that the battle in Bataan would turn the tide. Word was that the powerful U.S. Army only had to do some "mopping up," and the Japanese would soon be ousted from the Philippines, and things would go back to normal. Even so, a sporadic negative thought did creep in. *Would the fighting really be over so quickly? Could Bob come back to them so soon?*

BEFORE BECOMING A PRISONER OF WAR, BEN EDWARDS SPENT HIS last week of freedom as the all-expenses-paid guest of the Manila Hotel.

When Pan Am closed its Cavite facilities, its employees were moved into various hotels in the city. Ben drew the old, stately hotel overlooking the bay, where, since 1935, General MacArthur had kept a penthouse suite that had served as his command post until his move to Bataan. The hotel billed itself as "The Aristocrat of the Orient," and served such specialties as steamed lapu-lapu (MacArthur's favorite), a native grouper fish wrapped in banana leaves and served with calamansi sauce.

After spending a couple of days in a regular guest room, Ben moved to a luxury suite recently abandoned by a high-ranking aide to Philippine president Manuel Quezon, who had hurriedly left for the United States to set up a government-in-exile. The presidential aide departed in such a rush that he left behind much of his expensive wardrobe, including a dozen bespoke suits and shirts that fit Ben as if they were made for him.

Even with a competing event like a war—Manila was now experiencing daily air raids—the hotel still held its traditional Christmas Eve gala. As Ben strolled into the festively decorated ballroom, he felt as if he had stepped into another world. Military men who would the next day depart for Bataan and Corregidor wore their dress uniforms for a final time; businessmen donned dinner jackets, and women were in ball gowns and their finest jewels. As Ben dined and danced, other Pan Am employees were across the bay carrying out orders to destroy anything at the Cavite facilities that could be useful to the enemy—aircraft parts, spare engines, flight instruments. The celebrants in the ballroom could clearly see the resulting fires, adding to the evening's surreal, last-waltz-on-the-*Titanic* ambience.

For the next several nights, Edwards went to the docks and joined volunteers who were loading barges in the dark with food and medical supplies destined for Corregidor, an island at the entrance to Manila Bay fortified with coastal artillery batteries and an array of other defensive armaments, along with a network of tunnels filled with ammunition magazines. It was hot, dirty, back-breaking work, but the men felt they were contributing. As long as Corregidor stayed in American hands, the Imperial Japanese Navy would be denied the use of the bay, the finest natural harbor in the Far East.

Edwards and several of his Pan Am friends discussed the possibility of pooling their cash, driving into southern Luzon, buying a native sailboat (now selling for exorbitant prices), and striking out for Australia. Ben went to the bank to withdraw funds, and while inside he was caught in an air raid. A portion of the roof caved in, killing several people inside the building.

The idea of sailing to Australia was dropped when they learned that Japanese troops had landed in southern Luzon. Next, Ben and a couple of Pan Am mechanics contacted U.S. military authorities about joining the Army Air Corps, but they were told that all the planes based in the Philippines had been destroyed, so there was no need for aircraft mechanics.

Then just four days after the Japanese entered Manila, Ben became a prisoner of war when Japanese troops took over the hotel, evicting the guests and ordering them to pack three days' worth of food. He was taken by truck to Santo Tomás with other Americans from the Manila Hotel, and then two weeks later, he escaped.

Early one morning after roll call, he climbed atop a mound of dirt next to the twelve-foot concrete wall and hoisted himself over. Just a few blocks away he was stopped by a Japanese sentry. Ben began talking in Spanish, a language he'd only barely studied. The sentry clearly didn't understand him, but Edwards's rudimentary language skills combined with his dark complexion allowed him to pretend to be Spanish and pull off a bluff that doubtless saved his life. He made his way down to the docks, where he asked several fishermen if they would take him across the bay to Corregidor. Given that armed Japanese boats were patrolling the bay, intent on keeping men and supplies from reaching the fortified island, no one would take him.

With no place to hide in the occupied city, he decided it was safer inside Santo Tomás until he could come up with another plan. He also knew he had to get back before the Japanese noticed he'd been gone. Climbing over the high wall to accomplish this was not as easy as it had been getting out. Finally, by shimmying up a wooden pole and leaping across a six-foot gap, he landed painfully on top of the wall, which had broken pieces of glass embedded in the cement. Making sure no one was watching, he dropped down on the other side with a thud and quickly walked away.

A few weeks later, three young Britishers—Thomas Fletcher, Blakey Laycock, and Henry Weeks—made their own escape from Santo Tomás. They had a sailboat hidden somewhere by the bay and planned to sail to Australia. They waited until after the evening roll call, then in the darkness climbed over the wall. They were caught less than twelve hours later, only a few miles from camp, while at a store buying food and other supplies. Brought back by a squad of Japanese military police, they were led single file, their hands tied behind them with rope, into a room where they were beaten with wooden bats for several hours.

The next morning, the Japanese announced that the men had been found guilty by a court-martial and sentenced to die. Members of a newly formed committee representing the internees met hurriedly with the camp commandant, arguing that the Geneva Conventions code providing for the humane treatment of prisoners of war—military and civilian—did not include summary executions.

They followed with a written petition urging clemency. All attempts to win a reprieve for the three men failed.

On Sunday morning, February 15, 1942, Fletcher, Laycock, and Weeks were escorted to a vacant plot of ground adjacent to the Cemetario del Norte, one of Manila's largest cemeteries. A single, shallow grave had been dug. As two other prisoners watched—they had been brought to serve as witnesses—the three men, their faces horribly beaten and marked, were blindfolded and made to sit on the edge of the grave. From the opposite side, several soldiers with pistols fired shots into the men until they toppled into the grave. A Japanese officer stood over them and fired several more times as the men lay groaning in the bottom of the grave, then gave the order for it to be filled up. No effort was made to ensure that the condemned men were dead before they were buried.

When news of the executions spread throughout camp, Ben thought, *There but for the grace of God.* He said a prayer for the chaps he had known as good, courageous men who were unwilling to sit out the war in an internment camp.

For now, Ben Edwards crossed escape off his to-do list.

# TWO

# Prisoners of the Japanese

JERRY SAMS HAD ALREADY SERVED AS AN ENLISTED MAN IN two branches of the military, so being herded like cattle didn't bother him as much as it did some other prisoners. Determined to settle in, he "got organized rapidly" at Santo Tomás.

Jerry had a true knack for scrounging. Quickly realizing that a mosquito net was a dire necessity, he lifted one from an unattended guard's room. It was a square-shaped frame about two feet wide, with netting stitched over it. He was the first prisoner in his crowded room to have protection from the hordes of mosquitoes that came out at night. That first night he slept soundly, but when he woke up in the morning, he turned and saw two sleeping men had also placed their heads under the netting. During the day, he collapsed the wire frame and hid it in case anyone came looking for it.

A few days later, the camp commandant was driven through the gate in an older English sports car, which Jerry immediately recognized as the one he had bought shortly after arriving in Manila. The commandant went into his office while the driver and a soldier stood by. Jerry had been forced to abandon the car when he was picked up by the Japanese, but he had kept a set of keys and ran back to his room to get them.

Picture secretly taken by Jerry Sams of Japanese machine-gun practice at Santo Tomás Internment Camp, 1943. *Courtesy Gerry Ann (Sams) Schwede.*

He walked to the car, unlocked the trunk, and began rifling through the compartment. Seeing him with the keys, the Japanese soldiers standing nearby apparently thought he had permission to go into the trunk. He removed his electronics textbooks, magazines, his briar pipe, a can of tobacco, and the camera he had taken on his travels about Luzon. Cameras were strictly forbidden in camp, but none of the soldiers watching said a word. He closed the trunk and strolled away, taking his belongings with him.

On another day Jerry was summoned to a room where a Japanese Army officer waited behind a desk. He motioned Jerry to an empty chair across from him. The officer spoke in Japanese, which was then translated into English by a middle-aged Japanese civilian. The officer said Jerry's name had been found on a list of Navy electronics experts. They had located a partially destroyed radar site and wanted to salvage the equipment in order to build their own. They needed an expert's help and had apparently decided that Gerald Sams was their man.

To this point, the session seemed like a job interview.

But then Jerry asked innocently, "You mean *radio?*"

After an exchange in Japanese, the translator said, "No, *ray-dar.*"

Jerry was determined not to even acknowledge the existence of that top secret word, let alone discuss anything about the technology.

"I'm a *radio* man," he said. "*Radio.* That's the word in English."

He managed to confuse the Japanese enough that the officer switched gears. All the radio stations in Manila had been destroyed during the bombing, and the Japanese now wanted to set up their own station right away, no doubt for propaganda purposes. Since Jerry was a *radio* expert, the officer said, he could do that for them. He would receive a stipend and could live in his own apartment in Manila.

That's when it dawned on Jerry that this *was* a job interview. "Look, I'll do menial tasks and dig ditches, but I cannot work for you professionally. I would be treated like a traitor when the Americans come back."

The officer fired back in perfect English. "The Americans don't have an army!" he yelled. "They don't have a navy! They are cowards! They won't fight! They will never come back!"

Jerry felt his blood boiling. He knew he should keep his mouth shut, but he couldn't help himself. "The thing I have to look forward to is them coming back and kicking the hell out of you guys. They'll do it, too."

"You go! You go!" the officer screamed.

As Jerry got up and went out the door, he was struck from behind across his kidneys with a hose that felt as if it was filled with sand. He wobbled, but stayed on his feet and managed to stagger back to his room. Jerry was laid up with excruciating pain for days, and the camp doctor was concerned about damage to the kidneys or other internal organs. As Jerry slowly recovered, he realized he could have avoided the terrible blow if he had just kept his mouth shut.

Once he was back on his feet, Jerry soon found his own comfortable, furnished space, which he obtained without becoming beholden to the Japanese. While exploring around the camp, he discovered a third-floor landing outside a locked door to the old university museum, which since the occupation had been kept shuttered with all entrances padlocked. The six-by-six-foot landing was covered, and it opened onto the museum roof. Without asking for permission, Jerry moved in and built a bed platform on a scaffold so he would have even more living space.

He had volunteered for a work detail unloading firewood that came in by truck, which gave him the opportunity to bribe one of the Filipino drivers to bring him something hidden in the next load. That was how he became the only internee in Santo Tomás to have his own working refrigerator, which he smuggled past guards and brought to his landing. He built a wooden box to hide it, and tuned the compressor motor so it could barely be heard. He ran the power off a circuit in the museum after picking the lock. It was a coup to have refrigeration in the tropics, where foods quickly spoiled.

Jerry worked out a system with other prisoners to share the refrigerator, and as many as forty people labeled their items and stored them there. No one ever abused the privilege of communal refrigeration by taking someone else's food.

In his ongoing campaign to do just about anything the Japanese forbade, Jerry took his biggest chance in the summer of 1942 when he went over the wall to help a group of Filipino guerrillas set up a radio transmission station in the hills east of Manila. He had been asked for his expertise through some guerrilla contacts inside and outside of camp. He knew he'd be killed if he got caught but decided the project was important enough to take a calculated risk.

He climbed onto the roof of a camp building, dropped down on the other side of the wall, and dove quickly into a waiting horse-drawn buggy, which took him to the guerrillas.

Fellow prisoners inside Santo Tomás had agreed to cover for him during roll calls, and also, if his absence were discovered, to send out a prearranged signal. If that happened, he would stay with the guerrillas. If he wasn't discovered missing, he would reenter the camp.

Eight days later, after getting the new radio transmitter up and running, Jerry Sams managed to sneak back into Santo Tomás Internment Camp without getting caught.

Life in Santo Tomás had steadily improved for Margaret Sherk and her son, David. After two weeks, they moved to a building known as the Annex, which housed mothers with young children. Being with other mothers who were not so impatient with the sounds and cries of children made for a more congenial atmosphere. One woman who had had the foresight to pack two quilts before being taken prisoner loaned one of them to Margaret, which she spread out on the floor for her and David to sleep on. It was the first act of kindness they received at the camp but not the last.

Margaret had no money to buy from Filipino traders who were allowed to sell produce and fruits to internees. She and David— along with about two-thirds of the internees—got their only sustenance from a canteen set up by the Philippine Red Cross. The staple diet was mush, a cornmeal porridge, and mungo beans. The main vegetable was talinum, a local variety of spinach that the internees started to grow for themselves in a cleared patch of land between two buildings. Meat was seldom seen.

At first, few internees believed they would be held for long or even that the war would be lengthy, but such optimism eroded over time. And it ended for good when word circulated about the surrender of U.S. forces at Corregidor in May 1942.

Margaret knew then that it was likely they would be held at least two years. She was determined to do everything to see that she and David made it. Having a nature that required routine, she set up one for herself and her son, which included his time with playmates and kindergarten, taught by experienced schoolteachers in camp. She joined daily work details and played in a women's softball league; she had always enjoyed sports and had earned an athletic letter in college.

One September day, she went to see an outside basketball game. Sometime after the first half had been played, a latecomer arrived and stopped next to her.

"What's the score?" asked Jerry Sams.

Margaret pointed to the scoreboard across the way. She looked squarely at him but said nothing. Not recognizing him, she was sure she had never seen him around camp because she knew she would have remembered him. With thick blond hair, baby blues, and a chiseled jaw, she thought he was the most handsome man she had ever seen.

When the game ended, they both went their separate ways without another word being spoken.

A week later, Margaret was leaving a long line after getting a sliver of soap when Jerry appeared again, and this time introduced himself. They made small talk, then he offered to walk her back to the Annex, where he met David, who soon had his first piggyback ride in a long while. Jerry invited Margaret to his place for dinner that evening after David went to bed with the other children in the Annex.

When she found his third-floor landing, she was surprised to see it furnished with two chairs. He was playing chess with a friend but quickly gave up his seat for her. She hadn't sat in a real chair for eight months.

Over dinner, while Margaret attacked her pile of vegetables as if someone might suddenly take them away, Jerry told her he was now the official custodian of the adjacent museum, and that the guards had given him a key so he could serve as night watchman. He laughed at that, really laughed. She hadn't heard a laugh like that in a long time.

From that night on, Jerry began doing things for Margaret to make her life a little easier. For starters, he made her a laundry washboard from a wooden board, strips of cast iron, and a tin cracker can. A lot of thought and design went into it, and she couldn't imagine where he had gotten the supplies and the tools to make it. She loved that washboard as perhaps only a mother who had to scrub a child's mud-covered clothes could.

Next, Jerry made a little pail for David to carry his food from the canteen to the outside seating area at the back of the main building where most people ate their meals, a walk that even adults had a hard time making without spilling the soupy concoctions handed out. Jerry cut the top off an old cracker can, folded the edges over and made them smooth, and fashioned several compartments so that different foods would not run together into a mushy mess. He soldered a handle on it and painted David's name on the side.

Life for Margaret began to look up after she met Jerry. He invited her and David over—along with other friends—to eat meals he cooked on Bunsen burners from the museum, an improvement over the small charcoal fires others used.

Jerry was determined to make Christmas 1942 special for David. The university church's garden had a mature almond tree, and Jerry cut off two full branches, then cut them into shorter pieces, which he stuck into holes in a wooden pole. He placed the homemade Christmas tree in one corner, with a chair on each side for support, so it only needed foliage in front. He made a star for the top, and David cut out paper chains to hang around the branches. When Margaret brought David over on Christmas Eve, they were amazed to see lights on the tree. For their holiday dinner, Jerry had arranged for a special food parcel from the outside—sent by Filipino friends—which included turkey. Margaret had a flair for cooking, and Jerry had built a little tin oven she used to make a delicious "pumpkin" pie using squash, ginger, coconut milk, and brown sugar.

As the months went by, Jerry and life at the landing became more important to Margaret, as well as to David. Soon they were eating most of their meals together and spending a lot of time with each other. At night, Margaret and David always returned to the Annex to sleep. Although Margaret and Jerry were not lovers, only friends, she began to realize that she was developing strong feelings for him. She knew it had probably been inevitable, given his positive spirit, kindness, and generosity, combined with the dire situation she and David had found themselves in. Every day, she was reminded that they might not all make it out alive; the war could drag on, and they could die before being liberated.

No one could know what their captors, infamous for their cruelty, would decide to do with them. But still a part of her longed to appreciate and enjoy any pleasant moments she had because they might be among her last. However, there was one thing she couldn't forget: she was married.

Margaret had been brought up to believe that marriage was for life, with divorce "the work of the devil," and adultery unthinkable. When she married Bob, she had fully intended to make their marriage last a lifetime. In their five years together, she and Bob had gotten along well, and had a child they both loved. Bob remained the same guy she had always known: solid, dependable, and hardworking. She knew he valued his profession and getting ahead in the world over all else, but then, she thought a lot of men were like that. Bob had done nothing wrong, and she was sure they would still be together if the war hadn't come.

But the past year had pulled all of her normal support structures out from under her. The foundations she had built her life on and her sense of identity had vanished into the war, along with her husband. What had been simple truths about life and liberty were no longer true. That didn't mean she wasn't conflicted and guilt-ridden whenever she considered her growing attachment to Jerry, and she knew what the world—including her strict parents—would think of a woman who left her husband for another man while he was away at war.

Margaret's twenty-sixth birthday was on February 4, 1943, and she did not expect any kind of celebration. Since she'd left her parents' home, her birthdays had been mostly forgettable. Bob had never been sentimental or an enthusiastic celebrant. And anyway, what was there to celebrate this year?

Jerry went all day without mentioning a word about the event, and Margaret didn't say anything either. Jerry had not even invited her to come up to the landing to have a plate of mungo beans with him, but he did ask her to visit after she put David to bed. When she arrived, five or six other friends were there, and that wasn't unusual either. Then Jerry unlocked the museum door and ushered them all inside. That *was* unusual.

Once everyone was inside, he closed the door and everyone sang "Happy Birthday" to Margaret. Jerry had borrowed a record player and some records—some of Margaret's favorites. After putting one on the turntable, he asked her to dance. Later, they all made sherbet from sugar, water, and cake flavoring. Margaret thought it was her best birthday ever.

For his birthday on May 2, Jerry received a surprise of a different kind. The Japanese posted notices around camp announcing that due to the overcrowded conditions at Santo Tomás—which now had more than 4,200 internees with no space to expand—eight hundred able-bodied men were to be transferred on May 14 to a rural location forty miles south of Manila, where they would build a new internment camp to which the prisoners in Santo Tomás would be sent.

Jerry's name was on the list of men to be transferred.

His immediate concern was for Margaret and David. During his absence, he suggested they relocate to his landing so they could have more privacy and be more comfortable. Margaret agreed. Jerry got busy making modifications, including building a bed platform for David.

The commandant of Santo Tomás posted a notice in which he

exulted about the building of the new camp. "The new site is in Los Baños, an ideal health resort noted for its hot springs, where new buildings will be erected for your housing and where you will enjoy fresh air and find easy access to fresh meat and vegetables." It sounded like paradise.

Margaret was used to hearing the Japanese say many things that were not true, and she had no confidence in their promises about the new prison camp or about joining the men there. She knew it could be months, even years, before she saw Jerry again. Much worse was the thought of losing him forever.

Margaret had fallen completely and irrevocably in love.

AFTER THE JAPANESE ENTERED MANILA, DOROTHY STILL AND the other Navy nurses remained at Santa Scholastica until March 9, 1942, when they were ordered into the courtyard under armed guard and put on an open-air bus for the short ride to Santo Tomás. The Japanese really didn't know what to do with female U.S. military nurses, and eventually they decided to place them in civilian internment camps. At the same time, their male counterparts— trained Navy corpsmen—went sent to military POW camps.

The day before, the nurses had loaded two trucks with their belongings—personal trunks, mattresses, pillows, linens, luggage, pots, pans, canned goods, and medical supplies—which were waiting for them when they arrived at Santo Tomás. Luckily they found a medical clinic there, already in operation, staffed by civilian doctors and Filipino nurses. Surgical patients and the critically ill were sent to outside hospitals because there were no operating suites or facilities for intensive care. The nurses handed out emetine, carbazone, and bismuth to patients with dysentery and nonspecific diarrhea, and new sulfonamides to those with infections. They shaved and painted heads with potassium permanganate to get rid of lice, and treated scabies lesions with gentian violet.

When an amoebic dysentery epidemic hit, they conducted lab tests which revealed that the carriers worked in the main kitchen crew; the gastrointestinal parasite is most easily spread through contaminated food and water. Once the food handlers were isolated and treated, the epidemic ended and no new cases developed.

Two days before the men were transferred to Los Baños, Navy chief nurse Laura Cobb, forty-nine, from Wichita, Kansas, was asked by a missionary doctor at Santo Tomás if her team would be willing to accompany him to the new camp. After the July 1942 arrival of sixty-six Army nurses who had been working at the hospital on Corregidor, there were too many nurses at Santo Tomás. The men going to Los Baños would require their own medical services, and the Navy nurses would be leaving Santo Tomás in the capable hands of the Army nurses. After checking with her nurses individually, all of whom agreed to make the move, Cobb agreed that she and her nurses would go to Los Baños.

Before sunrise on May 14, the main courtyard at Santo Tomás was filled with friends and families saying goodbye. There were handshakes, pats on the back, hugs, kisses, and tears as the men climbed up into trucks that filed out the front gate in the dark. The last truck carried the Navy nurses. As they boarded, a group of wives and mothers came over to say farewell. "Take good care of our men until we get there," implored one of them. Suddenly, over the camp loudspeaker, came a scratchy rendition of "Anchors Aweigh." The onlookers broke out in applause as the departing nurses, tears streaming down their faces, were driven away.

Any good cheer was soon forgotten by the nurses at Tutuban train station when they saw the men being crammed like sardines into metal boxcars smaller than Western-style railcars. Then the Japanese soldiers started to close and padlock the doors. Several nurses ran over to the officer in charge and exclaimed that the men would suffocate in the heat and humidity. The officer reluctantly agreed to allow a door on one side of each boxcar to remain open but warned that anyone jumping out and trying to escape would be shot.

The nurses spread out among the line of boxcars, each of which held approximately seventy men crammed in so tight they were all standing shoulder to shoulder with no room to sit down or move around.

Dorothy and another nurse climbed up into a boxcar and could still smell the cattle that usually rode inside. The men insisted they sit in the open doorway, which they did, with their feet dangling over the side. Then, with several shrill whistle blasts, the train made a sudden jerk forward, then crept out of Manila's main rail yard. It didn't pick up much additional speed but continued to chug along slowly as if the cars were too heavy for the old steam engine to pull.

Within half an hour, the men in the back of Dorothy's boxcar were overcome by the heat, some convulsing and passing out. The outside temperature was its usual mid-90s with oppressive humidity, but inside the steel boxcars it was as hot as an oven: at least 115 degrees. The men decided to take turns rotating those from the back to the front and the open doorway, where an occasional breeze could be felt. The nurses rose to give up their prime locations, but the men, deferential even in such dire circumstances, insisted they stay put.

The rail trip took an agonizing seven hours and made countless stops onto side spurs to let other trains with a higher priority pass on the main track. Whenever the train halted, the guards closed and locked the boxcar doors to keep the prisoners inside. By noontime, everyone had emptied the bottles of water they had brought along. Soaked with perspiration and struggling to breathe, they soon became dehydrated. In the late afternoon, the train pulled into the Los Baños rail station at College Junction, and the men were ordered out of the boxcars and loaded into troop trucks.

The nurses rode in the back of a heaving, coal-burning truck. As they crested a hill, Dorothy had a partial view down into a bucolic valley bordered by a low-slung, forested mountain to the west.

Coconut and banana groves stretched as far as she could see. Compared to the gritty, urban setting of Santo Tomás, this was God's green acres under a blue sky with wildflowers blooming, birds chirping, and fresh air. They were also at a slightly higher elevation than Manila, and it seemed a bit cooler.

The paved road, shaded with acacias and bamboos, turned into a dirt road as it narrowed and crossed a wooden bridge over a meandering creek. Up ahead they could see a sign on a rustic, wooden arch above a wooden gate manned by Japanese soldiers. The sign read: LOS BAÑOS AGRICULTURAL COLLEGE.

Dorothy saw several school buildings—some of them bomb-damaged and vacant—as well as a soccer field, a baseball diamond, and a variety of building materials piled up in an open field: poles and boards, rolls of sawali—a woven, split bamboo mat used in the construction of nipa huts and fences—and countless coils of barbed wire.

Before leaving Santo Tomás, each person had been given a hard-boiled duck egg and a chunk of bread, their only food for the day. With their water long gone, they were all very thirsty. Once inside the main gate, they were herded into a field in front of the buildings. It would be dark soon, but rather than be allowed inside, they were told they would be spending the night in the open field.

While waiting for the men to find and boil some drinking water, the nurses, parched to the bone, sat on a patch of wild, tinder-dry grass, waiting patiently with empty cups. Rather than appear forlorn, some of the women pretended they were having a tea party, complete with clinking cups and playful poses.

The make-believe gaiety ended when the nurses realized a Japanese photographer was taking their pictures, presumably for propaganda purposes.

# THREE

# Los Baños Internment Camp

A T DUSK ON THAT FIRST NIGHT, THE INTERNEES FROM SANTO Tomás, still in the open field, were engulfed by swarms of mosquitoes that came in from the nearby swamps. By morning, their faces, arms, and legs were misshapen by hundreds of bites. It was an inauspicious welcome to their new home. Not only were they concerned that the bites themselves would become infected, but they all knew that mosquitoes in the tropics could be carriers of virulent malaria.

The railroad station where they had disembarked was located a short distance from the town center of Los Baños, which was situated on the southern shoreline of Laguna de Bay. Nearly ten thousand residents, scattered throughout several small barrios that composed the town, lived mostly by fishing and farming. From these lakeside shores, *bancas*—native boats shaped like canoes, most with sails— left in the morning and returned with their catch. Los Baños was nestled between the most dominant geographical features of southern Luzon: Laguna de Bay, the largest lake in the Philippines, with a surface area of 350 square miles; and to the southwest nearby Mount Makiling, a dormant volcano that rose to 3,580 feet.

The war had reached Los Baños just a week after Pearl Harbor when a Japanese plane bombed a train parked at the rail station, killing several passengers. Bombs also fell on the three-hundred-acre

University of the Philippines College of Agriculture campus a short distance away; a direct hit was made on Molawin Mess Hall, destroying it only minutes before a group of ROTC cadets would have been eating lunch there. By the end of December 1941, the college's military cadets had left to join the fight on Bataan. Many of those students who remained at the college, joined by numerous faculty members, would within months form the local nucleus of a guerrilla resistance force. Although most classes for the six hundred students (95 percent male) were suspended, the college had remained open with minimal staff to care for the crops and animals.

In mid-1942, the Japanese authorized the resumption of agricultural courses, as well as classes at the rural high school on the grounds of the college. Now, a year later, the Japanese were transforming about forty acres of the lower campus—which had been athletic fields and the college's animal husbandry compound—into an internment camp for civilian prisoners of war.

As the internees were divvying up scraps of food some had brought with them, a group of Japanese soldiers approached. A young officer, through an interpreter, began barking orders. He told them to take up picks and shovels from a stack and start making holes for fence posts around the perimeter of the camp.

No one moved toward the tools.

This made the officer furious, and his men raised their rifles.

Alex Calhoun had been selected as the chairman of the newly formed administration committee representing the internees, and he unhesitantly stepped forward. He had been a bank manager at the National City Bank of Manila, and he now calmly requested a meeting with the camp commandant.

The Japanese officer's answer was translated by the interpreter: "The commandant is not yet awake. I don't think he would talk to you anyway."

"The commandant at Santo Tomás always agreed to hear from the committee," Calhoun replied, as if discussing bank business.

"You had better check to see if the commandant won't see me as soon as he is in his office. We have a problem relating to the international rules governing the handling of civilian prisoners during wartime. In the meantime, these men have not slept or eaten, and are in no condition to do any work."

As the internees had learned at Santo Tomás, official Japanese policy allowed—even encouraged—prisoners in camps to elect representatives who would deal directly with the commandant and his staff. The Japanese still dictated the rules such as hours for roll calls, lights-out, curfews, and all security-related matters, but they left the running of the camp to the internees. This administration committee, which was made up of leaders in banking, government, education, and law, represented the internees in negotiations with the commandant, formulated and executed policies pertaining to their welfare, and supervised the operation of departments for the maintenance of the camp, which included allocating living quarters, assigning work details, and other functions.

As Calhoun spoke out on their behalf, the internees stayed slumped on the ground, making no move toward the tools. A work strike was on.

The interpreter excitedly explained the standoff to the officer, who cast threatening looks, then stomped off toward a nearby building.

As the men waited, they tried however they could to shield themselves from the tropical sun that was already beating down on them.

Calhoun was finally summoned to the commandant's office. When he returned, he called several men over and asked them to quietly explain the situation to the rest of the internees in small groups. Calhoun did not want it to look like they were organizing a mass protest, which might ignite a response from the soldiers. What internees soon learned was that their leader had raised three issues, pursuant to the Geneva Conventions: the lack of food and water, being kept outside all night without protection from mosquitoes, and being ordered to build fences to encircle the prison camp, work that was clearly of a military nature and therefore forbidden under the Geneva Conventions.

The commandant, Lieutenant Colonel T. Narusawa of the Imperial Japanese Army, had shown no signs of anger or resentment, and after listening to Calhoun dismissed him without comment. Calhoun didn't know if his protest would result in some sort of reprisals. He asked for a vote as to whether the internees supported the demands he had made. It would be a silent vote. He would ask for a show of hands while he was standing; that would be a vote in favor. When he sat down, any hands that went up were opposed. As Calhoun stood before the internees, virtually every hand went up. When he sat down, no raised hands were seen. With the Japanese watching, they waited another hour, then two.

No direct word ever came from the commandant. Instead, the bags the men had brought with them on the train were released to them, and they were taken into Baker Hall and an adjacent YMCA building, both now vacant except for stacks of canvas cots that had been shipped from Santo Tomás. They were told they would be living there until their barracks were built. The Japanese garrison and executive staff were housed in two nearby administration buildings.

The next day, Filipino workers began to erect the adobe brick barriers that supported large cooking vats covered by a thatched roof. Soon rice was boiling over woodburning fires. Crews of local workers also began building the barracks, and Japanese soldiers from a training camp arrived to dig postholes and start putting up barbed-wire fencing.

The men saw no reason to celebrate, but they knew that their work strike had been at least partially successful. A large number of them were ordered to do excavation work in advance of the construction, but after a few weeks, they were replaced by local laborers. They all then turned their attention to making the new camp as livable as possible. They built shelves and storage bins for the main cooking area, and footlockers where they could store their meager belongings. An available area was cleared and neat rows hoed in fertile soil for a large camp garden, and seeds—such as string beans, corn, tomatoes, squash, pepper, and eggplant—purchased from Filipinos, were planted and watered.

On May 31, 1943, Alex Calhoun and the other four committee members were called before an Imperial Japanese Army colonel—the director of general affairs for the prison camps in Luzon—who had arrived for a tour. Colonel Utunomiya spoke English as well as Calhoun.

"At the outbreak of the war, I was stationed in Brazil, where I was interned with the diplomatic corps," explained Utunomiya. "I received reports about the treatment accorded inside Japanese internment camps in America. It was with a great deal of regret that I learned their treatment is not in accord with the standards due to civilian internees.

"I need not repeat to you the causes of the war or why you are in this camp today. We shall continue to press the war to its conclusion until we have brought your government to its knees. I want you to feel assured of the continuance of your fair treatment under the magnanimity of the Japanese, no matter how long the war may last. You are especially fortunate to have Colonel Narusawa as the commandant of the camp. He was selected for this post because of his understanding and sympathy.

"I hope that you will continue to care for your health and improve the camp so that when your friends and families arrive from Santo Tomás you may all live as happily as is possible under the circumstances."

Through the summer and fall of 1943, the men continued to prepare Los Baños. The grounds, which had dissolved into muck during the summer rainy season, were green and leafy again. Everything was clean and newly built, and they didn't have to deal with the overcrowding they had experienced at Santo Tomás.

An allotment of uncooked rice in hundred-pound sacks was distributed by the Japanese, and prepared by internees in the cooking vats. The daily diet was supplemented with fresh vegetables from the camp garden, which was soon growing lush. The commandant also allowed the internees to run their own canteen. Calhoun used his banking connections to set up loans from the Red Cross and other charities to stock the canteen with various fresh foods that internees could purchase with their own money. Throughout 1943, whether internees had money or not, no one at Los Baños was starving. The breakfast from the camp kitchen—everyone took it back to their barracks to eat because there was no outside seating area—consisted of a coarsely ground cornmeal with coconut milk, and twice a week there was a spoon of raw sugar and ersatz coffee made from grain. Lunch was rice with either squash or mungo beans, and for supper usually a vegetable stew, sometimes flavored with bits of pork or carabao meat, rice, and occasionally a piece of fruit, usually a banana.

The original plan was for Los Baños to house up to seven thousand prisoners—including everyone interned at Santo Tomás—but those plans were scaled back to a projected two to three thousand. In all, more than twenty barracks resembling elongated Philippine huts were built. Single-story, wooden frames held up woven-bamboo sides and thatched roofs. Down the center of each was a dirt aisle that turned muddy whenever it rained, which was often during seasonal monsoons.

On either side of the aisle were bed platforms made of rattan slats. Each barracks, about 150 feet long and twenty-five feet wide, was divided into cubicles that could accommodate up to a hundred internees. The cubicles, with wooden-plank floors, were open to the center aisle; however, the view into adjoining cubicles was blocked by sawali partitions that stopped two feet above the ground, seemingly the only nod to privacy. Electricity ran to each barracks and bare lightbulbs provided minimal illumination. The barracks were constructed in pairs, parallel to one another. Each pair was joined in the middle by shared toilet and shower facilities; separate for men and women, with six cold-water showers and six toilets in each. With no partitions in the bathrooms or showers, it was said: "If you want privacy, shut your eyes."

View of nipa-style barracks for internees at Los Baños Internment Camp. *Courtesy American Historical Collection, Rizal Library, Ateneo de Manila University.*

The Japanese discarded their original plans for modern plumbing that included flush toilets and instead went with communal outhouses set over earthen ditches. This rudimentary concept was improved upon by a former civil service worker, George Messinger, who had built facilities at the Cavite shipyards before the war. The system he designed had a trough lined with sheets of galvanized iron, over which was laid a long plank. The plank had six circular holes, complete with seat covers. A twenty-gallon storage tank located at one end of the trough had a float inside, and whenever it reached a certain level (usually about hourly), a gush of water flowed into the trough, washing the contents down a five-degree incline into a cement septic tank at the other end. Each pair of barracks had their own septic tank and water-storage system.

Following the practice begun at Santo Tomás, the administration committee required every internee at Los Baños to work several hours a day for the good of the camp community. Some worked in areas in which they had experience, such as carpentry and plumbing, while others took on jobs they had never before performed, such as digging ditches, sweeping barracks, gardening, and cleaning lavatories. Departments were established to run the camp's internal operations, much like any municipality in America. The internees handled most everything that had to do with their daily lives. The departments included administration, medical, food preparation, grounds maintenance, social services, construction, and sanitation, which alone employed a hundred and fifty men. There were usually no more than a dozen exemptions from work granted, and most were temporary and due to illness.

The Japanese garrison at the camp maintained a strength of between a hundred and fifty to two hundred soldiers. Most were lower-ranked enlisted men, with a sprinkling of sergeants and officers; there were young recruits and older veterans, some assigned to guard duty while recovering from wounds, and a contingent of Formosans mixed in with Japanese. They were all in the service of the emperor's war machine.

After a couple of months, work was completed on two fences that encircled the entire camp, with approximately ten feet of barren ground between them. The outer fence was eight feet tall and covered with sawali matting to block the view from inside or outside the camp, and it was topped with rolled barbed wire. The four-foot inner fence had several strands of heavy wire strung between posts.

Soldiers with long rifles* walked back and forth inside and outside the fences. Much of the underbrush and tall grasses had been cut away for a distance beyond the outer fence. At strategic points, fortified guard posts with mounted machine guns and tall gun towers had been built. On-duty sentries numbered about thirty to forty at any given time on round-the-clock shifts; there were usually never fewer than two soldiers to any post, sometimes up to four.

There had not yet been any escape attempts at Los Baños.

After six months of work to prepare and organize the new camp, things were running smoothly by the end of 1943. Although the barracks were already decaying—the roofs leaked and the support posts were infested with termites—the internees agreed that the tranquil rural setting and living conditions at the camp were better than those at Santo Tomás.

The men waited eagerly for their wives, families, and friends to join them.

MARGARET SHERK WAS NOT IN THE FIRST GROUP OF WOMEN SENT to Los Baños. Two hundred women, single and married without children, went from Santo Tomás in December 1943. The next opportunity for families to transfer came in April 1944, and Margaret had conflicted feelings about it.

After the sign-up notices went up around Santo Tomás, Margaret went into a kind of trance for days. She well remembered Jerry telling her, a year earlier, "If you ever get a chance to come, I'll be waiting for you." But so much had happened since then, and she

---

* The Arisaka Type 38 bolt-action rifle was the standard rifle issued to the Japanese infantry. Supplied by a five-round box magazine, the Arisaka was four feet two inches in length—the longest infantry rifle used in World War II. A twenty-inch bayonet provided added reach when bayonet fighting; however, the average Japanese infantryman stood about five feet, three inches, and often had difficulty in handling such a long weapon in close-quarters fighting against U.S. troops.

wondered if he still felt the same. Even some of Jerry's close friends advised against her transferring because they had their own concerns that he might not honor his commitment to her under the circumstances. Hearing this from his friends added to her concern.

On Jerry's last night at Santo Tomás, after he had moved Margaret and David to the landing and the boy went to sleep, they had talked about their feelings for each other. What Margaret had long believed would never happen to her *had* happened: she deeply loved a man other than her husband, and a man who might never be her husband. She knew it would not be an easy path to follow, but she believed their love for each other would be worth the pain. That night, before they made love for the first time, they had discussed like level-headed adults the possibility of her becoming pregnant. Like most women in camp, she had begun to miss her menstrual periods, due to poor diet, stress, and weight loss. With sporadic and irregular cycles, pregnancy seemed unlikely, especially because Margaret and Jerry would have only the one night together. Still, Jerry had made a declaration that melted her heart. "If we do have a child," he said, "we'll be just that much ahead of the rest of the people in here." She knew he meant being ahead of others on their way to a postwar life together: having their own child—marriage—raising a family. She agreed with him and fell into his arms.

A month after Jerry left, Margaret knew she was pregnant. She waited another two months before she told her closest woman friend at Santo Tomás, and longer before she allowed a camp doctor to examine her. Feeling like a scarlet woman, she did everything she could to hide her pregnancy and avoid all the predictable questions. "Who is the father?" "What will he do about it?" "Will he marry you?" "*What about your husband?*" Also, the Japanese had a no-babies policy aimed at curbing the population of their prison camps. What would *they* do when they found out she was pregnant? Fathers of babies conceived in internment had been warned they would be punished, and several had already been thrown in jail.

The possibility that had seemed remote and romantic their one night together now felt much different. She alone would be appearing in front of an audience of thousands, many of whom would look on her with pity as well as disdain. She hated the idea of being a spectacle and kept her pregnancy a secret for as long as possible.

She knew there were two men she had to tell. The first letter she wrote was to her husband, Bob, who had been captured at Bataan and was being held at Cabanatuan POW camp sixty miles north of Manila. By then, they had been able to exchange a couple of notes, in which they both tried to be optimistic and hopeful. She had told him about her "new friend, Jerry," and how he had helped her and David. Now she knew she had to tell Bob *everything*: her love for Jerry and that she was pregnant with his child. Bob was the last person she wanted to hurt, and she knew he would be devastated. On top of that: he was a military POW, no doubt fighting to stay alive. But she felt he deserved the whole story from her before he heard it from someone else. Other women in Santo Tomás were writing to their husbands at Cabanatuan, and there was a chance they would spread the news. While trying to convey how sorry she felt about hurting him, she feared her words sounded trite. She promised to get a divorce "as quietly as possible," if and when they were ever liberated.

She next wrote to Jerry. Letters between Santo Tomás and Los Baños were carried by a rickety bus that made regular trips between the camps. All the internees were careful about what they said because censors read the mail. In his return note, Jerry wrote: "I love you. Keep your chin up." After that, his letters had been far apart. Then the bus broke down, and there were no more runs, and no more letters.

Margaret had received Bob's response after a few months. She fully expected a bitter and angry reply, and she knew she deserved it. Instead, he wrote what she thought must be one of the most beautiful love letters ever written. It was a letter she felt she did *not* deserve. He reiterated his love for her, promised to accept and raise the baby as if it were his own, and said he did not want a divorce. While his letter reinforced her belief that she had married a wonderful man, Margaret had made her choice, and there was no going back. She was no longer the woman she had once been. Jerry was in her heart, and she wanted to be with him. If he no longer felt the same, then she would raise their child alone.

What Bob gave her with his forgiveness was a new inner strength; what the rest of the world thought about her didn't matter so much anymore.

Margaret traded for some pink and blue embroidery thread and yarn, and knitted booties and a baby sweater. She also acquired a small wooden box to use as a bassinet. For diapers, she cut narrow, oblong strips out of cotton bird's-eye fabric that a friend gave her for the baby. Feeding the baby was her major concern, as she had no idea if she would be able to nurse. With David, she had been able to nurse for only three months before her milk dried up. And for this pregnancy while in captivity, she would gain only seven pounds.

After leaving David in the care of a good friend, she was taken to a Manila hospital after Christmas. Gerry Ann was born on the morning of January 23, 1944. When she awoke from sedation, Margaret's first view of her baby was at once joyous and heartrending. She was beautiful and perfect but tiny and thin; she looked to Margaret like a starved baby bird.

Two weeks later, Margaret returned to Santo Tomás with her baby. To her relief, the Japanese never questioned her about the father's identity. She was still too weak and wobbly to climb the stairs to the landing, so she settled back in at the Annex. Only a few friends knew that Jerry Sams was the baby's father, but that didn't matter anymore. People could talk about her behind her back if they wanted to. Everyone who saw Gerry Ann said she was *so beautiful.*

When the list for volunteers to move to Los Baños was posted in April, Margaret still hadn't been able to let Jerry know the baby had been born. His last note to her before the truck stopped running between the camps had been rather terse and businesslike, so she didn't know where she stood with him anymore. Maybe he wasn't interested in having a married woman with two children descend on him. And frankly, she couldn't much blame him if he did feel that way.

She ultimately decided to sign up to go to Los Baños because she thought she and her children had a better chance of surviving captivity in a rural setting than in the center of Manila, especially when it came to the availability of food. She had heard reports of Los Baños being located in a prime agricultural area; surely, that would bode well for them.

Administrative control over Santo Tomás and the other civilian prison camps had passed from a civilian department known as the Japanese Bureau of External Affairs to the War Prisoners Department of the Imperial Japanese Army. No one knew for certain, but it was likely there would be new restrictions coming now that they were under the control of an army known for its ruthlessness, especially with the war now going badly for the Japanese.

Since a new second-in-command, Army warrant officer Sadaaki Konishi, arrived at Santo Tomás, there had been steep reductions in food for the prisoners. Staples such as rice, wheat, bread, eggs, produce, fruit, even those products sold through the camp canteen to internees, were being reduced by up to 50 percent. It seemed so unnecessary as to be punitive, and the internees' committee made countless appeals, but they never got anywhere. The number of daily roll calls had doubled recently, and there were more guards patrolling with bayonets affixed to their rifles.

One day, dozens of trucks pulled into Santo Tomás carrying Japanese soldiers and hundreds of relief kits from the Red Cross. The boxes were dumped in piles on the ground, and Margaret watched in disbelief as a soldier went along stabbing his bayonet through tins of powdered milk, which spilled out on the ground. She had been able to hoard a few cans for her children, but all signs pointed to this being a good time for them to leave.

Margaret and her children were among more than three hundred men, women, and children loaded into troop trucks early on the morning of April 7, 1944. They drove as a caravan south for several hours over rough and pitted roads, bouncing and swaying with nothing to hold on to except one another. Even as the scenery changed from crowded, urban sprawl to picturesque, wide-open countryside, Margaret's mind was elsewhere. She steeled herself for what she might find at Los Baños. Would Jerry be waiting to greet her when they arrived? If not, she decided, his absence would answer all of her questions. She wouldn't go looking for him; she wouldn't push herself and the children on him.

As the procession passed under the Los Baños Agricultural College archway, two Japanese guards, rifles tipped with bayonets at their sides and scowls on their faces, held open the crude wooden gate. As she carried Gerry Ann in her arms, someone helped David down from the truck. She stood on solid ground for the first time in hours.

When the truck motors were turned off, everything went utterly silent. Then Margaret heard the cheers, shouts, whistles, and calls rising from a crowd of internees across a field. She recognized several of them, and smiled and waved halfheartedly. Jerry was not among them.

As some of the new arrivals moved to join the others, Margaret stood still. She decided she would wait for the others to go before she slipped off with her son and baby to find their new home.

Then she looked up and saw Jerry standing next to a truck. He was grinning widely, and his arms were open.

She did the first thing that came to mind and handed him Gerry Ann. Holding the baby in his arms, he looked down with wonder and disbelief. Then his three-month-old daughter stuck out her tongue.

Jerry howled with delight.

At that moment, Margaret was ashamed that she had ever doubted him.

# FOUR

# Sky Soldiers

THE 11TH AIRBORNE DIVISION, ACTIVATED IN FEBRUARY 1943 at Camp Mackall, North Carolina, was one of five U.S. Army airborne divisions in World War II and the only one that would see action in the Pacific.

Airborne divisions were structured similarly to other divisions except they were scaled down for quicker deployment and greater mobility. While infantry divisions operated with heavy artillery, armored tanks, and up to fifteen thousand men, the parachute divisions had half that manpower and fought with only light weapons that could be dropped with them from aircraft.

The German military pioneered the use of large-scale airborne forces during the invasions of France and Belgium in 1940, and their success is what led the United States and Britain to form their own. One of the first U.S. airborne assaults of the war, carried out by the 82nd Airborne Division in Sicily in July 1943, was disastrous. Paratroopers were scattered great distances from each other over hostile terrain, and many men were killed as a result. This caused General Dwight Eisenhower to decide that large-scale airborne assaults were too difficult to manage in combat, and he was prepared to break up the parachute divisions into smaller units.

Army chief of staff George Marshall persuaded Eisenhower not to make any decision about division-size airborne forces until there could be additional training followed by a large-scale maneuver. This took place in December 1943 in Knollwood, North Carolina, with a three-day war game that became known as the Knollwood Maneuver. It succeeded in changing Eisenhower's mind about the effectiveness of airborne assaults.

The idea of armed forces dropping from the sky was not new. Benjamin Franklin envisioned "sky soldiers" as early as the late eighteenth century, shortly after Louis-Sébastien Lenormand recorded the first public parachute jump off an observatory tower with a wood-framed, cloth-umbrella contraption he had designed. The Frenchman intended for *le parachute,* which he named from the Greek *para* (against) and the French *chute* (fall), to be used to help people escape from burning buildings.

The basic premise for the military application of airborne forces is that they come out of nowhere with such speed and stealth that no credible defense can be mounted against them. The downside is that they aren't able to arrive with heavy weapons, so the tactical advantage of surprise cannot be held for long against superior numbers unless supplies and reinforcements arrive soon.

When formed, the 11th Airborne, comprised of 8,300 men, was divided into three regiments. Two regiments—the 187th and 188th Glider Infantry Regiments—were trained to be deployed in gliders towed by aircraft. The nearly two thousand men of the division's third regiment, the 511th Parachute Infantry Regiment (PIR), were the paratroopers of the 11th Airborne. A number of smaller units, such as airborne engineers, airborne artillery, parachute maintenance, medical, and headquarters company, were also part of the division.

Volunteers for the 511th came from all over the United States, and volunteering was the *only* way to become an Army paratrooper. Most of the men were straight out of civilian life, often newly graduated from high school with no military training. They were made to pass tough physical tests such as running up Mount Currahee, a steep two-thousand-foot peak at Camp Toccoa, Georgia, in a specified time. The young men who made the grade physically had usually been high school or college athletes. Each applicant was given a battery of written tests and had to pass the Army IQ test with a score of not less than 110—the same score required for acceptance to Officer Candidate School.

Those selected were put through thirteen weeks of airborne basic training, followed by six weeks of jump school. Enlisted men and officers alike were required to make five practice parachute jumps from various heights. Pausing even momentarily in the aircraft's open doorway meant expulsion from jump school. While the dropout rate was high, there was never a shortage of volunteers. After graduation, the soldiers proudly wore the Parachutist Badge, referred to as "Jump Wings," on their paratrooper two-piece dress uniform with trousers bloused into new, shiny jump boots. They received an extra fifty dollars each month in jump pay, a windfall for a private making seventy dollars a month.

Earning "Jump Wings." *U.S. Army Signal Corps.*

These stringent qualifications and the arduous training convinced the 511th's first commanding officer, Lieutenant Colonel Orin Haugen—given the semi-affectionate nickname of "Hard Rock"—

that his men were the "cream of the crop" and represented the Army's finest group of volunteers.

Major General Joseph Swing, a 1915 West Point graduate, was in command of the 11th Airborne. That 1915 class—known as "The Class the Stars Fell On"—included future top wartime generals Dwight Eisenhower, Omar Bradley, Roscoe Woodruff, and James Van Fleet. Swing had surpassed them all in class ranking, finishing in the top 25 percent. Of the 164 graduates in the Class of 1915, sixty-one (or 37 percent) went on to attain the rank of general officer, a West Point record that will likely not be broken.

Joseph Swing, commanding general, 11th Airborne Division. *U.S. Army Signal Corps.*

After graduation, Swing married the daughter of General Peyton C. March, whose aide he was in France during World War I. In his younger days, Swing, who served in the horse-drawn artillery of the era, was considered one of the Army's best polo players, and most career officers with a future played polo during the country-club doldrums between world wars. Although by the 1940s he still had an affinity for horses and the former mounted officers who rode them, Swing was now "all airborne." Special dispensations were made for generals when it came to the rigors and dangers of jump training.* However, after Swing watched his men learn how to jump,

---

* Maxwell Taylor and Matthew Ridgway, commanding generals of the famed 101st and 82nd Airborne Divisions, respectively, each made only one practice parachute jump before taking part in the airborne assault at Normandy on D-Day.

tuck, and roll off platforms, he made five parachute jumps himself in five days with only a few hours training, earning his Jump Wings just like his men.

Swing was determined to prove that paratroopers were the world's most elite and versatile fighters. To that end, he pushed the 11th Airborne hard in training. As a commanding general in combat, he would be aggressive while rarely making a snap judgment or acting with false bravado. He always seemed to have deconstructed any possible problem, which he could then resolve swiftly because he knew the alternatives.

Although Swing was nearly fifty years old, he still had a lean, whipcord-straight carriage on his six-foot frame. With his prematurely white hair, tanned complexion, and Roman nose, his commanding presence was enhanced by a strong, square jaw and crystalline-blue eyes that could flash in fury or gleam mischievously. He had none of the affectations of rank, and he spoke to officers and enlisted men in the same direct manner. He could handle a spirited horse better than any general officer in the Army, and curse as colorfully as his paratroopers.

While the 11th Airborne was still training in North Carolina, its top intelligence officer was critically injured during a practice jump. This is a key staff position in an Army division, known as G-2, which not only supervises a significant part of the training to prepare for combat, but during battle is responsible for the collection and dissemination of combat intelligence. When the division's personnel people shuffled through their files looking for a replacement, they found only one officer in the 11th Airborne who had completed the postgraduate course at the Army's prestigious Command and General Staff College at Fort Leavenworth that prepared officers to serve as G-2s. His name: Major Henry J. Muller Jr.

Muller was twenty-six years old and a native of Santa Barbara, California. He had graduated from UCLA in 1939 with a degree in geology, a field he never worked in because he had also taken

ROTC and he soon accepted a commission in the U.S. Army. Two months after Pearl Harbor, Muller was one of the first to volunteer for the new parachute divisions being formed. After attending jump school at Fort Benning and completing the G-2 course, he had been assigned to the 511th Parachute Infantry Regiment.

A division's G-2 position was usually filled by an older and experienced ("mature," in the Army lexicon) lieutenant colonel, but with no other viable candidates, Swing went ahead and interviewed Muller. It didn't help that the slender, dapper Muller looked younger than his age as he stood stiffly before the gimlet-eyed general who questioned him about his civilian education and military training.

Then the general asked, "How old are you, Major?"

"Twenty-six, sir."

Following a long pause, during which Swing stared at Muller dubiously while drumming his fingers on the top of his desk, the general asked, "How long have you been a major?"

"One week, sir."

The oak leaf cluster on Muller's collar was as shiny as a new penny.

There was another long pause, icy stare, and renewed drumming.

"Tell you what I'm going to do," Swing finally said. "I'm going to make you *acting* G-2, at least until I can find someone more experienced. I want you to get started right away. I'll call your regimental commander and tell him of your reassignment. Any questions?"

"No, sir." Muller saluted and left the office.

Understanding what a general meant when he said "right away," Muller went down the corridor to the division's G-2 office and told the surprised members of the section that he was the new G-2. "Be sure to put *acting* in front of my job title," he cautioned them.

Finding his desk, he sat down in front of an overflowing in-box and went to work.

Swing made it a custom to take periodic, unannounced walking tours of his division's area during their training. He had a sharp eye for any kind of dereliction, and an equally sharp tongue with loud reprimands. He always brought along one of his staff officers who was to make note of any infraction of order or discipline, and follow up with the appropriate unit commander. Swing didn't ask Muller to join him for the walk for a month, but one day he stuck his head into Muller's office and barked, "Major. Come with me."

The general was out the front door before Muller could get his cap on straight. It was not easy keeping up with Swing's pace—somewhere between quick time and double time. The general said he wanted to see the new obstacle course being built by the division's engineers. When they got there, it was deserted but did appear to be completed. The first obstacle they saw was a long sawdust pit with a tangle of barbed wire above it. Next came a wooden wall, which trainees would have to get over by pulling themselves up on ropes. Then they came to an earthen incline. When they reached the top, they looked down and were taken aback at how high above the ground they were standing.

"This seems too high," Swing said. "What do you think, Major?"

"I agree, General," Muller said. "It certainly appears to be too high."

After a second or two, Swing announced, "I'm not at all sure about this. You're young and jump-qualified, Major. Could you jump off something this high?"

Muller knew if he responded with something like "No, sir, I don't think so," it would display doubt in his own abilities. Instead, he stepped to the edge of the parapet and leaped out into space. It was a long way down, and when he hit the ground—with his best landing position and front tumble as trained—the shock was jarring. Muller saw flashes of light dance before his eyes and felt sharp pains in his legs and ankles.

"Well?" Swing asked, looking down at the prone Muller.

"General—just as we thought—too high. If we send men off this jump, we'll have lots of broken ankles and legs."

"When we get back, tell the engineer I want to see him."

When Muller brought Lieutenant Colonel Douglas C. Davis, commander of the division's engineer battalion, into Swing's office, the general opened up on him with a fusillade.

"Dammit, Doug, are you sure you got those measurements right on the ramp? It is so high we'll break every leg in the division!"

"It's the prescribed height, sir. It's just not finished."

"Not finished?" Swing asked.

"No, sir. We're going to install firemen poles for the men to slide down into a sawdust pit. The poles are on order but haven't arrived yet."

Recovering quickly, Swing said, "I see. Well, dammit, put up some tape or signs before someone is tempted to leap off it and get hurt."

After Davis saluted and left, Swing said, "Well, Major, it appears we were a little premature. Are you sure you're all right?"

"Yes, sir. I'm okay."

Muller returned to his office, and minutes later was surprised when Swing's aide said the general wanted to see him again.

As he entered Swing's office, the general looked up from some papers. "Another thing, Hank. You can drop the *acting* in front of G-2."

Not long after, Muller undertook a month-long campaign to convince Swing that the division should have its own reconnaissance platoon to serve as the division's "eyes and ears" in combat, making patrols deep behind enemy lines to determine the whereabouts and strength of opposition forces. Combat intelligence fell under the command of G-2, which meant this platoon would be assigned to Muller.

Muller asked for volunteers to lead the new platoon, and Lieutenant James Polka stepped forward. He was an experienced platoon leader who was devoted to his men, and they to him. He and Muller set up a training regimen that stressed communications and survival. Recon's mission was to bring back valuable information from behind enemy lines, where they would spend most of their time, outnumbered and far removed from reinforcements and supplies. Consequently, they would have to travel stealthily, avoid fights whenever possible, and be self-reliant. If forced into a fight, they had to be deadly efficient. They had to neutralize any threats quickly and silently and get back safely to headquarters with their information. Members of the recon team had to be smart, tough, resourceful, with expertise in compass use, navigation, communications, living off the land for long stretches, and hand-to-hand combat. Recon was open only to volunteers who were unmarried. Muller called them "triple volunteers" because most had volunteered for the Army, and for the paratroopers, and for recon. Of the more than three hundred men who came forward, thirty-five were selected. They were, in Muller's opinion, the best of the best.

The recon platoon soon took on an aura of elitism: cocky, self-confident, courageous, and adventurous paratroopers who embraced the training that would make them even better. Muller made sure the platoon always bivouacked on its own so their training routine wouldn't be interrupted by the more mundane aspects of garrison life. Recon members operated outside the regular chain of command with Muller as their direct superior, and given that he worked for Swing, no questions were asked. It didn't take long before they were dubbed "The Ghost Platoon."

The 11th Airborne spent its last six months stateside training at Camp Polk, Louisiana. Deep in the bayous and backwoods, where pigs and cattle wandered unperturbed among the pup tents, the troopers held maneuvers in the rain and mud, not realizing they would soon be fighting in that same terrain. Although the scuttlebutt for months had them going to Europe, in spring 1944 they received orders to the Pacific.

This concerned Muller because the U.S. Army still knew so little about the Japanese, compared to the Germans. The Army had plenty of German experts who spoke the language and knew how they fought. The Japanese were an enigma; few in the Army could speak their difficult language, much less read and write it. Muller had heard stories about units that engaged with the Japanese only to find that they had suddenly disappeared into the jungle, and the Americans were unable to find them even when they were right on top of them. The war in the Pacific was being fought on unmapped islands covered with dense rain forests, which would make it incredibly difficult even to find, let alone accurately fix, the location of this elusive enemy.

Muller wondered how he was going to gather intelligence against the Japanese. It was a G-2's worst nightmare. Muller understood that the average soldier might not see much of a difference between fighting the Germans and fighting the Japanese; both were dangerous and disciplined foes. But there was a big difference when it came to gaining accurate intelligence for the division's battle plans. His job would have been less complicated if they were facing conventional forces in France, Italy, and Germany, where every landmark, road, river, bridge, and town had been mapped for years.

In April 1944, the division boarded trains for California, where they stayed for a week before the men started loading onto troopships in San Francisco Bay. Just days out to sea, the weather changed abruptly. Gone was the cool, crisp climate of San Francisco, and in its place was the heat of the tropics. Ordered to turn in their woolen uniforms—they would not see them again until after the war—and put on their khakis, the troopers ate Spam sandwiches and fought boredom for the several weeks it took to cross the Pacific.

The SS *Sea Pike*, a Liberty ship carrying the 511th Parachute Infantry Regiment, took twenty-eight days to reach Oro Bay, New Guinea, on the southeast tip of the world's second largest island. Off-loaded onto amphibious craft that came alongside their ship, the paratroopers found their designated camp a few miles away at Buna-Dobodura, a deserted Army Air Corps field. Hundreds of tents went up as quickly as a circus big top.

As they acclimated to the tropical heat and humidity, the division began intensive combat readiness training to learn jungle warfare. They sweated in the jungles and mountains of New Guinea, practiced amphibious operations at Oro Bay, and made several training jumps. For the first time, their training focused on the Japanese. They learned the tactics of the enemy they would face and how to defeat them.

Enlisted men of the 11th Airborne were used by port commanders for off-loading ships and stevedoring duties. In no time, they acquired a reputation for helping themselves to liquor, food, ice cream, ammo, and whatever else struck their fancy. "Joe Swing and his eight thousand thieves" became a common refrain. A bemused Swing halfheartedly came to the defense of his "boys," telling one complaining port commander who was missing supplies: "My angels couldn't possibly be involved in such shenanigans." And that's how the nickname "The Angels of the 11th Airborne" was born.

The heaviest fighting in New Guinea, a country without roads, had taken place in 1943 and early 1944. Though the United States and its allies now controlled the coastlines, Japanese forces were still scattered throughout the heavily jungled mountain range that transected the middle of the island that had a greater landmass than California.

The 11th Airborne, while still conducting jungle training and practice maneuvers at Oro Bay, was being held in reserve for one of the last major operations of the New Guinea campaign—thereby qualifying for a campaign battle star—but were never called into the fight.

While in New Guinea, Muller received a message from General MacArthur's headquarters ordering him to report to Brisbane, Australia, for a two-week orientation on intelligence operations in the Southwest Pacific. Privately, he really wanted to see Australia, and Swing appeared to have read his mind, declaring the trip a "boondoggle." Swing had no confidence in MacArthur's chief of intelligence, Brigadier General Charles Willoughby. Muller would eventually hear from other staff officers that Swing and Willoughby were bitter enemies dating back to prewar days. Nevertheless, this order came from MacArthur, and it wasn't an invitation Muller could turn down, so off he went in a C-47 transport to Port Moresby, where he caught a flight on a well-appointed Australian amphibious commercial aircraft to Brisbane.

Muller had grown increasingly confident about being able to gather intelligence against their enemy. A ten-man Nisei language team had been attached to the 11th Airborne; these first-generation Japanese Americans could read, write, and speak like native Japanese. Next came a counterintelligence team, a photo-interpretation detachment, and two order-of-battle specialists who had studied the Imperial Japanese Army and knew how it was organized and how it fought.

Now in Brisbane, Muller was exposed to a larger world of military intelligence. He spent days in the translator and interpreter section, where he observed specialists going through piles of captured documents and interrogating Japanese prisoners of war. A gold mine of information had already been gathered about the enemy. One example looked like a four-hundred-page phone book. Found in a beached Japanese lifeboat, it contained the entire roster of Imperial Japanese Army officers with their names, ranks, and unit assignments. Translated editions were being distributed to the intelligence officers in every tactical unit in the theater. They would only have to acquire the name of any officer from a prisoner or document and check it against the roster to identify the military unit confronting them. It was an easy next step—through the existing order-of-battle manual that had been put together detailing the strength of all the units in the Japanese Army—to determine its size and capabilities.

In another section, Muller was shown maps of Japan's home islands, which showed the locations of each factory that was producing war materials. Much of this information was obtained from an analysis of the nameplates from downed aircraft and ships, and captured weapons and other equipment. The Japanese had obligingly put the name and location of the factories on the nameplates, along with the date and serial number of each item, which permitted analysts to determine the rate of production of various plants. Once the United States had air bases that put long-range bombers within striking distance, it could use this information to destroy the heart of Japan's military-industrial complex.

Muller found the geographical section equally encouraging because of its impressive compilation of maps ranging from New Guinea to the Philippines, and many of the islands in between. Utilizing existing maps, aerial photography, and even old *National Geographic* magazines, they had prepared reports on potential areas of operations, covering terrain, weather, roads, rivers, landing beaches, tides, forests, and other basic information. Each report was illustrated with photographs collected in Australia, England, and the United States from tourists, missionaries, and businessmen who had visited or lived in these areas before the war.

On his last day in Brisbane, Muller was ordered to report to Willoughby for an exit interview. Over the past two weeks, Muller had gotten the impression that the intelligence chief—although described as "somewhat of a character"—was admired and respected by his G-2 staff. Muller was eager to meet the man who some people had already concluded had more influence on the course of the Pacific war than anyone other than MacArthur, who was thought to be so indispensable to the U.S. war effort that President Franklin Roosevelt had ordered him to leave his command at Corregidor in March 1942 and travel by PT boat and aircraft to Australia.

Shown into Willoughby's office, Muller was alone with the trim, soldierly looking general who towered several inches over six feet. He didn't smile and looked serious, even intense. He did not offer Muller a seat; instead he directed the young officer to "stand at ease."

After a few preliminary questions about his two-week visit, Willoughby asked about Muller's intelligence training; his postgraduate course at Command and General Staff College seemed to score points.

"And how old are you?" asked Willoughby.

*That question again.* "Twenty-six, sir."

This appeared to trouble the general and led to a long silence.

"Do you know how to use a two-way communications pad?"

"Yes, sir, I have been trained to use them and have practiced with them on some maneuvers."

A two-way pad filled with letters and numbers was a simple but secure method that let two individuals—holders of identical pads—communicate privately in code. Each pair of pads was unique, and no others existed with the same exact code.

Sometime during the coming campaign, Willoughby went on, he might communicate with Muller using a two-way pad, which Muller would be given before returning to his division. "Keep it locked in your field safe and don't identify me as the holder of the matching pad."

"Yes, sir. I understand."

"Sometime during future operations, you may receive a message directly from me, using our two-way pad. It will begin with the words 'Crystal Ball States.' What follows will be a report of coming enemy activity. You must believe it absolutely. You must not question it or inquire back for further details. Most importantly, you must not reveal the source of the report to anyone. Now, repeat what I just told you."

Muller repeated the general's explicit instructions.

"Very well," Willoughby said. "Now do you have any questions?"

"Well, sir—only one. Will my division commander know about this and be aware of the source of a 'Crystal Ball' report?'"

"No!" the intelligence chief exploded. "No, he will not! Only you will know that it comes from me. If something happens to you, I will brief your replacement. Is there anything else?"

Stammering a bit, Muller pointed out something Willoughby

certainly knew, that all military intelligence reports were evaluated both as to content and source. "If the report of a coming enemy action is significant," Muller said, "General Swing will want to know the source."

"Of course he will, and you'll have to contrive one. You'll have to use your imagination and intelligence to devise something logical."

"Yes, sir."

Then the meeting was over, and Muller was given his two-way communications pad. Soon he was on a plane back to New Guinea. For days, he remained troubled by his meeting with General Willoughby.

What would be so vital that he, a young major, would get a direct message from MacArthur's intelligence chief? And what could possibly be so important that he had been ordered to lie to his commanding general?


TERRY SANTOS WAS A PERFECT FIT FOR THE ALAMO SCOUTS.

An elite program organized in New Guinea in late 1943, the Alamo Scouts were trained to conduct reconnaissance and fast-hitting raids in the Southwest Pacific. The unit had been the brainchild of Lieutenant General Walter Krueger, commander of the U.S. Sixth Army, who believed that small teams of highly trained volunteers operating deep behind Japanese lines could provide valuable intelligence in advance of large-scale operations.

The Alamo Scouts' first mission was in February 1944 and was conducted by a six-man team that went ashore in the Admiralty Islands two hundred miles north of New Guinea. After learning the strength and disposition of Japanese forces, the team was evacuated by seaplane. A successful U.S. landing followed. Since then, before each major landing of U.S. forces, Alamo Scouts were put ashore by seaplane, submarine, or rubber boats for preinvasion reconnaissance.

Santos was born in Honolulu, and he had lost both his parents to a fire in a sugarcane field when he was just a year old. His father had been Filipino, born in Luzon, and his mother part Filipino, from Hawaii. Raised by an aunt and uncle in San Francisco, he grew up speaking Tagalog and English. He was working as a busboy when the Pearl Harbor attack happened, and two weeks later he had signed up at an Army recruiting station. He was ordered to Fort Benning, Georgia, shortly after New Year's. Following thirteen weeks of basic training, he was assigned to the 1st Filipino Infantry Regiment, a segregated U.S. Army unit made up of Filipino Americans based at Camp Beale, California. The regiment would become a major source of manpower for special forces in the Pacific.

After three months, Santos volunteered for the paratroopers. At five-foot-seven, he nearly failed the airborne physical for being two pounds under the required hundred and thirty. The doctor agreed to pass him if Santos promised to gain some weight. He was sent to Camp Toccoa, where he spent his days running Mount Currahee— three miles up and three miles down—on his own. (Instead of gaining weight, he lost five pounds.)

The airborne divisions were still being activated, and after two weeks Santos grew tired of running and waiting. He answered a call for volunteers for a "special unit" that turned out to be the Office of Strategic Services (OSS). He was accepted, and joined an OSS contingent for jump school and other courses, including underwater demolition (UDT) training at the naval amphibious base at Little Creek, Virginia. A forerunner to the SEALs, UDT learned how to plant underwater explosives. All the training was in preparation for paramilitary operations the OSS planned to conduct in the Pacific.

Santos shipped out with five other OSS-trained operators on an old World War I destroyer that seemed to rise and fall with every wave. The ship was met in New Guinea by an officer from MacArthur's staff, who told them that no OSS activities would be conducted in the Southwest Pacific. Distrustful of OSS director William Donovan and his close ties to Washington brass, MacArthur had decreed that he would retain control over all intelligence gathering in his area. The OSS personnel were released to other units, and that's how Santos, already wearing Jump Wings as a qualified paratrooper, was assigned to the 11th Airborne shortly after its arrival at Oro Bay. Santos, still inclined to volunteer for anything that "sounded exciting," quickly found his way to the recon platoon. Only four members of the 11th Airborne were accepted for Alamo Scouts training, all of them from recon. The twenty-three-year-old Santos, who was officially a corporal but was serving as an acting sergeant in the recon platoon, was one of them.

Terry Santos, lead scout, 11th Airborne Reconnaissance Platoon. *Courtesy Terry Santos.*

Santos entered the fourth Alamo Scouts training class on July 31, 1944.* The training center, also used as a base for the operational teams already in the field, was located midway up the island's rugged northern coastline at Cape Kassoe near Hollandia. The isolated location was ideal for the six-week regimen that included maneuvers and exercises in the sea, on the beach, in the jungle, and in the mountains. This was no basic course— those accepted into the program were assumed to be well-trained soldiers. But what they learned went beyond anything they had ever known.

---

\* Between late 1943 and September 1945, nine Alamo Scouts training classes graduated 325 officers and enlisted men. Of those, 138 were assigned to one of the twelve Alamo Scout teams that conducted 108 missions behind enemy lines. The rest returned to their units to pass their newly learned skills on to others.

The training class was divided into teams that resembled operational teams, with an officer and six to ten enlisted men. The teams remained together unless dropouts made a team too small to function, in which case its members were combined with another team. The class had a dropout rate of nearly 40 percent.

After drawing their equipment—including a first-aid kit, compass, binoculars, machete, rain poncho, canteen, pistol belt, and cartridge pouch—they were taken a mile offshore in a rubber boat, dumped over the side, and told to swim to shore. Anyone who had to be pulled out was dropped that day and sent back to their units.

The training only intensified after that, including a live-fire drill that taught the recruits how to avoid enemy gunfire while in the water. Again everyone went into the water offshore, only this time they were approached by a boat with an instructor holding a submachine gun.

"Duck now!" he yelled seconds before he started firing at them.

They dove down as far and as fast as they could, and seconds later the surface of the water where they had been erupted with bullets.

When the instruction moved onshore, they learned how to use different types of radios and walkie-talkies in case the team's designated radioman was ever knocked out of action. For the same reason, they all learned advanced first aid in the event that a team's medic went down. They were also taught basic Japanese words and phrases so as to make sense out of overheard conversations while on reconnaissance. They learned how to plan a mission from beginning to end, everything from how many men to take to how much food and ammo they needed.

Next they set off into the jungle to learn reconnaissance and patrolling skills. The rule, Santos soon learned, was *go quietly*. That was not easy to do when you were moving through dense foliage. The trick was to go underneath vines and reeds rather than through them, which caused a loud rustling and snapping of branches. The men learned how to move silently in short intervals of five to ten yards at a time, recognizing and avoiding booby traps as they went. For one drill they were blindfolded and told to move through the jungle without being caught. They also learned to use mud, grass, and other natural ways of concealing themselves and blending in.

A team of seasoned Australian special forces along with local native hunters taught the trainees about surviving in the jungle. They pointed out which plants and bugs were edible and showed them a method for tapping drinkable water from vines that grew in the jungle. They also showed them how New Guineans, some of them headhunters, had tracked prey—animals as well as humans—through the jungle for centuries.

Although the Alamo Scouts' main mission was to gather information and report back, they also had to be prepared to fight. Since they would almost always be outnumbered, they had to be able to fight efficiently, quickly, and ruthlessly. The Scouts were given their choice of weapons from a bountiful armory. Carbines were the most popular, especially with the folding wire stock designed for paratroopers, although some men preferred Thompson submachine guns and others liked M1 Garand rifles. M3 .45-caliber "grease guns" were available as well, along with Browning Automatic Rifles (BARs), a handheld machine gun with a twenty-round magazine of .30-06 rounds and an effective range up to fifteen hundred yards. Scouts also carried a sidearm, usually a Colt .45 automatic pistol, as well as a personal knife. And they were also given grenades: the standard Mk 2 fragmentation, the M15 white phosphorus called "Willie Peter," and the AN-M14 incendiary that burned up to two thousand degrees and melted steel.

The Scouts practiced hand-to-hand combat daily. They learned ways to use their hands to bring down, disable, and kill in seconds. Santos, the smallest in his class and the quickest on his feet, excelled at this.

By the fourth week, half of Santos's class had dropped out. They were all able to swim five miles now, and continued to be pushed and tested—physically and mentally—on everything they had learned. A final test of endurance: a twenty-six-mile jungle hike with full packs.

They were now taking everything they had learned and putting it into practice in the jungle. One team would be assigned to disappear and another to go find them. Sometimes, natives were employed as their elusive prey.

For a final test during the last week of training, each team went into an area where Japanese forces were known to be operating in order to get a taste of what they would be facing in their work behind enemy lines.

Inserted into a coastal area, Santos's six-man team went inland about ten miles without seeing anybody. Then, in the soft sand along a riverbank, Santos came across footprints with water seeping into them. He knew they were fresh prints. The team spread out and moved forward silently.

They heard the Japanese patrol before they spotted them.

It was the sound of chopping, then *crack* and *thump*—followed by excited Japanese voices.

Coming in low through the underbrush, the Scouts saw an enemy platoon—of about twenty men—in a small clearing. They had chopped wood to make a fire to boil their afternoon rice. *Rather brazen*, Santos thought. The Scouts could sit and watch them eat or take them out. Even if the Scouts tried to slip away, they might eventually be followed, which could not be allowed. Or they might stumble across the patrol again in a less advantageous position. Given the enemy's larger numbers and increased firepower, the Scouts might not win such a firefight. Santos decided to follow a basic tenet of combat: *he who strikes first, strikes hardest.*

After a few whispered exchanges and hand signals, the Scouts dispersed to set up opposing fields of fire. Some moved to a place where they could engage the enemy troops in a crossfire while keeping a clear field of fire so as not to send rounds into other Scouts. When they sprang the ambush, the fight was not quiet, but it was quick and decisive.

Carrying an M3 submachine gun with a thirty-round clip, Santos turned it sideways so the recoil would not bring the barrel up. Instead, the gun swept to the side on its own. Using short bursts of three or four rounds, he "walked" his blistering fire across the clearing.

The Japanese desperately returned fire, but with rounds coming from all directions fired by unseen shooters, they were confused and their volleys were off target. One by one they fell, dead or mortally wounded.

When it was over, the Scouts drifted out from their cover and went through the clearing kicking bodies to make sure none were playing possum. Then, quickly and without conversing, they dissolved back into the bush and headed away before enemy reinforcements showed up.

Back at camp at week's end, Santos's team was debriefed. The options for what they could have done when they came across the enemy patrol were discussed. Santos said nothing was to be gained by leaving the Japanese soldiers alive to kill Americans another day. The commander of the training center, Major Homer "Red" Williams, finally declared his support for their actions with: "Good job, fellows." To Santos, he added a private aside: "Terry, why do you always find trouble?"

A grinning Santos replied, "Red, trouble always finds me."

Santos could tell that the trainers who had drilled them for the past six weeks were proud that his team had wiped out a larger enemy force without any casualties of their own. It was a historic pregraduation exercise. In the nearly two years the Alamo Scouts Training Center was in operation, no other team in training would engage and kill the enemy during its final exam.

September 9, 1944, was graduation day for Santos's class of

thirty-seven trainees. Of these, thirteen graduates were assigned to operational Scout teams and the rest were returned to their units to teach what they had learned to others.

Santos was one of those chosen for the Scouts, but on the final day he met with Major Williams and said he wanted to return to the 11th Airborne because he had heard the division would soon be part of a big operation he didn't want to miss out on. Williams said he understood, shook his hand, and wished him good luck.

Terry Santos did not want to miss the U.S. Army's return to the Philippines. He was determined to help liberate his father's homeland.

# FIVE

# "You'll Be Eating Dirt"

UPON THEIR ARRIVAL AT LOS BAÑOS INTERNMENT CAMP, Dorothy Still and the other Navy nurses immediately began looking for a place they could turn into a medical facility. They found a pink stucco building that had been the agricultural college's dispensary and set about transforming it into the camp's medical clinic and a twenty-five-bed hospital with four-bed wards and a few private rooms for patients who needed to be isolated. Starting without furniture or even any beds, the nurses found the place stripped to bare walls, with shelves and cupboards missing, too.

The Japanese had not allowed the nurses to bring anything other than a few medical supplies from Santo Tomás, which meant they had to improvise in their new location. They would have to scrounge, jerry-rig, or build whatever the hospital needed. Using an old pedal sewing machine, they turned a bolt of unbleached muslin into bedsheets. The first patients admitted to the hospital had to bring a sleeping cot with them, but soon the carpenters built wooden-slat beds, and laced them with bejuco, a tropical, woody vine. (Similarly constructed beds were built for the new barracks going up.) The same craftsmen built tables and chairs, and fashioned basins, cups, and eating utensils from pieces of corrugated tin.

The nurses concocted a syrup of onion juice and sugar that

soothed hacking coughs, and they made a tea from guava leaves that relieved bacillary dysentery. One of the prisoners had been a pharmaceutical representative before the war, and he figured out a substitute adhesive for homemade dressings and bandages. He tapped sap from a rubber tree growing near the hospital and thinned the thick solution with oil to form a sticky paste. Before putting a dressing on a patient, a nurse dipped a ladle into a jar of the goop, spread a thin line on either side of the wound, then placed a piece of gauze or cloth on top.

Whenever one of the guards was brought in for treatment—the Japansese garrison had no doctor, only a medical orderly who was always seeking the advice of the American nurses—the nurses negotiated a trade for suture materials and medicines, such as sulfanilamide drugs to treat bacterial infections. That was how the nurses acquired for the hospital a surgery table old enough to be in a museum.

The only piece of equipment left over from the old college dispensary was an electric autoclave used to sterilize instruments, but it had shorted out when someone tried cooking rice in it. Fortunately, camp electricians were able to fix it, as well as rewire and repair a gaping hole in the kitchen wall where an electrical outlet had been yanked out.

The front door of the infirmary—a U-shaped building tucked into the camp's northeast corner not far from the main gate—opened into a waiting room that led into a long hallway, off of which were numerous rooms that the nurses turned into examination rooms, a laboratory, a pharmacy, an operating room, an office, and storage space. The kitchen overlooked a weedy front courtyard. Out back was a one-bedroom apartment attached to the rear of the structure. Some of the nurses moved into the small apartment and others into a windowless basement, while Dorothy and a few others settled into a newly built barracks across the street.

The men at the camp were all relatively young and healthy,

so for the first few months the nurses' workload was light. Most of the early admissions to the hospital were for dengue fever and recurring malaria. The nurses were accustomed to being assisted in Navy hospitals by male orderlies, who gave baths, changed sheets, and helped move nonambulatory patients. Anticipating that busier times might loom ahead, they decided to look for likely candidates to volunteer for these chores. Each patient who came into the clinic was judged on the basis of his demeanor, empathy, and enthusiasm. Soon several young men, who clearly liked the idea of being around the nurses—for seven months the only women in Los Baños—were raring to go.

Dorothy was to be their teacher, something she had never been before. One of the nurses had a copy of the *Handbook of the Hospital Corps,* the bible for Navy corpsmen, which Dorothy used as a general guidebook for training. She had to regularly remind herself to simplify some of the book's language for these young men who lacked medical training. Much to her surprise, the classes were a hit, and soon the nurses had an enthusiastic team of trained orderlies working with them.

The camp's medical unit received a setback when its missionary doctor, who had accompanied the nurses from Santo Tomás and was associated with the Rockefeller Institute, made the short list of twenty-seven internees from Santo Tomás and Los Baños who were repatriated to the United States in September 1943 aboard the Swedish liner SS *Gripsholm,* chartered by the U.S. government as a prisoner exchange vessel. That left a Polish doctor, whose doctorate was in chemical research and who headed the camp's sanitation department, as the lone doctor at Los Baños. He wouldn't be of much help in the hospital or clinic. Until another qualified MD arrived, the nurses were on their own.

But soon a burly new physician named Dana Nance arrived. He had been imprisoned in the mountains in northern Luzon at the Baguio Internment Camp since early 1942. He made friends quickly at Los Baños and was soon elected to the internees' committee. He came to his new camp prepared, carrying an ax in one hand and a baseball bat in the other. Both would be put to good use, as he would become one of the camp's best woodchoppers and a star in its softball league.

Nance had a boyish grin that made him appear younger than his thirty-eight years. With thick hair combed back without a part, he bore more than a passing resemblance to tough-guy actor James Cagney. He was born in Nashville, Tennessee, but grew up in China, where his Methodist missionary father was cofounder and president of Soochow University. One of three sons—his two brothers also became doctors—Dana was home-educated through high school by his mother, an avowed agnostic and devotee of Chinese culture and arts. He was inspired by an American missionary doctor with a practice in Suzhou both to pursue medicine as a career and to live abroad as an expatriate.

Nance earned his MD at Vanderbilt in 1929 and interned at a hospital in New Orleans, where he met Anna Boatner, a recent Wellesley graduate from a prominent Louisiana family. They were married in 1931 and soon left the United States for Nance's new post as a public health doctor in Manila. In 1934, they moved to Shanghai, where he opened a surgery practice that catered to foreigners and wealthy Chinese. In 1937, when the Japanese bombed Shanghai in the opening days of their invasion of China, Nance spent seventy-two hours at the hospital patching up survivors. Dana and Anna stayed on even after Shanghai fell to the Japanese, as life for many in the expatriate enclave went on as usual for a time.

In January 1941, after the U.S. State Department ordered women and children dependents of American citizens to leave China, Anna sailed for New Orleans with their three children. That summer, Nance accepted a position as chief medical officer of a mining company based in the Philippines, which he thought was safer from the threat of war since it was under U.S. protection. Nance hoped his family would soon join him, but then came Pearl Harbor and the Japanese invasion of the Philippines. He was sent to the Baguio Internment Camp, where he assumed a leadership role as head of that camp's committee and medical director, helping set up the hospital and overseeing several other physicians, until the Japanese decided his services were required at Los Baños.

Dr. Dana Nance and his wife, Anna, at the tenth reunion of his Vanderbilt Medical School class in Nashville, Tennessee, 1939. They were on a six-month leave from his Shanghai surgical practice. *Courtesy Vanderbilt University Special Collections and University Archives.*

The nurses who were staying in the hospital's attached apartment cleared out and relocated to the barracks across the street so Nance could move in. They were pleased to have not only the new physician but also the medicines and equipment he brought with him, including his own set of surgical instruments. Stainless-steel scalpels with a variety of blade shapes; large and small scissors, curved and straight; hemostats for clamping blood vessels; forceps in a variety of shapes; probes for dissecting and separating tissues—all finely crafted instruments. They would soon be put to use because this broad-shouldered doctor whose hand-eye coordination allowed him to swing a bat and ax with power also had the fine and precise motor skills required of a skilled surgeon. And as the nurses soon learned, the affable Dr. Nance, who kept his scalpels sharp with a honing stone and leather strop, *loved* to cut.

The first appendectomy performed at Los Baños was not done on an internee but on a Japanese civilian who worked in the commandant's office. Summoned by some guards, Nance found the man in pain from a "hot appendix." The Japanese were considering moving him to a hospital in Manila, a rough road trip Nance said would most likely result in his death from a burst appendix.

"Let me operate," he said.

The commandant thought it over for several hours before deciding to put his valued assistant in the hands of the brash, internee surgeon.

At the hospital, Nance and three nurses scrubbed for surgery. One of the nurses handled the ether can; the powerful liquid anesthetic was administered by dropping it onto a gauze mask placed over the patient's mouth and nose. The other two assisted Nance, one next to him and the other opposite him.

It was a hot, humid night, but that was not the only reason for Nance and the nurses to sweat as he made his initial incision in the man's lower abdomen. They had been warned that if the patient died on the table, one of the nurses would be shot. Two soldiers stood with rifles in the already cramped operating room.

As Nance suspected, once he cut through layers of muscle and tissue in the man's lower abdomen, he found an inflamed and infected appendix attached to the beginning of the large intestine. It was precariously close to bursting. He carefully tied off the end of the hollow, worm-shaped pouch considered one of the few useless organs in the human body, gripped it gently with forceps, and cut it free. He did so without the organ rupturing. He then asked for sutures, and stitched up the site where the appendix had been attached. Then he sewed the peritoneum and abdominal muscles back together. A few stitches in the skin completed the operation, leaving only a thin, three-inch scar. The patient woke up alert and recovered without complications.

Nance's skill as a surgeon was obvious to the nurses. They would soon discover he could be impetuous and impatient, but they trusted him and knew the camp would be well served by his doctoring. From his competence, the nurses would benefit personally as well as professionally, as Dorothy Still soon found herself under his sharpened scalpel for the same surgery.

BEN EDWARDS HAD BEEN AMONG THE FIRST GROUP OF MEN transferred to Los Baños, where he joined the camp's woodchopping detail. Some thirty to forty men left camp several times a week, escorted by Japanese soldiers, who watched as the men felled trees, chopped them up, and hauled the logs back to camp to be used as fuel for the cooking vats. It was a much-sought-after job for many of the younger men because it involved physical exercise and being outside the camp.

Ben, who had escaped from Santo Tomás only to sneak back when he realized he had no place to go, liked the job for those reasons and another one as well. The excursions outside camp gave him the opportunity to scout the terrain. Los Baños was not escape-proof, but the Japanese knew there was no place for the internees to go, and the prisoners knew that if they left and were caught, they would be killed. That's why Ben wanted to have a sense of the surrounding territory should he ever decide it was time to plan another escape.

After the men cleared much of the bamboo and deciduous trees on the southwest of the camp, the Japanese took the detail into an uncut area outside the northwest corner. After they cut down several trees, the lieutenant in charge of the guard detail pointed to a tall tree he wanted down.

Ben pointed out that the tree was standing on a hillside with a decided list toward the camp's barbed-wire fencing. When it went over, he explained, the tree was sure to land on the fence.

The lieutenant was not happy that his orders were being questioned. Speaking rapidly and angrily, he demanded that it be cut.

The prisoners chopped down the tree, and it fell downhill, where it flattened about forty feet of fencing. Furious, the lieutenant took the detail back to camp. Once they arrived, he ordered the internees to wait until he returned from the commandant's office.

Fifteen minutes passed.

When the lieutenant returned with the interpreter, he ordered the entire detail arrested. Their crime? When the internees had refused to build the fences upon their arrival at Los Baños, the Japanese had them built by Filipino laborers. This made the fence the property of the emperor, said the lieutenant, his voice rising to a feverish pitch, and by destroying the emperor's property, they had earned the death penalty.

An astonished Ben and the other men were taken away.

The internees committee was outraged, and immediately protested to the commandant in person and in writing. They argued that Ben had told the lieutenant what would happen to the fence if the tree were cut down, something the officer had failed to mention to the commandant.

For the rest of that day and into the night, the woodcutters were held in the camp jail, where other internees smuggled food to them. The men judged that the committee's protests were making some progress when the interpreter showed up in the early evening with two soldiers and told them the commandant had decided to release half the detail. Only the other half would be punished, he explained.

"Half you men leave now," ordered the interpreter.

No one moved.

"All right, I will tell you who is to go."

He spoke rapidly to the soldiers, and they used their bayonet-tipped rifles to divide the prisoners into two groups.

"This group will leave," the interpreter said, pointing to one group of prisoners. "As you leave, give me your names."

The internee in the lead, a tall, red-bearded Scotsman, followed the instructions with a variation.

"My name is Heinrich Himmler," he said.

The interpreter wrote down the name.

The next internee stated, "I'm Joe Stalin."

Again the name was noted.

The third man identified himself as Simon Girty, who, only a student of U.S. history might recall, was the Scotch Irishman liaison between the British and their Native American allies during the Revolutionary War.

The interpreter looked confused. "Why you say that? I know you are Mr. Anderson."

Realizing something was amiss, the interpreter ordered all the internees back into jail and left with the soldiers.

An hour later, a member of the internees committee visited the jail. "We appreciate the way you men are hanging together," he said. "We feel we're winning in our discussions with the commandant, but please go along with them dividing up your group as they wish.

It's a face-saving way of erasing the problem a little bit at a time. Okay?"

The internees reluctantly agreed.

"But if things change one bit," said the big Scotsman, "we want to rejoin our gang so we can all sweat it out together."

The committee member agreed. "But I think we'll soon be able to forget the whole thing."

At the end of the next day, the order came from the commandant to release all the men from jail without charges. The lieutenant responsible for their incarceration was transferred and never seen again in Los Baños.

The sudden shock of realizing how close they had come to mass executions lingered. While for a time some of the guards seemed to make an effort to be friendlier, the internees and their leaders retained a keen awareness of how quickly and tragically their fates could change.

The internees had found some sporting gear in the old gym, and the committee convinced the commandant that some recreational activities would be good for morale. They laid out a soccer field, held track-and-field competitions, hit golf balls, and began using the baseball diamond.

The baseball games soon caught the attention of the commandant, who announced that a team of his soldiers would play against the internees. Ben, the camp's best pitcher, quickly put together an all-star team. A day or two before the game was to be played—the camp was already abuzz with the us-versus-them challenge—Ben was called before the administration committee. Some members thought the camp would be better served if the internees lost to the Japanese.

"You mean throw the game?" Ben asked.

He had faced a similar situation during a game against the guards at Santo Tomás, when some committee members told him he should take it easy with his pitches against the commandant, a man of great pride but lackluster hitting abilities. "Let him get a single," Ben was urged. "You know how they are about saving face."

This did not go far with Ben, although he did ease up enough to allow the commandant to hit two foul tips before fanning him with a blistering fastball he missed by a mile.

Now, when it came to losing a game so their captors could save face, Ben thought, *The hell with that.* But he knew the issue shouldn't be just his to decide, and so he checked with the rest of the team. They all agreed that there was only one way to play the game.

The game was played before hundreds of spectators—internees and Japanese alike—with a hard rubber ball the guards insisted on using. The Americans hit everything thrown at them, racking up runs in the double digits. But the Japanese couldn't hit anything off of Ben, and they couldn't field either. After a few innings of watching his team being badly beaten, the commandant stopped the game and marched his players off the field.

Nothing more was said about the internees playing baseball against the Japanese.


IMPERIAL JAPANESE ARMY WARRANT OFFICER SADAAKI KONISHI arrived at Los Baños in August 1944 to serve in the same post he had previously held at Santo Tomás. As quartermaster of the camp, he was in charge of finances and supplies, which made him second-in-command. The internees at Santo Tomás had loathed him because of his oppressive policies, especially the reduction of their food rations. He not only decreased what they were given but curtailed their access to outside vendors.

Konishi, who was twenty-eight years old, five-foot-four, and 135 pounds, had a shock of coal-black hair and deep-set brown eyes. Born and raised in Fukuoka Prefecture on Kyushu, the southwest-ernmost of Japan's four largest islands, he had a high school education and had been a farmer before the war. As a member of the

65th Infantry Brigade, he had landed at Lingayen Gulf on January 2, 1942, and with his unit marched to Baguio, where he was soon diagnosed with pulmonary tuberculosis and hospitalized for two months. Instead of returning to the infantry, he was assigned to a headquarters group commanded by Lieutenant General Ko Shiyoku, who had been put in charge of overseeing all the prison camps in the Philippines. Santo Tomás had been Konishi's first assignment with his new unit.

Konishi had been admitted to a Manila hospital with recurring TB on the same day that more than three hundred men, women, and children—including Margaret Sherk and her children—left Santo Tomás and transferred to Los Baños. After five months, he was discharged and sent to Los Baños, though he was left with a chronic rattle in his chest that was not helped by a chain-smoking habit that had stained his teeth a nut brown.

Most internees thought the first two Los Baños commandants had been reasonable and competent administrators. Either of them might have stopped Konishi from instituting his severest policies, but a new commandant had already taken over.

Major Yasuaka Iwanaka, an older, bowlegged reserve officer who spoke no English, showed little interest in running the camp. Those who dealt with him thought he was befuddled, doddering, and possessed an "inferior mentality." He spent most of his days in a kimono and sandals, puttering around in the garden outside his office, potting geraniums, painting watercolors of the surrounding countryside, and writing haiku.

Into this command vacuum rode the strong-willed Konishi, who issued orders and directives to the guards as well as the internees as if he were the one in charge. For months, some internees thought Konishi *was* the commandant. He was in effect its self-appointed dictator because Iwanaka was never known to countermand a single order of Konishi's. Under his directive, guards again had bayonets attached to their rifles, which gave them an extra element of menace. Konishi displayed an incredibly disagreeable manner and an open contempt for Caucasians and Westerners, especially Americans. He seemed to revel in their subjugation and humiliation. But even those who came to despise Konishi did not question his innate intelligence.

Under his rule, the internees were now subjected to spontaneous searches of their barracks and belongings. There were two roll calls per day, one in the morning and one in the evening. Communication between guards and internees was to be strictly limited. The internees were required to bow to any member of the Japanese military, regardless of rank. The penalty for not doing so—for men, women, and children—was a stern reprimand and a hard slap across the face. The Japanese saw a slap—the *binta*—as an act of ultimate disdain. The Americans rebelled against bowing to a member of the same military that had carried out the sneak attack on Pearl Harbor. And the Japanese insisted that it couldn't be just *any* bow; it had to be the *correct* bow.

"From the hips, not the waist! Head to ground! Back stiff!"

Everyone looked for ways to avoid this act of obedience, including veering off from the direction in which they were heading or dropping an object and bending down to pick it up so as to avoid eye contact. Some mothers pinched their babies to make them squall at the exact moment they would have to bow. A bawling baby was usually enough to send the Japanese away without receiving a bow or delivering a rebuke.

Those familiar with Konishi's rule while at Santo Tomás were not surprised that his first official act at Los Baños was to reduce internee rations by 20 percent, followed by prohibiting Filipinos from selling food to internees. The next month he ordered two more reductions in their food allotment. He suspended for a time the salt ration, claiming the mineral was needed in Japan in order to manufacture ammunition; then he inexplicably reinstated it, but at a smaller amount. He then cut in half the rations for the children, and reduced the amount of powdered milk for babies and nursing mothers. By the end of September, the food shortage was so grave that internees were beginning to show signs of malnutrition.

Dana Nance, as medical director, was required to submit a monthly report to the commandant. In his report for September, he wrote: "The average daily meat ration declined to five grams. The ration of dried beans has fallen to a paltry three grams per person—a negligible figure. The plain fact of the food situation at Los Baños is that everybody is HUNGRY!" Nance termed the daily average caloric intake served that month by the camp kitchen "starvation rations." He warned that internees would be increasingly debilitated by sickness and other symptoms of malnutrition unless they had more to eat.

The internees were particularly maddened by knowing that there was no reason for hunger at Los Baños. It was situated in the center of a rich agricultural area, and they could see in the surrounding countryside countless trees filled with coconuts and bananas, and fruits rotting on the ground in plain view. They were even able to watch small monkeys gorge themselves while they remained hungry.

These conditions had not existed under the previous commandants. What the detainees were now suffering, Nance knew, had to do with repeated acts of deprivation by one man: Sadaaki Konishi.

His cruelty was extraordinary. Konishi once turned away a delivery of meat because it had arrived late, and on another occasion he confiscated a shipment of seeds for planting. He ordered that a wagonload of fresh fruit—brought to camp by Filipinos for the internees—be dumped on the ground, then waited hours until the hot sun and swarming flies turned it into a putrid mess before he let the internees scavenge in the pile.

One day, quite unexpectedly, Konishi let the internees carry away as many of the hundred-pound sacks of rice from the Japanese warehouse as they could store at the camp kitchen. The shed was unlocked by guards, and Konishi stood by watching as the internees, struggling and sweating from the effort under the midday sun, spent more than an hour moving sacks. When they finished, Konishi said he had changed his mind. Apparently it amused him to watch starving prisoners struggle to lift and move the heavy sacks because he promptly ordered them to carry all the rice back to the warehouse.

The food situation worsened in October. Nance reported that the daily average intake of food the kitchen served fell to the "appalling figure" of 881 calories—a 65 percent decline from September. The clinic had seen 380 new cases of beriberi, an illness brought on by protein deficiency that causes joint swelling, difficulty walking, and mental confusion. Nance reported more than a thousand cases. He said more than half of the camp showed clinical signs of starvation.

Nance continued to provide medical services to the guards—by then he had performed several emergency appendectomies on soldiers. He saw no signs of vitamin deficiencies or malnutrition in any of them. Observing the guards at mealtimes on many occasions, Nance estimated that they were being given between three and four thousand calories a day.

Nance was unflinching in his assessments of how the internees were being mistreated, no matter whom he was addressing. He also kept a copy of all his reports. The war would be over one day, and regardless of the number of prisoners who survived, he wanted to have a record of how the Japanese had treated them. Nance knew world history; he understood that brutal conquerors throughout the ages had used hunger as a weapon to make people submissive and to weaken their spirits and bodies. It was a despicable form of warfare practiced against innocent people, and he wanted the world to know it had taken place at Los Baños in 1944.

"These reports," he wrote to the commandant on November 1, 1944, "serve as an indictment of the inhuman treatment of civilian internees by the Japanese authorities. Continuation of the present food policy can only result in ever increasing suffering of all internees. THE CAMP URGENTLY NEEDS MORE FOOD."

At Thanksgiving, Konishi blocked the delivery of a load of Red Cross packages that contained holiday meals. When members of the camp committee went to his office to complain, he cut them off. "Before I'm done," he promised, "you'll be eating dirt."

Internees now picked through the garrison's garbage for scraps, choking down rotten vegetables and fruit cores and finding stripped carabao and fish bones to boil. Every weed or plant was put to use, as people stewed pigweed, lily bulbs, morning glory, and tomato leaves. Someone put up a sign, KEEP OFF THE GRASS. WE EAT IT. They had taken to grazing like pastured cattle. Some internees unwisely consumed slices of cacti, which they found had a fresh, applelike flavor; it also caused internal lacerations. Fried banana skins became a delicacy. Slugs, snails, and worms were cooked with their daily rice, and camp dogs and cats, once plentiful, began to disappear. Word soon spread that cat meat was tastiest.

When the committee met with Konishi in late November to discuss the alarming conditions, Nance delivered the same blunt message.

"If you fail to remedy this situation," warned the physician, "it can only mean that you are deliberately adopting a starvation policy."

Konishi was unmoved. "Nothing can be done," he replied.

Nance was not surprised that fall when internees began to die.

# SIX

# Return to the Philippines

A FTER DAWN ON OCTOBER 20, 1944, U.S. SIXTH ARMY IN-
fantry divisions began amphibious landings on the east coast of
Leyte, one of the Philippine archipelago's larger islands three hundred miles southeast of Luzon.

All around the area were the deafening sounds of warships hurl-
ing rounds and aircraft diving to bomb and strafe enemy positions
inland. Hundreds of flat-bottomed landing craft churned through
pounding surf to get as close as possible before dropping their front
ramps to send infantrymen on their way across the sandy beaches
toward jungle-covered hills.

Within an hour of the first wave of U.S. troops coming ashore at
several locations along a twenty-mile stretch of coastline, most sec-
tors had secured beachheads wide enough to land more troops and
matériel. At only one landing beach—designated Red Beach, near
the coastal town of Palo, just south of Leyte's largest city, Tacloban—
did enemy resistance force a delay.

Amid the rattle of small-arms fire aimed at rooting out snipers
hidden in trees and dense undergrowth, General Douglas MacArthur arrived at 1:30 P.M. with the third assault wave at Red Beach.
The coxswain steering his landing craft dropped the ramp in shallow water about fifty yards from shore. Accompanied by staff officers
and Philippine president Sergio Osmeña, MacArthur waded ashore

for his dramatic return to the Philippines two and a half years after President Roosevelt had ordered him to leave Corregidor and go to Australia.*

"I Shall Return." MacArthur keeps his promise on October 20, 1944, at Palo, Luzon. *Courtesy MacArthur Memorial.*

A radio mobile unit was waiting for MacArthur a short distance from the beach. The tap-tap-tapping made by a Japanese Type 92 heavy machine gun, which American soldiers had nicknamed the "Woodpecker," could be heard in the distance, and smoke billowed from nearby burning palms. As MacArthur was handed a microphone, the sky let loose with a tropical shower.

"People of the Philippines, I have returned!" he announced in

---

* Correctly anticipating that reporters would be awaiting his arrival in Australia, MacArthur had a fifty-word statement ready that ended with: "I came through and I shall return." When that quote made headlines in the United States, MacArthur's bosses in Washington asked him to change his patriotic prophecy to the more inclusive "We Shall Return." MacArthur ignored the request.

the melodious voice that had become recognizable to so many. "By the grace of Almighty God, our forces stand again on Philippine soil—soil consecrated in the blood of our two peoples. We have come dedicated and committed to the task of destroying every vestige of enemy control over your daily lives, and of restoring upon a foundation of indestructible strength the liberties of your people."

MacArthur had memorized his statement so he could speak without notes. It was recorded and would be beamed to the Filipino people over a more powerful broadcasting unit aboard a ship in the harbor.

As he walked off the beach, the rain stopped as suddenly as it had begun. Passing the bodies of dead Japanese soldiers, he recognized the insignia of the 16th Infantry Division on their uniforms. This had been General Masaharu Homma's ace unit, the notorious division that carried out the Rape of Nanking (1937–1938), in which an estimated forty thousand Chinese military POWs and 250,000 civilians were murdered. In April 1942, members of this division committed widespread atrocities on the Bataan Death March, during which weakened and famished POWs—American and Filipino soldiers under MacArthur's command during the defense of Bataan—were force-marched seventy miles in six days and were bayoneted or shot when they fell from exhaustion. Many thousands died before reaching POW camps.

MacArthur had returned, with a score to settle against old enemies.

THE 11TH AIRBORNE WAS NOT INVOLVED IN THE LANDINGS ON the Leyte coast, and did not arrive on the island until three weeks later. Its commander, Joe Swing, had lobbied to be a part of this initial campaign to retake the Philippines, but MacArthur and his staff as well as the Sixth Army's were concerned about the combat capabilities of the lone airborne division in the Pacific versus regular infantry divisions. The 11th Airborne had seven battalions and infantry divisions had nine, giving the latter the advantage of being able to put thousands more soldiers into battle. Also, infantry divisions could bring in heavy artillery with greater range and destructive force, whereas paratroopers had to carry lighter, mobile artillery pieces.

Although it was the largest amphibious operation in the Pacific to date, Leyte was seen as the springboard for a more decisive Luzon campaign. MacArthur wanted to take over three airfields the Japanese had built on the eastern side of Leyte, which would put the main island of Luzon, four hundred miles away, and the capital of Manila, within range of land-based U.S. bombers for the first time in the war.

The men of the 11th Airborne had trained for many long and often tedious months stateside and in New Guinea, and finally they left for war on November 11, 1944, aboard nine transport ships. A week later, they sailed into the Leyte Gulf for an unopposed landing at Bito Beach, a long, narrow spit of land located halfway down the island's eastern seaboard.

The next day, as the division's gear was still being off-loaded from the crowded holds of cargo ships, a lone enemy plane approached from the north. Anticipating an attack, the men on the beach dove for cover. Instead, the plane turned sharply seaward and began a final dive at a ship anchored a mile offshore. Antiaircraft fire from the assembled ships boomed, filling the sky with bursting shells and shrapnel. The plane appeared to be hit several times, but stayed on course and impacted below the bridge. Rocked by secondary explosions, the ship soon sank.

It was on Leyte that kamikaze attack pilots made one of their first appearances, and the men of the 11th Airborne who had witnessed the event were shocked and bewildered at the willingness of the Japanese to carry out suicidal missions. What kind of die-hard enemy did they face?

The Japanese had not aggressively defended the beachheads during the Sixth Army's initial landings, but they put up a tough fight inland. Still, the Japanese lacked the manpower to halt the U.S. drive. Unbeknownst to U.S. planners, the Japanese high command, aware of Leyte's importance to the United States in staging an attack on Luzon, had decided the island must not be lost.

Four days after its arrival at Bito Beach, the 11th Airborne was assigned to hold the U.S. positions along a fifteen-mile front that extended from Dulag south along the coast to Burauen and to "destroy all Japanese troops in the sector." This Burauen-Dulag area of operations included the three airfields that Army engineers were working to make usable for U.S. bombers. The Japanese had built them on swampy lowlands that were susceptible to flooding, and soon after the U.S. landings, the worst typhoon in a decade hit Leyte. Torrential downpours accompanied by violent winds produced "horizontal" rain and turned the ground into a sea of mud.

The 11th Airborne set up its headquarters just outside Burauen, at the small barrio of San Pablo, which was next to one of the half-flooded airfields. The steep, heavily forested mountains looming to the west were thought to be so impassable as to provide a natural barrier against an attack by any large force on the other side. Even maps captured from the Japanese did not show any roads going over them. Other U.S. units were skirting around to the north in a drive to reach the enemy port of Ormoc on the opposite coast.

The day after the division moved to San Pablo, Muller received an A-1 intelligence report, meaning its source was considered reliable. It said the Japanese 26th Infantry Division from Luzon was landing at Ormoc Bay and would be crossing the mountains to attack the U.S. forces holding the three airfields at Burauen. It was a trek of fifteen miles as the crow flies, but longer on foot through difficult terrain with no roads. Swing and Muller agreed that it would be a stupid idea for the Japanese to throw a fresh division into the impassable mountains in an effort to reach the opposite side of the range when they were barely holding on elsewhere and could put those reinforcements to better use.

But they couldn't ignore the intelligence evaluation, so Swing agreed when Muller suggested sending the recon platoon into the foothills of the uncharted and unphotographed mountain range, where they could speak to inhabitants and hunters about possible routes and crossing sites. They were also to scout trails they came across and to report on any enemy troop movements.

Bad weather from the typhoon continued to limit the effectiveness of aerial reconnaissance missions flown by the division's unarmed, light observation planes. High-wing Stinson L-5 Sentinels, which had room for only a pilot and an observer, could land and take off on short fields. To accommodate the flights, a patch of runway was cleared at one end of San Pablo airfield.

Muller went up in an L-5 to see for himself what could be observed. As his pilot dipped the plane below a broken cloud layer, he saw a thick emerald-green canopy of trees and not much through it. As they crossed over the mountain range, he had a panoramic view to the west of the horseshoe-shaped Ormoc Bay and its ring of white beaches. Muller counted nine large Japanese troopships and several smaller vessels lying offshore. Landing craft were ferrying troops ashore.

As he was observing the vessels, a Japanese Zero—the Rising Sun visible on its fuselage—streaked by them. The enemy fighter whipped into a tight, high-speed turn to come back around. Muller's pilot quickly plunged their plane back to the other side of the ridge, dove through a break in the clouds, and flew between the walls of a narrow, twisting canyon. They made it back without seeing the Zero again.

Muller went immediately to Swing and reported what he had seen in the harbor. "We can safely conclude," he said, "that a new enemy infantry division is landing in the southern part of Ormoc Bay, directly across the mountains from us."

The 11th Airborne's planners began urgent discussion about what course of action to take. Should they wait for the Japanese to come down the slope of the mountain range and fight them in the valleys and plains near Burauen? Or should they head into the mountains and engage the enemy? Waiting for the enemy, Muller knew, had distinct advantages. They would have time to set up on ground of their choice to fight an enemy that had made a long and difficult march from the opposite coast. Surprising them in the mountains, however, could throw them off balance and keep them farther away from being able to attack the airfields.

Swing heard out both scenarios, then surprised no one on his staff when he said they would meet the enemy head-on in the mountains. He had been looking for a fight, and anyone who thought Joe Swing was going to let his paratroopers wait for the Japanese to come get them didn't know Swing very well. After meeting with his boss, Major General John Hodge, XXIV Corps commander, Swing was given the mission he wanted. He ordered the 511th Parachute Infantry Regiment under "Hard Rock" Haugen to push westward into the mountains, destroying any Japanese units in its path.

The lightly equipped and superbly conditioned airborne troopers turned out to be ideal for the fight in the rugged mountains. They were organized to move quickly on foot and trained to fight at close quarters. It would turn into a mano-a-mano brawl in the worst topography and most unforgiving conditions in the Pacific. There were, however, lessons to be learned for men with no combat experience facing Japanese units that had been at war for years.

Since their earliest days in training, Henry Muller, who had recently been promoted to lieutenant colonel, had stressed the value of retrieving paperwork found on enemy soldiers. Japanese paybooks, in particular, were prized because they were signed every payday by the unit's paymaster. In the Imperial Japanese Army, a soldier could not draw pay without one. The Japanese usually destroyed letters and other papers for security reasons, but the emperor's soldiers always held on to their paybooks.

About a week after his flight over Leyte, Muller was handed two recovered paybooks brought to divisional headquarters by a runner from the 511th PIR, which had engaged Japanese forces in the mountains. He turned over the books, which had been found on dead Japanese soldiers, to his Nisei translation team, who soon gave him the names of the paymasters who had signed the books. Muller looked those names up in the order-of-battle book on the Japanese Army and saw they were the paymasters for two infantry regiments of the Japanese 26th Infantry Division. Muller rushed into Swing's office without knocking.

Startled, Swing said, "Well, I guess you have something hot, Hank?"

"Yes, sir," said Muller, explaining that the two paybooks confirmed the presence of the Japanese 26th Division coming across the mountains to engage them.

"I'll be damned," Swing said. "Still stupid of 'em."

Knowing the enemy's order of battle revealed much about its capabilities. U.S. Army intelligence already knew the 26th had fifteen thousand men, most of them veterans of Manchuria. Swing immediately ordered his other two regiments—the 187th and 188th Glider Infantry—into the mountains to reinforce the 511th.

In the face of terrible terrain, a lack of mapped trails, and unrelenting rainfall, the progress of the 11th Airborne's three regiments against the newly committed Japanese reinforcements proved slow. Resupplying the U.S. units in heavy combat with adequate food and enough ammunition was a logistical nightmare. At first, carabao were used to haul supplies up the steep grades, but they moved too slowly on trails soggy with knee-deep mud. Some places were too narrow for the large animals burdened with packs to squeeze through. Hand-carrying mortars and ammunition was tried next, but that took too long as well. Fighting men, out of K rations, went days without eating.

During November and December, twenty-eight inches of rain inundated Leyte. The paratroopers in the mountains lived in soaked fatigues that began to rot, and their always wet boots were falling apart. With no replacements, they went a month without taking off their socks. The heat of the day turned to a piercing cold by night. The men got only an hour or two of rest each night in their muddy, rain-filled foxholes because they had to defend against the Japanese human-wave attacks. The enemy soldiers would scream *"Banzai! Banzai! Banzai!"* and charge forward to try to break through the Americans' perimeter.

SERGEANT TERRY SANTOS WAS NOW RECON'S LEAD SCOUT. He and the other two recon members had returned from the Alamo Scouts Training Center in September (1944) and trained the rest of the platoon on what they had learned. Traditional fire and movement tactics were still emphasized, but stealth, patience, camouflage, and living off the land became the primary focus.

The recon team learned they could cut a foot-long section of a "water vine" in the rain forest and fill their canteens with its potable water, and that when they ran out of K rations—which happened on long patrols—it was safe to eat whatever birds and animals ate, including worms, grubs, and plants. They were also taught that in the jungle the enemy could be hiding nearby, and thus talking or making noise could get someone killed. This became so important they even favored soft fatigue caps over metal helmets, which pinged when hit by heavy rain. And though the caps offered little protection from enemy fire, they blended into the background better. The men devised their own "brevity signals" for nonverbal communication, using hand signals and soft knocks on the butt of a rifle. During several extended treks in the jungles of New Guinea, the recon platoon had become a cohesive unit. Now they were doing their job in an environment on Leyte even more inhospitable than New Guinea, which a few weeks ago they wouldn't have thought possible.

Although the mountain range peaked at only four thousand feet, its treacherous passes were nearly impenetrable. Narrow, circuitous animal paths went alongside cliffs, through steep gorges, and around blind corners. In many places, there were no trails through heavy rain forests, dense jungles, and narrow slits in rocky outcroppings that even the carabao did not use. Every step was muddy and slick from torrential rain, and nerve-racking in that the enemy might be only a few feet away.

While leading a recon patrol up a narrow, winding trail, Santos, whose eyesight was sharp enough it was said he could see a leaf move at a hundred yards, came face-to-face with an enemy patrol emerging through a rainy mist not more than twenty feet away. The leaders of the two patrols saw each other at the same instant. Santos swung his Thompson submachine up as the other guy brought up his weapon. Santos squeezed the trigger first, nearly cutting his adversary in half. The rest of the enemy patrol turned and ran back up the trail. As they fled, Santos chopped down three more. He had been taught never to chase the enemy in the jungle because they could have comrades hiding not far away.

When a private in his squad, Paul Iden, became sick and feverish and couldn't continue, Santos hid him in some heavy vegetation and set him up with his back against a tree. Santos had learned in the Alamo Scouts that this was the best sleeping position when on patrol because it was more difficult for someone to sneak up on you from behind.

Santos unhooked a grenade from Iden's web belt. It was a fragmentation grenade that would kill anyone within fifteen feet by launching dozens of small metal fragments in every direction when it exploded. While holding down the strike lever on the grenade's side so it wouldn't explode, he pulled out the safety pin. Then he handed the live grenade to Iden. Santos did the same thing with a second grenade, which he placed in Iden's other hand. When the strike levers were released, the grenades would go off within four to five seconds.

"One is for the enemy," Santos explained. "The other is for you, Paul. I don't want you captured."

Iden looked up at Santos. "Are you coming back?"

"Of course I'm coming back."

Santos and the rest of the patrol were gone all night. When they returned early in the morning, Iden was still sitting against the tree, holding the grenades in a death grip. Santos had the safety pins in his pocket. He replaced them in each grenade, rendering them safe.

"Okay, you can let go now," Santos said.

For several minutes, Iden wouldn't loosen his grip on the grenades.

Upon Santos's return to division headquarters, Muller told him that Swing was waiting to get a report from recon. Santos soon found himself facing the general, explaining that there were no improved routes through the passes and what few trails existed were little more than animal paths. He pointed out enemy positions on a table map.

"Are you certain about those locations?" Swing asked.

After several days in the mountains behind enemy lines, Santos was hot, filthy, and exhausted. Wanting only to get some hot chow and a few hours of shut-eye, he had little patience, even for a two-star general.

"They are on the move, and the situation is fluid," Santos said. "But if you don't believe me, sir, I'll take you out there."

Santos considered Swing a good man and an inspirational division commander, but he had also seen the general turn nasty in a flash. He was known to have demoted and relieved the messenger if he didn't like the message, and that went for officers as well as enlisted men.

Swing nailed the recon sergeant with his patented ice-cold glare. "You're irascible and irreverent!" Swing barked.

Santos waited for the hammer to drop.

"You have no respect for authority!" Then the general's expression softened, and he added: "But I'm glad you're on my side."

Even after a few days back at headquarters, Paul Iden's nerves were still so shaken from his night alone in the jungle holding two live grenades that he requested a transfer to another unit. Just asking to leave recon was all it took, no questions asked.

It was much more difficult to get into the elite, all-volunteer unit. One of its newest members, Corporal Martin Squires, a lean and strong six-footer, had been volunteering for recon since North Carolina. Squires was twenty-four years old and from Bellingham, Washington. By 1942, he had finished two years of college when he volunteered for the Army. Soon after completing basic training, he received a letter from an old friend who was in the paratroopers. "Mart, this is the outfit! The morale of the men, the thrill of the jump, it just can't be matched. Plus, you get an extra 50 bucks a month, no KP duty, and the girls see our shiny jump boots and they chase after us!"

That had been enough for Squires, and he volunteered for the airborne. But Squires wore prescription glasses, which the airborne allowed if one could pass an eye test with 20/30 vision, uncorrected. Squires could not. However, the doctor giving the exam left him alone in the room long enough to memorize the various lines of letters. Having grown up on the Olympic peninsula, Squires was an avid outdoorsman. He had owned his first rifle at age twelve and was an excellent shot. His familiarity with guns led to the Army training him in infantry heavy weapons and demolitions. He liked the idea of being a reconnaissance scout, and had tried for months to get into the Recon Platoon but was repeatedly turned down because he wore glasses, which could be a hindrance in rain and steamed up in the humidity of the South Pacific. Finally, once the division arrived in New Guinea, his persistence paid off and Lieutenant Polka gave him his shot at recon.

Martin Squires of the 11th Airborne Reconnaissance Platoon. *Courtesy Margaret (Whitaker) Squires.*

Squires tried to improve his vision with eye exercises and by taking vitamins and drinking carrot juice. Before leaving for Leyte, he gave himself an eye test to determine if his vision had improved enough that he could leave his glasses behind. There was only a slight change, and the glasses still gave him a sharper focus. He decided in combat he should have every advantage, so he kept his glasses with him.

Squires found a home in recon; like him, most were outdoorsmen who grew up hunting, hiking, and camping. Each was a buddy to the others, Squires wrote home, and "our bond is such that we all look out for one another." Notwithstanding the fact that they were all "crazy as hell," they were devoted to their leaders, Lieutenant Polka as well as G2 Henry Muller, whom everyone considered "the brains of Recon."

Santos had quickly become a mentor to the new guy in the squad. The lead scout was concerned that "Martin the thinker"—Squires was soft-spoken and contemplative by nature—was more inclined to ruminate than react.

Indecision, Santos knew, could get a person killed in combat.

IN THE AFTERNOON OF DECEMBER 6, 1944, ONE DAY BEFORE THE
third anniversary of the attack on Pearl Harbor, Henry Muller received a radio communication he had hoped would never come: a
coded Crystal Ball message.

Muller went to the division's field safe, where classified documents were kept, and removed the two-way pad he had been given
several months earlier in Brisbane, Australia. Sitting behind a map
board that gave him some privacy, he decoded the message sent
directly to him by Brigadier General Charles Willoughby, MacArthur's chief of intelligence.

> FOR MULLER G2 11ABN DIV EYES ONLY
> CRYSTAL BALL STATES
> JAP FIRST PARACHUTE BRIGADE FROM
> LIPA COMMA LUZON WILL MAKE PARACHUTE
> ASSAULT BURAUEN AIRSTRIPS SEVEN DECEMBER
> 1800 HOURS SIGNED WILLOUGHBY G2

Muller's pulse quickened as he checked the order of battle
book. The Japanese First Parachute Brigade, organized with two
light regiments, was made up of about three thousand men. *Three
thousand enemy paratroopers would be dropping into their backyard within
twenty-four hours?* Not only was 11th Airborne headquarters adjacent to one of the targeted airfields, but it was their responsibility
to defend *all* the Burauen airstrips. Yet its three regiments were
engaged miles away in the mountains. In the immediate area, they
had only the headquarters company and some service units with
mechanics, cooks, and drivers. A battalion of 1,500 paratroopers
was being held in reserve about five miles away.

Muller's first impulse was to go to General Swing's tent and let
him know about the message. Perhaps the Japanese 26th Division's

Henry Muller Jr., 11th Airborne's
G-2 intelligence officer. *Courtesy Henry
Muller Jr.*

move over the mountain was not so "stupid" after all, and was meant to draw the American troops away from the air bases, leaving them open during a jump there by Japanese paratroopers. But Willoughby had strictly ordered Muller not to reveal the source to anyone. So how was he going to tell Swing they were about to be attacked by a Japanese parachute brigade at a specific time the next day?

Muller knew Swing would see through any phony source he offered, and either disregard the report or wring the truth out of him. He checked his watch. It was already 4 P.M. and his daily G-2 report was due in an hour. A roundup of all known enemy activities, contacts, and unit identifications, the report ended with an estimate of the enemy's capabilities. Under Army doctrine, a G-2 should never predict the enemy's course of action; however, it was permissible to evaluate the relative probability of each enemy capacity. Muller realized that this was the answer. He would list a brigade-sized airborne assault on San Pablo airstrip as a new but valid enemy capability— even providing a day and hour—and then proceed to justify this capability in his relative-probability comments.

Not long after the report was delivered to Swing, the general's aide stuck his head in the door and said, "Sir, the Old Man wants to see you right away."

As Muller entered the general's tent, Swing had the report in hand. "Damn it, Hank," he said, waving the report. "Have you lost your good judgment? Where do you get this dumb capability of a brigade jump? I doubt the Japs can even assemble that many transports."

"Well, sir, the last air order of battle for the Philippines does give them an adequate troop carrier capability. Of course, they can fly in more from Taiwan or Japan for a special operation."

"Nonsense! Even if they did, why would they expend a good airborne brigade to take back these mud flats?"

Swing had a point. They had already abandoned two of the dilapidated airfields as beyond salvage, and even with all the effort going into fixing the third one, it was still unusable for heavy bombers.

After several more exchanges, Swing ordered Muller to retrieve every copy of the report so it wasn't circulated to Corps or Army headquarters.

"This could make us the laughingstock up there," he said. "I want you to rework this report and delete the airborne assault part."

Muller couldn't pretend he hadn't received the Crystal Ball message. "General, there's something I have to tell you."

"What is it, Hank?"

"The report on which I based my estimate was sent to me direct from General Willoughby. I was not to reveal that to anyone at all. Not even you."

"Oh, dammit, I might have guessed this was one of Willoughby's harebrained reports. Do what I told you and rewrite the report."

Muller decided to take one last shot. "Sir, since this is a valid capability, and we have been specifically warned, shouldn't we make the appropriate troop deployments to meet such an attack?"

"No! It isn't a valid capability, and I am not about to move the reserve battalion through five miles of mud on the basis of such a far-fetched possibility."

Muller saluted and left. Returning to his office, he dispatched an enlisted man to retrieve all the copies of the report that had gone out and had the sergeant retype the report without the airborne assessment.

Muller didn't sleep well that night. He had failed to convince Swing to take the steps necessary to counter an enemy attack, even after disobeying Willoughby's direct order not to disclose the real source to anyone. And now, if the Japanese didn't jump tomorrow, he would lose credibility with Swing. Of course, if they *did* jump and there were U.S. casualties, he worried that the 11th Airborne's failure to heed this warning from MacArthur's intelligence chief would result in a court of inquiry, and perhaps even his own court-martial when it came out he had revealed the source of the Crystal Ball message.

He somehow got through the next day as the clock ticked down to 6 P.M. At five thirty, he joined Swing and several other staff officers for the evening meal in the small tent set up as the general's mess. He pretended to be interested in the tactical and strategic discussions that always took place whenever one dined with Swing, but all Muller wanted to do was look at his watch. He didn't dare for fear that Swing or someone else would make a comment. *Waiting for the enemy paratroopers, Hank?*

Finally, he purposely dropped his paper napkin on the ground so he could bend over to pick it up and furtively glance at his watch. It was exactly 6 P.M.

Sitting back up, he heard what sounded like a swarm of bees in the distance. Then the drone grew steadily louder.

No paratrooper could mistake the reverberating sound of a formation of troop-carrier aircraft. Someone outside the tent shouted, "Aircraft!"—followed by cries of "Jap transports!" and "Paratroopers!"

Swing and his officers ran outside and looked skyward.

A dozen parachutes were coming down directly above them. Muller drew his .45 sidearm from his belt holster and emptied two seven-round clips at the targets. Most of the enemy paratroopers—

there were a few hundred rather than thousands—were floating down well beyond the division's headquarters and landing in and around the nearby airstrip.

Muller rushed into the communications tent to send out alerts concerning the enemy attack. When he went back outside, it was dark. He could hear rifle fire and occasional explosions coming from the airstrip, where the only U.S. personnel were an aerial supply detachment.

During a long night, Lieutenant Colonel Douglass Quandt, the division's G-3, who was responsible for planning operations, prepared for one field artillery battalion to fight as infantry along with some members of the division's ordnance and quartermaster companies, to counterattack across the airstrip at first light. Quandt's ad hoc plan worked, and they cleared the airstrip with little resistance other than a few snipers. Most of the Japanese paratroopers withdrew into a wooded area after destroying several light aircraft on the ground and torching some stores of aviation fuel and supplies meant for the troops in the mountains.

Muller went with Swing to check out the situation at the airfield, and Swing began shouting directions to the commander leading the counterattack.

It was soon apparent that the Japanese assault had been a complete debacle. Not only would it come out later that the Japanese had not been able to gather the transports needed for the whole brigade and had dropped only a few hundred men, but most of the paratroopers who jumped were strung out well beyond the airstrip in an area of tall trees, the bane of parachutists everywhere. One entire planeload jumped to their deaths when the anchor line that was supposed to pull open their chutes failed or was severed by gunfire. Many other enemy soldiers just wandered about without direction and were easily found and killed.

Back at headquarters, Muller was relieved. The enemy jump had indeed happened, but there were no serious U.S. casualties. His credibility with his general was not in danger. As to his unauthorized disclosure of the source of the Crystal Ball message, only Swing and he knew of his breach. It would be in both their best interests to keep the incident to themselves. In fact, Muller waited all that day, sure that Swing would comment about his correctly forecasting the enemy parachute attack. But the general said nothing. Muller did not think he could say anything to Swing that didn't have an I-told-you-so ring to it, so he kept silent. But the division's other staff officers and G-2 staff were not as quiet.

"Hey, Hank, how the hell did you call that jump?"

*It was a logical capability.*

"Wow, how did you nail the day and even the hour?"

*Oh, Pearl Harbor Day and the advantage of a jump before dark . . .*

Muller felt like a "wretched charlatan" for taking credit he didn't deserve. The G-2's credibility had been greatly enhanced, and he was seen as a soothsayer. Muller knew he was going to be pressed to live up to what was now expected of him.*

On the same day as the enemy parachute attack, the U.S. Army's Seventh and 77th Infantry Divisions made amphibious landings on Leyte's west coast south of Ormoc. As the units pushed to the north in order to capture the port, others went eastward toward the mountains. The remaining Japanese troops were caught between U.S. forces coming at them from several directions.

Swing recognized that his division's final effort on Leyte would

---

* The December 6 Crystal Ball message was the only one Muller ever received. Only after the war did he learn the real source of the information: the U.S. Army and Navy developed a machine that was able to break the Japanese high codes. This capability was closely held in Washington and was revealed to only a few officials, and in the field went no lower than MacArthur and Admiral Chester Nimitz and their top intelligence officers. The asset was used sparingly so as not to alert the Japanese that their codes had been broken. It was used to defeat the Japanese fleets at Coral Sea and Midway, and to intercept and shoot down the aircraft carrying Admiral Isoroku Yamamoto, the Supreme Commander of the Imperial Japanese Navy, who had planned and carried out the attack on Pearl Harbor.

be to link up with the reinforcements that had landed on the west coast, so he ordered his paratroopers in the mountains to push forward at breakneck speed toward Ormoc. The 511th left a trail of enemy dead, and on December 25, 1944, after they completed their mission, Swing ordered them to return to base camp at Bito Beach.

High on one desolate mountaintop pass, a long line of bearded, filthy paratroopers who couldn't remember their last hot meal plodded through ankle-deep mud toward the coast ten miles away. A whisper passed from one to another down the line of weary soldiers who had lived for thirty-one days straight with the violence and anguish of combat.

"It's Christmas."

*Hey, buddy, it's Christmas.*

*Pass the word. Christmas.*

(It also happened to be the twentieth birthday of one of the paratroopers, Private Rodman "Rod" Serling, of Syracuse, New York, who would return home after the war to nightmares and flashbacks, which he tried to get off his chest by turning to screenwriting. He went on to have a successful career in television as the creator and producer of *The Twilight Zone*.)

A lone monotone voice somewhere up in front started to sing. Soon everyone was joining in to sing "O Come, All Ye Faithful" as they led the walking wounded and carried the litters with the nonambulatory injured. Some of the men looked back through the foggy mist at a row of American graves with handmade crosses. Others did not.

The 511th lost 128 paratroopers in the mountains of Leyte, and they were credited with killing thousands of Japanese. Yet the troopers who walked out of those mountains thought it was a steep price to pay for the lessons learned: to use more reconnaissance, cover, and concealment, and to better ration their food, water, and ammo. But they had also discovered about themselves that they were every bit as rough and tough as they'd thought, and more than equal to their enemy.

On December 26, MacArthur announced: "The Leyte campaign can now be regarded as closed except for minor mopping up."

The 8,800-man Japanese 16th Division from Bataan had been reduced to five hundred men. The newly arrived Japanese 26th Division had been annihilated in the mountains by the 11th Airborne.

With the Leyte fight over, the liberation of Luzon came next.

"The Japs are reinforcing their garrisons in Luzon to an extent that will make almost every attack a frontal one," Swing wrote to his father-in-law, General Peyton March, the former Army chief of staff, on December 30. "The chances of seizing an undefended beachhead from which an assault can be launched are nil. We're going to have to fight for every inch."

DURING THE SECOND WEEK OF JANUARY 1945, THE POWERFUL U.S. Sixth Army under Lieutenant General Walter Krueger was to land on the shores of Lingayen Gulf, a hundred miles north of Manila. This was to be the main thrust of infantry, heavy artillery, and armored tanks into Manila, which was expected to be heavily defended by the Japanese. The 11th Airborne, less the 511th Regiment, was to follow with an amphibious landing at Nasugbu, fifty miles southwest of Manila. Seventy-two hours later, the 511th paratroopers were to make their first regimental combat jump of the war at Tagaytay Ridge, thirty miles inland. The 11th Airborne units were then to link up and hold their ground well south of Manila, preventing Japanese troops in southern Luzon from moving north to meet the Sixth Army's advance on Manila as well as cutting off the retreat of any Japanese fleeing Manila.

Henry Muller spent the last days of 1944 gathering information for this upcoming Luzon campaign. When he was told that waiting outside was a Filipino who had recently left Manila and traveled through Luzon, Muller had him shown in.

As G-2, he was responsible for amassing intelligence from all sources, whether from captured Japanese soldiers or aerial reconnaissance photos or from the debriefing of eyewitnesses.

The man was a middle-aged, well-to-do grower from Mindanao, the southernmost major island in the Philippines. In excellent English, he explained that his wife suffered from a chronic illness and he'd gone to Manila to get needed medication. Now, as he made his way back home, his journey had included a trek through Luzon by *banca*, oxcart, and on foot.

Before Muller started the debriefing, he asked a couple of questions he knew the answers to and was satisfied that the man was not an enemy collaborator trying to pass disinformation.

"Let's start at the beginning," Muller said. "When you left Manila, what routes did you take? Tell me everything you saw en route."

As the man began his detailed travelogue, Muller took notes.

After a few minutes, the grower said in passing, "When I was heading south on Highway 17, I went by that big POW camp."

Startled, Muller looked up. "What camp?"

"The one at the old Los Baños agricultural college. Civilians, not military. Men, women, and children. Looked like mostly Americans."

This was the first Muller had heard of an internment camp filled with American civilians south of Manila. "How many do you think?" he asked.

"Oh, I'd say about two thousand."

*"Two thousand?"*

"Yes, sir," said the Filipino, who seemed surprised that the U.S. officer didn't already know about the large prison camp.

By the time he went in to see General Swing, Muller had pumped all the information he could from the grower. He had pinpointed the camp's location on a map. It was forty miles east of Tagaytay Ridge and across a steep mountain range that was infested with Japanese troops.

Swing knew nothing about the Los Baños Internment Camp either. Given how far it was outside the 11th Airborne's planned area of operations on Luzon, the general wasn't surprised they hadn't been told about it. He told Muller to go ahead and prepare a report, and send it up the channels, but beyond that not to concern himself with the matter.

"Hank, that's not in our area," Swing said. "We've been told we're going to stay on Tagaytay Ridge and go no farther. Don't waste your time on something like this. We have plenty of other things to worry about."

But not long after leaving Swing's office, Muller reached several conclusions: rescuing American prisoners was an appealing mission to anyone brought up on tales about the cavalry coming to the rescue. Also, the mission was suited for a surprise airborne operation behind enemy lines, and the 11th Airborne was the only parachute division in the Southwest Pacific, so it might become their mission at some point. He had been taught that a raid behind enemy lines, possibly more than any other type of military operation, required precise and complete intelligence to succeed.

Muller was determined to gather all the information he could about Los Baños—surreptitiously, of course, given the rebuke General Swing had given him. If the 11th Airborne was ever assigned to undertake a Los Baños rescue mission, he wanted to be ready.

Muller couldn't stop himself from replaying the words the Filipino grower had said about the POW camp and its prisoners.

*They are in pitiful shape. They're dying.*

# SEVEN

# Freedom Week

D R. DANA NANCE AND THE NAVY NURSES STRUGGLED TO fight the diseases that swept through the Los Baños camp with devastating effect. The Japanese often took whatever medicines the Red Cross sent, and sanitation was so poor it was hard to prevent the spread of contagions. Mosquito-borne tropical diseases like malaria and dengue fever flourished.

Nance estimated that more than 1,900 of the people in the camp—nearly the entire population—were suffering from the debilitating effects of malnutrition and vitamin deficiency that could only be cured by food. Beriberi was now widespread, resulting in badly swollen faces, limbs, and feet; some internees could no longer wear shoes. Many people had tropical ulcers due to poor nutrition. These were painful, open lesions that developed primarily on their legs. These and other ailments such as edema, intestinal parasites, pellagra, dysentery, pernicious anemia, and scurvy were treatable if only Nance had the right medications, and his patients weren't also malnourished.

No one in the camp had much energy, so life slowed to a standstill, with all but the most essential activities cut back. As a starved body quits functioning gradually, mental acuity suffers as well. For a while former teachers had taught courses in their particular subject areas—as a way of keeping people occupied—but even these popular classes were canceled because everyone was too hungry to focus on schoolwork.*

Food dominated most conversations. The other two major subjects discussed were the war's progress and "When are the Americans coming?" Young children drew pictures of foods they heard adults talk about but had not seen or tasted. Men and women obsessed about recipes, and traded pictures of delicacies torn from old magazines. Beef roast with droplets of fat. Turkey with mashed potatoes and gravy. Ham and eggs. Crispy bacon. Pork sausages. Fried chicken. Apple pie à la mode. Mouthwatering conversations took place about breads and cakes, macaroni and cheese, fruits like crisp apples and juicy oranges, and how great a tall glass of cold milk would taste.

The prisoners' reality was two sparse meals a day; a noontime meal was no longer served. The Japanese handed out food supplies every ten days, and the kitchen staffed by internees had to make it last. For breakfast, they served a thin, rice mush called *lugao*, consisting of four or five parts water to one part rice—usually along with worms and other debris—boiled into an ill-tasting paste that had the consistency of wallpaper glue. Supper was more *lugao*, and sometimes a thin, watery stew.

The internees supplemented these meals with whatever greens they could pick—mostly leaves, vines, and edible weeds—and vegetables from their own small gardens. The large camp garden they had tended so laboriously for more than a year had been off limits to the prisoners since Konishi decreased the camp's perimeter and increased the number of guards on patrol.

At the same time that hunger and diseases began to take over the camp, the first wave of babies were born after couples were re-

---

* At the insistence of the camp commandant, a Japanese-language class to be taught by one of his civilian interpreters was scheduled. Not a single internee showed up for the course.

united when women arrived at Los Baños a year earlier. Unlike at Santo Tomás, married couples were allowed to live together at Los Baños, and the no-babies rule became unenforceable. The wails of hungry babies whose malnourished mothers had no milk in their breasts were heartbreaking. Newborns soon dropped half their birth weights, and infants were kept alive with doses of Klim, a dehydrated whole-milk powder first developed in the 1920s for use in the tropics, where dairy milk tended to spoil. The nurses had collected and saved it for such emergencies.

The supply of general anesthetics was gone, although the hospital still had morphine and local anesthetics, which allowed Nance to continue to perform necessary surgeries. He was still the only medical-surgical physician in the camp, and everyone knew his worth. On call day and night, he had professionally seen most of the internees at one time or another, and had saved countless lives.

Since arriving at Los Baños, he had performed some three hundred major operations, among them appendectomies; perforated gastric ulcers; cholecystectomies (gallbladder); exploratory laparotomies; excision of semilunar cartilage (knee); hemorrhoidectomies; cesarean sections; thyroidectomies; hernioplasties; hysterectomies, and the removal of ovaries and a brachial cyst.

One young girl came in with a cut on her foot that required stitches. Nance said he couldn't use precious local anesthesia for such a minor wound and asked her to be brave. He put in three stitches, although normally he would have used twice as many. Commending her for her courage, he told her he was sorry he did not have a lollipop for her.

Nurse Dorothy Still was left with very little body fat on her slim frame. She and the other nurses were often as weak and sick as their patients, but they still worked twelve-hour shifts treating up to two hundred patients daily, assisted by two dozen aides and orderlies.

With so many malnourished patients with low resistance to illnesses and a hospital without medications, people died in increasing numbers. The aged and those weakened by chronic diseases went first. Then young people began dying, too.

Dorothy was horrified when she saw that twenty-four-year-old Betty Lou Gewald's waif-thin abdomen was swollen due to acute appendicitis. Nance had no choice but to remove the diseased organ even though he knew that with no postoperative medicines infection would set in during her recovery. The nurses and doctor worked nonstop to drain the infection coursing through the young woman's body, but Betty Lou died. All Dorothy could do was weep. The entire medical team was left shaken and feeling helpless when a popular seventeen-year-old, Burton Fonger, died suddenly from a virulent form of malaria.

The next to die was a crusty, ex–merchant seaman whom few of the internees liked. He succumbed to tertiary syphilis. He was followed by Hugh Williams, a kindly old character and retired British Navy captain nicknamed "Skipper." He was a favorite of the children in camp for his swashbuckling sea stories. With internal bleeding from acute colitis, his starved body was too weak to respond to treatment.

When "Pinky," a professional piano player, died suddenly, Nance's autopsy revealed that his stomach contained pieces of a wool blanket and a leather belt he'd eaten. Hungry people were willing to eat almost anything, and there would be more deaths from intestinal obstructions; one man died when he ate a piece of his canvas cot and mosquito net.

Dorothy was certain that one patient, a fifty-year-old man, died because of love. He had given his children so much of his sparse daily rations that he starved himself. His passing served as a warning to other parents who regularly passed part of their food to their offspring so they would suffer less from painful hunger pangs.

The heat and humidity meant that dead bodies had to be buried quickly before decay set in and rodents found the remains. With the death rate now averaging seven people per week, the carpenters had trouble getting enough lumber from the Japanese to build coffins. The number of gravediggers had to be doubled to six. It was an ordeal for men with skeleton-like frames to swing picks and shovel into hard, claylike soil in an overgrown cemetery next to the college chapel. The names of the deceased were burned onto the wooden crosses that served as markers.

One day Nance became so furious that his patients were dying because they lacked food that he took one of his sharp scalpels and went outside looking for the fat, old shepherd dog that belonged to a woman who kept it alive by feeding it from her rations. In a place where it was now suicidal for a rat or snake to be caught out in the open, the dog had been the cause of much derision in camp. Even the woman's family had begged her to put the dog down. Konishi, with his sly grin that exposed a shiny gold incisor, had taunted Nance several times about the dog whenever the physician begged that food rations be increased.

Now the doctor saw the dog as forty pounds of protein for himself and his medical staff, all of whom needed to keep up some strength so they could help others.

Nance found the dog outside.

The owner realized what was about to happen and began screaming. Her two grown sons—large men well over six feet—came running.

By then, Nance had the dog behind the barracks, and with one swipe of the razor-sharp blade, he slit the dog's throat. Without even a whimper, it fell to the ground dead. Driving the instrument into the dog's sternum, Nance opened the stomach and began to clean the animal.

The woman's sons lunged at the doctor and several blows were struck before bystanders broke up the fight, which had also attracted the Japanese guards.

"You dumb bastards!" Nance hollered. "People are starving!"

His nose bloodied, the doctor picked up his scalpel and stalked away.

The dog ended up being buried, but not before the carcass was smeared with rat poison to prevent anyone from digging it up.

Soon after, when another man killed and ate a pet dog, the owners charged him with "inhuman and barbarous conduct." The case was brought before the internees' court, which was composed of experienced lawyers and judges. After they heard testimony, the case was dismissed on the grounds that the charge of stealing was unfounded because dogs could not be considered "private property" in a wartime internment camp.

Anything from the animal kingdom was fair game for the stewpot.

MARGARET SHERK AND HER TWO CHILDREN WERE ASSIGNED TO A women-only barracks when they arrived at Los Baños. She and Jerry Sams were not married, so they could not live together in family quarters.

Jerry, who was in a men's barracks across from Margaret and the kids, spent most of his time with them, returning to his own cubicle only at night. A born nest builder, he got busy making improvements for his extended family. He planed and sanded the rough edges of their cubicle's wooden floor so the children wouldn't get splinters, and for Margaret he made shelves in one corner and a small closet in another. He fashioned wire hangers for her "best clothes," which she was saving to wear when they were liberated, as many of the women did in order to boost their morale.

He cut a doorway on the outside wall of the cubicle—and hung a wooden door he made from the camp's building supplies—so they would have a shorter route to the toilets and washroom and wouldn't have to use the barracks' central corridor. Jerry used his know-how with electronics to make a built-in electric hot plate, recycling the ceramic top from a burned-out hot plate he had scavenged and winding the steel strand of surplus telephone wire around a dowel for the heating unit.

To obtain electricity—this part seemed like magic to Margaret—he spliced into the line that brought power into the barracks, which he discovered still carried juice at night after the guards turned off the lights. He buried about forty feet of copper wire along the outside of the barracks to run the power into their cubicle under the floorboards.

Jerry found another use for electrical power in the cubicle. Making his own resistors by mixing charcoal and salt in a hollow piece of bamboo and sealing the ends with candle wax, Jerry, the radar and radio expert, built a small shortwave receiver by fashioning condensers out of paper and tinfoil, and using coils from magnet wire taken from an old call-bell system in the hospital. If the Japanese found out he'd done this, he would have first been brutally interrogated then executed.

Although he had built the radio set before Margaret came to the camp, she understood the chances they were both taking by keeping it in the cubicle, and whenever he put on the headset at 6 P.M. to listen to the latest war news, she kept watch on the corridor for the Japanese soldiers. This is how they had learned about MacArthur's return to the Philippines—*"They've landed!"* Jerry announced joyously, and it was all Margaret could do to stop him from telling everyone—and the recent victory of U.S. forces at Leyte. They told only a few trusted friends what they knew, but to help with camp morale, Jerry sent out some vague "rumors" about the war's progress. If the Japanese overheard current war news being passed around among the prisoners, they would know there was a radio in camp and would do whatever was necessary to find it and punish those who had it.

As frightened as she was by this—and she was often *terrified* by Jerry's ability to eye death face-to-face and scoff at it—she was proud of his ability to do something when others seemed trapped by circumstances and their own inertia. He was fearless when it came to doing things others only dreamed of doing, which she wished she could do but lacked the nerve. Although at times he worried her with his bold actions, she was proud of him.

There was no other man like Jerry Sams, she decided. But even though she had given birth to his daughter, there was still a lot she did not know about him; the kind of things a couple normally learn about each other. Did he sing in the shower? How did he like his eggs cooked? But she knew about his character, and most important, she knew he accepted her and the children when other men in a similar situation might not have. To Jerry, she was his wife, and his place was at her side regardless of what anyone else thought or said.

Together, they found ways to hide the radio from frequent inspections of the barracks and their cubicle. Up to now, Jerry had painstakingly dismantled the radio after each time he used it and stowed the pieces in various hiding places. Margaret was always scared a guard would pop in unannounced and catch him assembling or disassembling the electronic pieces scattered about the cubicle.

Margaret did a lot of mending and patching of their worn-out clothes, using needles and pins they had bartered for and some Jerry had made out of splinters of bamboo. She gathered thread she painstakingly unraveled from old clothing and miscellaneous pieces of fabric. Jerry decided to make a wooden sewing box and let the Japanese see that's what it was during numerous inspections as Margaret sat sewing next to it. Jerry proudly pointed out to the guards the "wonderful little sewing box" he had made. They would look over the box, peer inside, and nod appreciatively. After a while, he stopped talking about the box, and the guards stopped looking inside. At that point, he placed the intact radio at the bottom and covered it with Margaret's sewing supplies. Jerry was able to easily pull the radio out of its new home and quickly stash it away.

One afternoon, Margaret returned from doing some wash to find a Japanese soldier in the cubicle with Jerry. They were both standing up. The sewing box was in its usual place in one corner. The guard's rifle was lying on top of it!

For a moment, she thought she would faint. She was certain the radio had been found and her and Jerry's time had come. Then she realized that the conversation was amiable, and nothing unusual was happening. Quite the contrary, Jerry was smiling and laughing as he chatted away. Margaret willed herself to take her eyes off the sewing box.

When the soldier looked in her direction, she smiled.

Then it hit her. They were getting away with something very dangerous right under the noses of the Japanese, and Jerry was loving it.

Surprising her even more was the fact that she was enjoying it, too.

TWO WEEKS BEFORE CHRISTMAS 1944, THE LAST GROUP OF PRIS-oners was transferred from Santo Tomás to Los Baños, bringing its total population to more than 2,100 men, women, and children.

Margie Whitaker, a rosy-cheeked eighteen-year-old brunette, arrived with her parents and younger sister, Betty. Their day began with a three-hour, predawn ride in the crowded boxcar of a rickety train, followed by an arduous walk from the train station carrying bags with their worldly possessions. Margie's father, who had recently recovered from tuberculosis and was so thin he appeared cadaverous, passed out just as they entered the camp's front gate. Margie thought they had lost him right then and there, but he was carried to the clinic, where the nurses revived him.

Margie had been a sophomore at Manila's Bordner High School when Pearl Harbor was attacked, an event for which her teenage ego had accepted a measure of responsibility. On her way to school that morning, she had prayed for divine intervention to keep her history class from having a scheduled test she hadn't studied for over the weekend. She arrived at school and found that all classes were canceled and students were being sent home due to the shocking news of the surprise Japanese attack. Since then, the only classes she had attended were at Santo Tomás, where some dedicated teachers who were also being held prisoner had taught her and other schoolchildren so they wouldn't fall too far behind in their studies.

The Whitaker family moved to the Philippines a few months after Margie was born in Spokane. Her father, Jocelyn "Jock" Whitaker, became a top administrator in the Philippines Sugar Administration, and when she was six years old, her father and his brother bought a plantation in northern Luzon, and the family moved there from Manila.

Margie Whitaker. *Courtesy Margaret (Whitaker) Squires.*

When it was time to plant rice, the fields were flooded and shallow dikes were built to make checkerboard rice paddies. After the rice was harvested, the fields were dried up and sugarcane was planted. The Whitakers lived in a two-story, six-bedroom home with a wraparound veranda that had been built during the previous century on the banks of a meandering river. Margie and her sister—homeschooled by their mother—spent many afternoons in a large, oval swimming pool set in a shady mango grove. For the Whitakers, the years on the plantation were among the happiest of their lives. The family had moved back to Manila when it was time for the children to go to high school.

The Whitakers were separated at Los Baños due to what they were told was a shortage of family quarters. Jock was assigned to a men's barracks, and Margie, fourteen-year-old Betty, and their mother, Evalyn, moved into Barracks 20 with a group of Franciscan and Maryknoll nuns in a section of the camp known as "Vatican City" because some five hundred members of the clergy—two bishops, a monsignor, a hundred and forty priests, more than a hundred nuns, and two hundred Protestant missionaries—had arrived and were placed there months earlier.

The family already knew many of the Los Baños internees from Santo Tomás. One of Margie's best friends brought her talinum starts from her own little garden. Margie and her mother planted the fast-growing lettuce in a patch of dirt outside their cubicle between the barracks and inner fence. The nuns continued to wear their order's traditional habit and veil despite the heat, and they were friendly and gregarious, though it was a bit ominous to hear so many of them going through the day reciting Hail Marys.

Margie hadn't thought anyplace could be worse than Santo Tomás, but in no time she discovered she was wrong. She wondered who had started the rumor that life in Los Baños was healthier than in Santo Tomás. That hope had caused her family to volunteer to transfer to the "country club camp." Yes, the setting was an improvement; now, instead of being inside the walls of urban Santo Tomás, they were in a lush countryside environment, surrounded on three sides by coconut groves and banana trees; to the west was a beautiful, forest-covered mountain. There was a feeling of space and beauty here that was far removed from Santo Tomás.

Even so, the barbed-wire fences, gun towers, and patrolling soldiers with bayonets affixed to rifles were demoralizing. Margie and the other newcomers were immediately struck by the fact that the official policy here revolved around purposely keeping food from the internees and starving to death as many as possible before the camp could be liberated. All the wan, pale faces, emaciated frames, and lagging steps among the prisoners showed that the Japanese were succeeding.

Margie volunteered to work in the Japanese garrison's vegetable garden so she would get an extra hundred grams of uncooked rice each day. The job consisted of five hours of work daily in three shifts starting at 7:30 A.M. If her mother hadn't taken the early shift, Margie probably would have quit or been fired during the first week. Even with the extra rice, which equated to about a cup of cooked rice that she shared with her family, Margie was hungry all the time. She had little energy for physical labor, which was rendered even more difficult by a blazing-hot sun.

Soon after arriving at Los Baños, Margie's mother passed a patrolling guard and didn't bow as she was supposed to. She was stopped and reprimanded but still refused to bow. The soldier apparently decided against striking the older woman and let her off with a stern warning. Back at their cubicle, Evalyn, a stubbornly independent woman by nature, said she had no intention of ever bowing. Margie had a friend who had bowed improperly, and the officier struck her with his sheathed sword and made her bow from the waist fifty times without stopping. Margie begged her mother not to give the Japanese reason to single her out for such physical abuse.

Eventually, a member of the administration committee showed up and told Evalyn that if she didn't cooperate, things would go badly for the entire camp. He said the last thing they needed was further restrictions. He had a form for her to sign stating she would follow the rules. Evalyn did so only because she didn't want others punished for her actions.

Margie Whitaker, far right, helping her mother wash her hair at Los Baños. *Courtesy Margaret (Whitaker) Squires.*

Margie also worried about what might happen if she or her sister met up with a soldier in the dark or in an isolated part of the camp. She and Betty and their girlfriends talked it over, and decided not to venture far alone and to walk with others whenever possible.

As Christmas approached, everyone began to hope that relief supplies or Red Cross "comfort kits" would arrive for the holiday. But if any were sent, the Japanese kept them. For the holiday, the camp cooks who prepared the meager daily rations served an extra portion of corn-rice mush with traces of banana and coconut milk. The administration committee had asked Konishi to give them some sugar and coffee from the garrison's well-stocked warehouse, but he denied their request. Families broke out a cherished can of Spam or corned beef they had been saving and celebrated as best they could. Things had become so desperate at the camp that many wondered if this would be their last Christmas.

Everyone's spirits were given an uplift when they spotted overhead the first large formation of U.S. land-based planes on the day after Christmas. They had already been seeing fighter planes that operated from aircraft carriers at sea, and even dogfights between U.S. and Japanese planes. But to see an entire formation of American aircraft, with their white stars gleaming in the sun as they roared through the sky, was a joyous event for all. Those internees who were outside began shouting and waving frantically at the planes. Adding to their enjoyment was the sight of terrified Japanese soldiers diving into ditches to take cover or running to their barracks.

Several internees knew enough about aircraft to identify the planes as Army Air Corps P-38s, which meant U.S. forces had airstrips within flying range of Luzon, likely taking off from Leyte or the island of Mindoro, only twenty miles south of Luzon. This was visual confirmation for the prisoners at Los Baños that MacArthur had in fact returned and the retaking of the Philippines was well under way.

Eight days later, twenty-five B-24 bombers flew over the camp in formation at about ten thousand feet, headed north toward Manila. Word excitedly spread among the internees that each of the four-engine bombers carried an eleven-man crew, which meant more than 250 U.S. airmen had flown overhead!

As exciting as these developments were, the internees all had the same questions. How long would it take the U.S. Army to land on Luzon? To defeat the Japanese? To reach Los Baños? Most important, how many of them would still be alive when the Americans finally did arrive?

Shortly before 4 A.M. on January 7, 1945, Margie, her sister, and her mother were awakened by jubilant shouting and yelling coming from the men's barracks next door. The Whitaker women rushed over to find out what was going on. Outside, a Catholic priest told them the Japanese had packed up and were pulling out of camp. Several men began singing "God Bless America" at the top of their lungs, but they were hushed because not all the soldiers had left yet.

George Gray, one of the committee members, had been awakened at midnight by one of the Japanese staff members who said that the commandant wanted to meet with the committee right away in his office. The meeting was short. They were ordered to have all the picks and shovels in camp delivered to the commandant's office as quickly as possible. (Six shovels were kept hidden so that new graves could be dug.) Once that was accomplished, the commandant explained, the garrison would pull out.

"By sudden order of my superiors," said the commandant, "I release all the internees to the committee. You will be in complete charge. I suggest you keep all the prisoners inside the camp. That is all I want to tell you."

One committee member saw Konishi hurriedly clearing out his office. He had a towel wrapped around his head and on his desk was an empty sake bottle. Among his belongings were "bale after bale" of Japanese-printed occupation currency, which the internees called "Mickey Mouse money" because it bought so little. Outside, the office staff was tossing documents into fires blazing inside two large trash drums.

As dawn approached, people began pouring out of their barracks and congregating in front of Barracks 15, where the administration committee had its office. As everyone was milling about—still looking out for Japanese soldiers—word spread that an announcement was about to be broadcast over the loudspeaker system. Soon the entire camp was standing by to hear what was said.

Martin Heichert, the chairman of the administration committee, a forty-seven-year-old native of Los Angeles who had been a Manila-based administrator of General Motors Corporation when war broke out, came over the loudspeaker just before 6 A.M.

"Ladies and gentlemen, earlier this morning this internment camp was officially released to your administration committee," Heichert said. "As of now, your committee declares you free!"

Pandemonium broke out. Only after the cheering and yelling quieted down was he able to resume. "The committee wants you to know that we have no news of actual landings by U.S. forces on

Luzon. While the Japs have left the camp, we have no knowledge that they have abandoned the surrounding area. Consequently, we continue to be in a war zone, and remain subject to all the dangers and risks of warfare. It is the committee's plea that you remain calm and maintain the same organization and some sense of discipline in order that the camp may continue to exist as a unit and function properly for the benefit and protection of all. Further announcements will be made giving details of our new administration setup for the camp, which as of now is designated—Camp Freedom!"

More wild cheering, clapping, and whistling.

Heichert went on to say that he and other members of the camp committee had searched the Japanese warehouse and found that it contained an estimated two months' worth of food. An early breakfast would be served right away, he continued, and starting today the camp kitchen would serve three full meals a day. He was again interrupted by waves of applause.

"Please stand by for a flag-raising ceremony," Heichert said. "It is our intention to lower the flag immediately thereafter as we don't wish to incur the risk of any type of enemy retaliation."

The Japanese flag had already been hauled down the camp's flagpole. As dawn broke over the camp, a large, wrinkled U.S. flag— cherished and hidden through years of captivity—was hoisted to the top, accompanied by a recording of "The Star-Spangled Banner."

Many internees, including Margie and her family, cried openly.

The British produced a smaller Union Jack, and soon it was being sent up the flagpole to an instrumental rendition of "God Save the King."* Overcome with emotion, an Englishwoman next to Margie fainted.

---

* Ten nationalities were represented at Los Baños, with Americans (more than 1,600) and British (329) accounting for the vast majority. Others were: Dutch (89), Canadian (56), Australian (33), Polish (22), Norwegian (10), Italian (16), French (1), and Nicaraguan (1). Included among the American prisoners were a few hundred wives and children of U.S. servicemen.

Despite the call for calm and discipline, a stampede of internees—men, women, and children of all ages—broke through the fences on the northern perimeter of the camp and rushed the Japanese barracks and headquarters. They ransacked whatever had been left behind, including bags of rice and sugar, as well as mattresses and furnishings. One man came out with a pair of knee-high leather boots and another waving a Japanese dagger in the air for all to see. Members of the committee quickly restored order by assigning internee guards to provide security. "No Looting" signs went up with warnings that violators would be brought before the internees court and punishment could include being held in the camp jail, which was used for serious offenses.

That first day, some families and other internees could not resist the temptation to leave camp and stroll into the town of Los Baños or one of its small neighboring barrios, where they traded with friendly residents, offering clothes, pens, and other personal items for eggs, chickens, firewood, salt, sugar, even gin and rum. In addition to this plethora of outside food, the camp kitchen served more generous portions of old and new dishes, which was possible because they could include ingredients such as milk, eggs, poultry, and meat they were now able to get from local markets and farms. Filipino traders brought oxen-drawn carts into camp loaded with freshly picked vegetables and ripened fruits. One farmer walked a young steer into camp and left it for the internees. It was skinned and butchered, and went into a savory stew that very night.

At 6 P.M. the next day, a broken AM radio left by the Japanese was repaired and connected to the camp's public-address system. A huge crowd gathered to hear the first voices most of them had heard from America since New Year's Eve 1941. The popular radio commentator Gabriel Heatter opened with his catchy trademark, "There is good news tonight," even though the war news from Europe was not so good.

Heatter reported that a battle between U.S. and German forces was nearing a decisive resolution, but was still in doubt. Much hinged on the Americans holding a small Belgian town called Bastogne, where a U.S. paratrooper commander, whose unit had been urged to surrender by a German force that had them surrounded, replied with a famous one-word refusal: "Nuts!"

Then President Roosevelt spoke for a few minutes on the overall state of the war. He sounded characteristically optimistic, though cautiously so, about the big battle taking place in Western Europe. He made no mention of the Pacific war, which was disappointing to those listening in the Los Baños Internment Camp.

After that, a variety show came on the air. To the wild delight of the internees who had just passed their first day of freedom after more than three years in captivity, the first song was a new release of a 1930s Cole Porter hit sung by Bing Crosby and the Andrew Sisters.

*Oh, give me land, lots of land, under starry skies above,*
*Don't fence me in.*

Glorious days of eating followed, as shrunken stomachs were filled for the first time in ages. There was roasted and stewed carabao, and pork and beef served with gravy and molasses. Rich coconut milk was ladled over the morning mush. Mouths lovingly held bites of food as the taste and texture of every morsel was savored.

Everyone was given a kilo of uncooked rice, which they could prepare whenever they wanted. Initially, some people became sick because their bodies were not able to handle such quantities, but within days everyone had gained ten to fifteen pounds.

After hearing distant explosions all day, internees on January 10 received the news they had been waiting for. The evening broadcast played over the camp's loudspeaker reported that the U.S. Sixth Army had landed the day before at Lingayen Gulf, 150 miles away in northern Luzon. The report indicated that around two hundred thousand U.S. soldiers came ashore along a twenty-mile beachhead and were rapidly moving south toward Manila against light Japanese resistance, liberating towns in which crowds of celebrating Filipinos flocked to the streets waving tiny U.S. flags.

The battle for Luzon was taking place at long last.

The internees continued to celebrate, certain that they would be liberated any day now. Talk of home filled the night, as few could find sleep.

Three days later, many internees were awakened in the middle of the night to the sound of trucks outside the camp. Certain that the conquering U.S. Army had arrived, some rushed to the gate to greet them.

The trucks were filled with disembarking Japanese troops.

Konishi and the entire garrison had returned.

Imperial Japanese Army officers in charge of Los Baños Internment Camp. Photograph was taken January 10, 1945, at New Bilibid Prison. Commandant Iwanaka is seated; Konishi is believed to be standing second from right. *Courtesy Yale Divinity Library.*

# EIGHT

# Under the Cover of Darkness

Major Jay Vanderpool, recruited and trained for a "highly hazardous mission," beat the U.S. Sixth Army to Luzon by three months.

In many respects, he was the perfect man to organize and co-ordinate the Filipino guerrillas prior to the U.S. forces' landing on Luzon. As assistant G-2 of the 25th Infantry Division, he had been asked in the summer of 1944 to nominate an officer of field rank (major or above) for a dangerous mission behind enemy lines. Intelligence officers of several other divisions were asked to do the same. The desired attributes included combat leadership experience and being adept at backwoods hiking, camping, and living off the land. Vanderpool came up with only two names—another officer and himself—and decided finally that he was the best suited for the job.

Soon after, he was ordered to report to MacArthur's headquarters, recently moved from Australia to New Guinea.

Vanderpool was twenty-seven years old, five foot eight, and stocky like the high school football player and Army boxer he had been. He had enlisted in the Army in 1936 at the age of nineteen. The scion of Dutch and Flemish immigrants three generations earlier on his father's side and with mixed American Indian blood from his mother, Vanderpool spent his childhood moving around the country following his father's seasonal construction work. He attended high schools in three different states. After his parents divorced, he and his mother returned to Oklahoma, where he had been born.

When his mother died unexpectedly during his senior year in high school, he dropped out without graduating. This was during the Depression, when finding a job was not easy for a teenager, so he signed up with the public works relief program, Civilian Conservation Corps, and worked at hard labor for a year. He also spent a lot of time in the mountains and backcountry, often taking off on his own for days with a pack, his rifle, and a fishing pole.

He joined the peacetime Army primarily so he could travel and was sent to Schofield Barracks, Hawaii, for basic training. He graduated at the top of his class. When he was asked to choose an assignment, he volunteered for artillery and was assigned to a regimental battery of the Schofield-based 25th Infantry Division.

Vanderpool's unit offered a course for enlisted men who wanted to become officers and whose commanders thought they were officer material. He eventually enrolled in the course, learning communications, tactics, map reading, land survey, trigonometry, and topographic survey. Excelling to the extent that he was soon teaching some classes, Vanderpool became a second lieutenant in the spring of 1941.

He thought Hawaii was idyllic right up until December 7, 1941. Schofield Barracks, some twelve miles from Pearl Harbor, was adjacent to Wheeler Field, which the Japanese hit in the first wave, destroying or damaging more than a hundred U.S. planes on the ground. Rumors about an impending invasion were flying around for days—fishing boats hurriedly returning home were misreported as approaching enemy troopships—and the 25th Infantry Division moved out to beach positions to defend Honolulu and Ewa Point on Oahu's leeward coast against a Japanese invasion that never happened.

A period of intensive training followed to prepare the 25th Infantry for combat, during which the division received new arms and equipment. All the units received new communications gear, which the Army had sorely needed for years but in its peacetime budget never had the money to buy.

In November 1942, the 25th Infantry deployed in a large convoy to Guadalcanal in the Southwest Pacific, where they reinforced U.S. Marines who had been taking heavy casualties. The division participated in some of the worst combat yet in the Pacific, and after a brutal fight that cost more than seven thousand American lives and wiped out the thirty-six thousand Japanese holding the island, resistance on Guadalcanal ended in February 1943. The 25th Infantry remained on the island several more months while they received replacements and resupplies.

Vanderpool, a captain at the time, was out one day with a small party on a training exercise. While climbing over a ridge formerly defended by the Japanese, he noticed a hidden bunker. The body of a dead enemy soldier was lying halfway inside the entrance. Vanderpool moved in to get a closer look at the bunker's construction and kicked loose a stone that rolled down the hole. This caused the "dead" soldier to quickly try to move farther down into the bunker.

Vanderpool pulled his Colt .45 from the holster and yelled, "Hey, come out of that hole!"

The Japanese soldier slowly came up holding a rifle. He had a bandolier of ammo and four hand grenades attached to a chest harness.

Vanderpool continued pointing the pistol at the soldier even after he remembered that it was empty. With the fighting now largely over on the island, his peacetime training had kicked in. *To avoid accidents while training, keep your gun unloaded until ready to fire.* The ammo magazine was in his jeep's glove compartment down the hill.

"Cover him!" he yelled to his men as his hand started to shake.

Luckily, the enemy soldier decided not to be a hero, dropped his rifle, and threw his hands in the air. Vanderpool took his prisoner to the jeep, reached into the glove compartment, and snapped the seven-round magazine into his gun. He would always remember the astonished look on the soldier's face. He was surprised later when he received his first combat medal, a Bronze Star, for "capturing a heavily armed Japanese soldier with an empty pistol."

During this time, Vanderpool also took part in a joint training program instituted by Admiral William "Bull" Halsey, the commander of air, land, and sea forces at Guadalcanal. The program, for officers from the Army and Navy, emphasized combat scouting and patrolling. Instructors taught skills such as map reading, first-aid and medicine, compass navigation, scouting techniques, pidgin English, and bivouac construction. As a graduation exercise, each officer led a platoon-sized unit across the mountain ranges of Guadalcanal from coast to coast, a patrol of about a week to ten days.

At the end, the program's instructors held a secret ballot, and Vanderpool was selected as the most outstanding patrol leader. When the division went back to New Caledonia to prepare for its next campaign, he was promoted to major and made assistant G-2 primarily because he could teach scouting and patrolling to young Americans, few of whom had any experience in the woods or mountains and were now being asked to fight in such terrain.

His main themes were that "the jungle is not going to eat you" and "the Japanese are not nine-foot-tall Supermen." He taught his men how to keep from getting sick in the jungle, how to care for their feet in the wet environment, how to make a fire in a rain forest, how to set up a lean-to and dry out their clothes at night, and tricks such as not stopping to rest after crossing a river—which would stiffen cold muscles—but to get to the next ridge before taking a break. But it was more than being trained for the jungle—it was also about developing the confidence to face an enemy experienced in jungle fighting.

When he reached General MacArthur's headquarters in New Guinea, Vanderpool finally found out what he'd volunteered for:

he was to sneak into the Philippines by submarine in advance of U.S. landings and work with the Filipino guerrilla forces. He entered an intensive cycle of briefings by military personnel and civilians who had spent time with Filipino guerrillas. They were not allowed to take notes and had to commit everything to memory because they could not take the chance of carrying notes in the event they were captured. After a few weeks, they received their individual assignments.

Vanderpool headed a team of several trained Army technicians to set up weather stations, and handle radio communications and demolitions. Their destination was Lingayen Bay, one hundred miles north of Manila. For their ride to the Philippines, they were assigned to USS *Cero* (SS-225), one of the newer diesel-electric submarines, which in the fifteen months since her commissioning had completed five wartime cruises and sunk a number of Japanese freighters, tankers, and cargo ships.

Loading each of the sub's four tubes with a single Mark 14 torpedo, the sailors had removed the remainder of their torpedoes to make room in fore-and-after spaces for Vanderpool's party and supplies—much of it earmarked for guerrilla forces—including weapons, ammo, radios, batteries, and medical supplies. Landing the Army patrol held priority over all else. The submarine's captain, Navy Commander Edward Dissette, had been ordered not to attack enemy shipping until delivering Vanderpool and his men.

This was Vanderpool's first time on a submarine, and he thought the quarters were warm and comfortable, and the hot chow served by the Navy mess cooks beat the Army's K rations. After a few days, the sub's radio officer began overhearing traffic from other submariners about having spotted a large Japanese fleet. Soon scores of greenish images filled *Cero's* screen representing four or five battleships, heavy and light cruisers, destroyers and destroyer escorts.

When the *Cero* reached Lingayen Bay, they spotted scores of enemy transports unloading thousands of Japanese troops. Vanderpool had the captain send a message to Pearl Harbor asking for instructions. Then they waited for an answer.

Pearl relayed the message to MacArthur's headquarters, and then the response back to the sub. *Cero* was to make its way north around Luzon and land Vanderpool's party on the opposite coast at Infanta, some fifty miles east of Manila. Vanderpool was told that he would meet up with Air Force Major Bernard Anderson, who since escaping Bataan in early 1942 had lived in the Zambales Mountains with Negrito natives. His guerrillas would help unload the submarine.

At night, they cruised on the surface around to the other side of Luzon, and stayed submerged during the day to avoid detection. There was a danger in being spotted even by U.S. planes, whose pilots often couldn't tell the difference between American and Japanese subs because they looked so similar in the water—sleek, black, and unmarked.

One night while proceeding on the surface, they crossed paths with a squadron of five Japanese Chidori-class destroyers that spotted *Cero* as she hurriedly submerged. The captain brought the sub down to a very deep three hundred feet—considered its maximum depth—and rigged for silent running. But the enemy destroyers had gotten a sonar fix on *Cero*. While four of them took "pings" to fix the sub's latest position, the fifth would speed directly over it and drop explosive depth charges into the ocean. Taking turns making the depth-charge runs, the five ships did this all night long.

The Army party's primary task was to keep out of the way of the crew and stay quiet. The bridge continued to keep them informed, but no one needed to tell Vanderpool when a destroyer was making a depth-charge run. First came the deep growling of the engines, then the thrashing propellers, and finally the rhythmic concussion waves of the underwater explosive charges as they came closer, then moved farther away. Vanderpool had heard plenty of artillery and bombs at close range, but the sound of a depth-charge blast against a metal hull was a different and more sinister sound. Finally, at day-break, the destroyers gave up.

*Cero* waited until nightfall before surfacing. They were then able to pump fresh air into the hot, stuffy compartments below and re-charge the batteries. They chugged around to the other side of Luzon without incident. When they knew they were offshore of Infanta, they flashed a prearranged signal, which was quickly acknowledged.

Under the cover of darkness, they off-loaded.

Vanderpool and his team were taken to Major Anderson's well-hidden camp and Anderson briefed him on recent enemy movements in his sector. Anderson had set up an efficient intelligence-gathering operation using guerrillas, who also did some sabotage work. Al-though he didn't run a combat unit, Anderson maintained contact with various guerrilla units on Luzon that had been fighting the Japanese for years.

Vanderpool received a radio dispatch from MacArthur's head-quarters with his new orders, and they were about as broad a directive as a young army major could be given by the supreme commander.

VANDERPOOL FROM MacARTHUR: DO WHAT
WILL BEST FURTHER THE ALLIED CAUSE.

Vanderpool folded up the message and slipped it into his pocket. Given MacArthur's popular standing in the Philippines, this order would function like a "passport from the Almighty" whenever he showed it to guerrillas and other Filipinos, all of whom idolized MacArthur and were eager to assist in his and the U.S. Army's long-awaited return.

Vanderpool met with Anderson to determine where he was most needed; preferably in a region where U.S. military officers were not yet operating. The handful of other Americans working with guerril-las in the Philippines had established radio contact with Anderson, and he spoke with them almost daily and knew their whereabouts.

Anderson suggested Vanderpool locate in an area south of Manila. There were a number of promising guerrilla units operating around Laguna de Bay that needed improved communication and coordination, he explained. One group in particular, Hunters ROTC, was a first-rate outfit with solid leaders who employed the military order and organization missing in other guerrilla units.

Vanderpool's party started out in *bancas,* sailing south along the coast for several miles until they went ashore where Anderson said they could pick up a trail into the mountains. He sent out couriers to scout ahead and make contact with any guerrillas they came across, then followed with the main party bringing the supplies.

Native *banca. Courtesy Paul Shea.*

Within a week, they had reached the eastern shore of Laguna de Bay. Arriving at a small barrio about dusk, they were told to spend the night because when it got dark the Japanese used the paved road along the coast, and during the day, they hid out to avoid being attacked by U.S. planes that now controlled the skies over Luzon. While the other Americans scattered into houses around the neighborhood, a priest took Vanderpool up to the belfry of the Catholic church. On the way to the top, he passed two small rooms used as bedrooms by several nuns.

Vanderpool was awakened at dawn by voices below. A platoon of Japanese soldiers was searching the church, and several were on their way up the narrow steps to the belfry. The only other way out involved making a thirty-foot leap from the steeple, but more Japanese troops lingered in front of the church.

Suddenly he heard the loud protests of the nuns, who were defending their modesty and complaining about men in their domain. The soldiers withdrew downstairs.

But the Japanese did not leave the area until nightfall, at which point Vanderpool quickly gathered his party. Deciding to stay off the road, he hired several *bancas* to sail them across Laguna de Bay. At one point, they heard Japanese patrol boats and saw their searchlights sweeping the waters, but they were not challenged.

Once they made landfall, they holed up in a barrio, and Vanderpool was told there was a seldom-used trail about ten miles down the road that went through rice-paddy country, where they would be met by a guide who would take them the rest of the way to the Hunters ROTC's camp near Nasugbu, a coastal town sixty miles southwest of Manila.

Vanderpool had to consider how to proceed ten miles on a road used by the Japanese. The Filipinos with him would have no problem being seen walking on the road, but he couldn't take such a chance with his own men and their equipment. He thought, *What would I do if I were home? Hell, I'd call a taxi!* He asked a local resident to summon a taxi, and eventually a big, old black sedan for hire came down the road. However, when the driver saw the group of Americans, he was reluctant to take them because if they got caught, he would be killed, too. Vanderpool gave the cabbie a choice. If he didn't take them, Vanderpool would take his car. If he gave them a lift down the road, he would be rewarded from a wad of bills the officer flashed. The driver decided to accept the fare.

In a few miles, they came to a Japanese sentry post.

The taxi had a small Japanese flag atop its radiator cap. Instead of being made to stop, they were saluted and allowed to drive through.

When Vanderpool and his exhausted party marched into the Hunters ROTC camp, the guerrillas were stunned to see that he had made the long trek through enemy lines in his complete U.S. Army uniform.

TWO WEEKS BEFORE JAPAN'S IMPERIAL ARMY ENTERED MANILA in January 1942, MacArthur closed the Philippine Military Academy (PMA)—the country's West Point—and disbanded all ROTC programs. He did so "to preserve the younger generation from the ravages of war." This disbandment directed all military cadets to return home, and that was bitterly disappointing to many of them. A group of these PMA cadets decided to recruit other volunteers to join them in opening up a "second front."

A few weeks later, they had recruited sixty followers, including ROTC cadets from different colleges. They trained secretly in the handling of assorted weapons collected by breaking into armories and waylaying Japanese soldiers on bicycles. They then graduated to acts of sabotage, such as cutting phone lines.

Days before U.S. and Filipino forces surrendered on Bataan—and with their surrender the suspension of organized military action in the Philippines—this group of young resistance fighters took to the mountains of Luzon's Sierra Madre. Their motto was "Only those who are not afraid to die are fit to live in freedom," and they began to carry out small-unit, hit-and-run raids to harass the Japanese and cause them to lose men and matériel. They also liquidated spies, pro-Japanese collaborators, and other traitors in their midst who had gone unchallenged up to then.

Eventually, Hunters ROTC grew to a force of more than twenty-five thousand officers and men willing to die to free their homeland. More than other guerrilla groups, they remained true to their military training, maintaining the command structure, training, and communications necessary to be an effective fighting force. They were also masters in the art of jungle warfare, and had established a valuable intelligence network on Luzon. Hunters ROTC was active in Manila and southern Luzon, notably in the Laguna de Bay region, while many other guerrilla units were active throughout Luzon and the rest of the Philippines.

The guerrillas were aware of the cruel and inhumane treatment their countrymen had received from the Japanese military, so they never took prisoners. For the most part, they fought on their own as autonomous units. They found their own weapons, ammunition, food, and targets, and made their own plans. At times, they competed with one another and were even antagonistic. Their primary loyalty was to their country, though they had emotional ties to the United States. But there was no central guerrilla control or allegiance.

Their leaders often acted as independent warlords; some imposed taxes on local residents to fund their operations, though others did not. Some were geographically situated, and others were spread over large regions. No two were alike, except that they were all supported by locals who supplied food, clothing, and other assistance. The civilian population was not only the economic base for the guerrilla movement, but also the main source of new recruits: fighters as well as couriers, doctors, and nurses.

Early in the war, the lack of coordination between the groups was beneficial when a unit was overrun and its members captured. Even under the worst torture, the men knew little about the makeup and location of other units. But as MacArthur was planning to invade Luzon, this lack of coordination became a liability. For the Filipino guerrillas to help the U.S. Army with timely intelligence and reconnaissance, they had to coordinate their movements with those of the Americans. It was up to U.S. intelligence officers like Jay Vanderpool to see that they were functioning this way before the Luzon landings.

The first thing Vanderpool did when he entered the Hunters ROTC camp was have his radioman set up the big and powerful shortwave set they had lugged across the sea and over the mountains. Encoding a short message and using a designated call sign (JU-4), he went on the air to let MacArthur's headquarters (KAZ) know his location.

After a rest and a meal of boiled rice, bananas, and sugarcane, Vanderpool met with the overall commander of the Hunters ROTC, Colonel Eleuterio "Terry" Adevoso, a twenty-three-year-old from a province in the Calabarzon region east of Manila. Adevoso was young, but Vanderpool was impressed with his reserved and soft-spoken leadership style.

Vanderpool told Adevoso and his staff officers that as MacArthur's personal representative in southern Luzon—he showed them MacArthur's extraordinary one-sentence message—he controlled the distribution of U.S. military, medical, and communications supplies the other guerrillas in the Cavite, Batangas, and Los Baños areas would receive. Asked if he would be commanding the guerrillas, he said that was not his intention. He pulled out of the air his self-appointed title, "guerrilla coordinator," which he hoped sounded nonconfrontational and made it clear that he would only act as liaison between the United States and guerrilla forces. He realized that his job was not to reshape or revolutionize the resistance effort that had been in place for years, but to give its members the tools to fight the enemy as a cohesive force when the time came to do so.

Adevoso's staff was smart, well trained, and highly motivated. His four top planners were: a former secretary to the president of the Philippines, as G-1 (personnel); Major Marcelo Castillo Jr., a twenty-nine-year-old 1938 graduate of the U.S. Naval Academy, as G-2 (intelligence); Major Rigoberto "Bert" Atienza, who had military experience with U.S. forces before the war and spoke fluent English, as G-3 (operations and planning); and a graduate of the French war school, the École de Guerre, which Napoleon and every great French general after him had attended, as G-4 (logistics). They all held the same staff positions for Vanderpool when he set up his own General Guerrilla Command to act as go-between for U.S. and guerrilla forces. He and Adevoso, who served as Vanderpool's chief of staff, conversed regularly about strategy and tactics, and whenever Vanderpool traveled to meet with other guerrilla groups, Adevoso made sure the American was escorted by Hunters ROTC members.

Vanderpool could see that the resistance fighters on Luzon were excited about the impending arrival of U.S. forces, and they were ready to jump into the larger fight to liberate their homeland. That spirit was great, but he had the same message for them all: "Let's not jump the gun. Don't try to take on the Japanese Army alone because if you are wiped out you'll be no good to anyone. Wait until the Americans get here and be ready to coordinate your work with U.S. ground forces."

Throughout November and into December, Vanderpool strove to set up a communications network that could carry messages from one isolated barrio to another. He even instituted a pony express right out of America's Old West. Two or three ponies were placed in every barrio so couriers could come in, dismount, and quickly be off on a fresh mount. The indigenous ponies weren't that fast, but they were faster than walking. Every barrio in the region had a local security and warning system, and word of enemy movements would reach guerrilla headquarters through a combination of runners, riders, and walkie-talkies.

Vanderpool organized a downed-pilot retrieval program. Any guerrilla unit that saved a U.S. pilot and gave him back—Vanderpool would arrange to have a U.S. submarine or PBY amphibious plane arrive offshore to pick them up—would receive a load of guns, ammo, and supplies. The incentive was so great that in December alone, twenty-two U.S. pilots who had been shot down over Luzon were returned by guerrillas.

That same month, Vanderpool received a message from MacArthur's headquarters to get himself down to Tacloban, Leyte, for a conference. This was not a small request because fulfilling it involved a three-hundred-mile journey through enemy-held territory. He knew it must be important to be summoned from such a distance, and figured it concerned final plans for the Luzon landings. He radioed a U.S. intelligence officer operating in Mindoro and told him he was coming and would require transportation from there to Leyte.

The only way to get from Luzon to Mindoro was by boat. Vanderpool and his guerrilla escorts visited a small fishing village on Manila Bay where they found a sturdy, seagoing sailboat. They took it out of the bay into the channel, past Corregidor Island, and into the ocean. The weather looked pretty good to the American's untrained eye, but when it got dark that night, they found themselves in a storm packing furious winds and thirty-five-foot waves that threatened to capsize their boat.

The crew took down all the canvas and threw out a sea anchor to try to steady the boat. The next day was just as bad. Even the experienced sailors were so seasick they could barely work the boat. The second night no one got more than an hour's sleep, but the storm lessened the next day. They had no idea where they were other than someplace west of the Philippines. Vanderpool reasoned that if they maintained an easterly course, they would eventually come across land.

The land they hit was a little island chain between Mindoro and Luzon called Lubang, which had a Japanese airfield on it. As their boat sailed past, a scout plane was launched to check them out.

When the plane swooped over them, the three Filipinos left on deck waved to the plane. The pilot waved back and flew away.

Vanderpool referred to the only chart he had—an eight-by-ten-inch map torn from an old *National Geographic*—and figured that if they headed to the southeast they could not miss Mindoro. He was correct, and they came in right where they were heading: Abra de Ilog, on the north coast of Mindoro, near where the American officer who came out to pick up Vanderpool's party in *bancas* had his camp. Once ashore, Vanderpool found out that American forces had landed at San Jose, in southern Mindoro, and they had taken over the harbor and an airfield.

The Navy dispatched two PT boats to pick up Vanderpool and take him to San Jose. After being on the sailboat during a storm, zipping along at 30 mph and enjoying a mug of hot coffee was like passage on an ocean liner. That is, until an armed Japanese patrol plane appeared on the horizon.

As the plane swung around to approach them from behind, the PT skippers kept their positions, with one boat in the lead and the other slightly behind. They held their course and speed as the plane came in low at three hundred feet. As it released its bombs, the two boats made sharp outboard turns, one to the left and one to the right, and the bombs exploded harmlessly into the water. As the plane flew by, the twin .50-caliber machine guns on both PT boats opened up. Hit multiple times, the plane crashed into the water half a mile ahead.

At San Jose, Vanderpool boarded a C-47 for a flight to Leyte.

The briefing and meeting at general headquarters lasted a couple of days. As Vanderpool had suspected, it involved commanders and senior staff who were planning for the final offensive in Luzon. Every operation was outlined in detail. When it was time for his briefing, Vanderpool said their intelligence estimate showing a Japanese infantry division defending the beach at Nasugbu was incorrect.

"So, Major, what is at Nasugbu?" asked one senior officer.

"A rifle company minus one platoon, plus two extra machine guns."

Raised eyebrows and furtive glances all around.

"How old is this information?" he was asked.

"About four or five days," Vanderpool said.

"And just how do you know this?"

"I was just in Nasugbu," Vanderpool explained. "I saw for myself, and I talked to the town mayor and other residents."

"What happened to the Jap infantry division and its tanks?"

"The main force went north toward Manila," Vanderpool said.

Some of those present believed him, and others did not. It was decided that the landings at Nasugbu would be considered a "reconnaissance in force." If Vanderpool was correct, and the landing there faced scant opposition, the corridor south of Manila could be rapidly secured as the U.S. Sixth Army rolled down from its Lingayen Gulf beaches with the goal of liberating the capital. If Vanderpool was wrong, and a division of Japanese infantry was defending Nasugbu, then U.S. troops would at least have another beachhead from which to fight their way inland.

Shortly after concluding his briefing, Vanderpool heard that his name was being added to the "no-capture list," which meant he knew too much to take the chance of being captured. He got the word that they were planning not to send him back to Luzon.

That sent Vanderpool directly to the office in charge of operations, hoping word hadn't reached them that he was not to return to Luzon. He asked if he could borrow a C-47 for a flight back to San Jose. They didn't have one available, but they did have a Navy PBY, which could land in the water. That meant he didn't have to land at San Jose but could be dropped off on the north coast of Mindoro.

"Even better," he said.

Vanderpool, who had not yet received a direct order about not returning to Luzon, quietly grabbed his things and snuck out of Leyte that night, compliments of the U.S. Navy.

The PBY landed in the river at Abra de Ilog, Mindoro, and Vanderpool borrowed a boat from the U.S. intelligence officer for clear sailing to Looc Cove, just above Nasugbu. He walked up a hill, found his guerrillas, fired up his radio set, and reported to headquarters that he was back in position. Since he was already back in Luzon, he figured he couldn't be ordered not to go there.

He did know too much—such as when and where the U.S. landings on Luzon would take place—to allow himself to be captured. He resolved to do everything in his power to make sure he wasn't taken alive.

Vanderpool started a mental countdown to January 9, 1945, the day when the Lingayen Gulf landings were scheduled to take place. Once an operation of this magnitude—one that involved the moving of thousands of ships and planes and tens of thousands of troops—went into final staging, last-minute changes weren't possible. *It would be January 9.*

On that morning, after he and his senior staff finished breakfast, Vanderpool announced that the Americans had landed that morning at Lingayen Gulf. His men knew he'd had no outside communications, and none of them had heard anything of the sort. They looked at him in silence, with disbelief on their faces. Vanderpool even detected some concern, as if they thought he had lost his marbles.

A few hours later, there was a radio report that said U.S. forces had landed at Lingayen that morning and were moving south to Manila. The U.S. Sixth Army, under General Walter Krueger, had come ashore at 9 A.M. following a devastating naval bombardment.

Meeting little opposition on the beaches, more than two hundred thousand soldiers landed over the next few days. The assault forces secured a twenty-mile-long beachhead and penetrated several miles inland, liberating towns where they were greeted by cheering Filipinos who waved U.S. and Philippine flags.

Three weeks later, Vanderpool was still near Nasugbu, waiting to hook up with U.S. forces. He had a bad feeling as they settled down for the night. *We've been here too damn long. Time to find a different location.* He roused his staff, and they got everyone packing and moving. They were gone so fast they left a couple of small campfires still burning.

Carrying their heavy gear through wooded terrain, they dropped into a canyon and came up on the other side. Around midnight, by which time they were on the opposite ridge, all hell broke loose on the other side. Japanese machine guns, mortars, and rifle platoons were attacking their empty camp.

At sunrise, they heard a naval bombardment hitting Nasugbu, and a short time later, U.S. troops came ashore. Japanese resistance was light overall, although some determined defenders were dug into caves that had to be cleared.

Vanderpool knew the next step for his guerrilla liaison command was to be attached to the 11th Airborne's G-2 section. Later that morning, he introduced himself to Henry Muller, and the two experienced intelligence officers shook hands.

Muller asked Vanderpool to tell him everything he knew about enemy strength in the area, and also about the guerrillas: What could be expected from them by way of intelligence and other assistance?

Vanderpool did so, but added that he had already deployed the Hunters ROTC to protect the 11th Airborne's flanks, and what he anticipated would be the division's main supply line as they headed inland.

Muller was impressed with Vanderpool's preparedness and his grasp of the situation as they went over some charts and aerial photographs.

Even though the Los Baños Internment Camp still remained outside the 11th Airborne's area of operations, the planning of any raids to free friendly POWs, as well as capture enemy prisoners, came under the purview of a division's G-2. Muller well remembered that General Swing had told him not to waste his time on the matter and to keep his "eye on the ball," but the intelligence officer fully intended to be prepared in case the paratroopers were given the job of liberating the camp.

"What do you know about Los Baños prison camp?" he asked.

Vanderpool said he knew of the camp and estimated it held about two thousand men, women, and children, most of them Americans.

"I want you to find out from the guerrillas everything you can about Los Baños," said Muller, explaining that he wanted to know the current situation and how the prisoners were faring.

Muller said to report only to him because his interest in Los Baños was unofficial—"Call it bootleg intel," he said. Vanderpool knew that meant Muller had no business gathering information on the prison camp. As someone who had skirted the rules in carrying out his own duties, he had no problem helping Muller do so.

"One other thing," Muller said, his curiosity piqued. "I see you're in full uniform, Major. Did you wear it the entire time you've been here?"

Vanderpool nodded a bit sheepishly.

"Can I ask why you took such a chance?"

"Well, I decided early on that if I got caught, I wanted to be shot not as a spy but as an American soldier."

NINE

# The Killings

A N OMINOUS SILENCE HUNG OVER LOS BAÑOS INTERNMENT Camp as the men, women, and children who had enjoyed seven days of freedom began Sunday, January 14, 1945, as prisoners of the Japanese.

The Japanese soldiers looked tired, disheveled, and defeated. Major Iwanaka had taken his men closer to Manila because he feared the U.S. forces might land on the Batangas coast south of Los Baños. But then headquarters ordered them back to Los Baños. Some of the soldiers were limping and wore bandages and head dressings, so it seemed likely they had engaged in a skirmish or two with guerrilla forces.

The soldiers, having lost face with their hasty retreat and return, appeared angry and vengeful. Matters only got worse when they found that their storehouse, offices, and barracks had been ransacked.

An interpreter came over the public-address system to announce an unusual midday roll call. All internees—even children, the sick, and elderly as well as those on working parties—were to line up in front of their barracks at 2 P.M. Before the Japanese left, the regular 7 A.M. and 5 P.M. roll calls had always been taken outside each barracks by internee monitors who gave the count to a member of the administration committee, who turned it in.

The guards ordered the internees to return everything they had taken. This included food, bedding, clothing, personal effects, a missing AM radio, even the commandant's personal rice bowl, hand-painted with the Rising Sun flag. The Japanese made it clear that failure to return the property meant the entire camp would be severely punished.

In the hours following the return of the Japanese, several internees wandered back from town only to find the gate and perimeter again manned by soldiers. The Japanese soon realized that during their absence internees had been streaming in and out of camp. The returning internees were immediately taken into custody and questioned about their activities outside of camp, with the Japanese particularly concerned about their having had any contact with guerrilla forces. Afterward, they were allowed to return to their barracks, but the Japanese were even sterner in making it clear they would tolerate no more transgressions. A final threat came over the loudspeaker for all to hear: "The commandant has issued orders that anyone attempting to escape or communicate with outsiders will be shot on sight."

Konishi asked that the administration committee come in for what turned into a stormy session. First, he warned that one of their members would be shot unless the rice and other foods taken from the storehouse were returned. Then he said he was immediately cutting food rations in half, which meant a daily allotment of less than four hundred calories per person; meals were now reduced to two scant portions a day. Furthermore, food from outside the camp would again be halted. When committee members tried to protest these policies, Konishi abruptly ended the session.

When Filipinos came to the main gate that day pushing carts filled with fruits, vegetables, eggs, and meats—as they had done for the past week—the Japanese soldiers ran them off with orders not to return. A working party of internees hauled the bags of rice and other food back from the camp kitchen to the Japanese storehouse, where soldiers put everything under lock and key.

Every man, woman, and child in Los Baños was now aware of a dark fact: plenty of food was available in and around Los Baños to keep them alive, but the Japanese—and Konishi, in particular—refused to let them have it. The only reason for this was cruelty. It was not clear if this was dictated by higher-ups or if it was Konishi's own agenda, but there was a deliberate plan to starve the internees at Los Baños.

At 2 P.M., the guards ordered the internees to fall into formation in front of their barracks. A search party led by the commandant and Konishi went into each barracks looking for contraband, and emerged with stashes of U.S. money, axes, large Filipino bolo knives, and other disallowed loot.

When the search party got to a barracks that housed single men, about fifty of them blocked the entrance to protest having their quarters searched without their being present. This was about more than the search; it was about the starvation rations, so much sickness and death, and this latest loss of freedom. The Japanese guards drew and leveled their bayonets and rifles at the young men, who, though pitifully thin, towered over most of the soldiers. There was yelling and posturing on both sides, and at any moment a bloody row could have erupted. Then, in defiance of the order to remain outside, the men filed back into the barracks even while the soldiers shouted for them to halt. The Japanese finally capitulated by following them inside the barracks, where they took roll call and conducted a quick and superficial inspection. Word of the men's victory soon spread through camp.

The next day, twenty women from Barracks 16 marched down to camp headquarters and pushed their way into Konishi's office, demanding that rations be increased and the camp kitchen be given enough food to serve three meals a day. Only one woman spoke at a time, and another was prepared to pick up where she left off, keeping a continuous stream of complaints flying at Konishi.

*We know it's available! We got plenty when you weren't here!*

*If you don't give us more food, wait until the guerrillas get here!*

Konishi, red-faced and sputtering, let out a bellow.

Ignoring his anger, Jan De la Costa, who had tuberculosis and was all skin and bones, demanded that the internees and their committee be allowed to buy food from local Filipinos.

"Quiet!" shouted Konishi, shaking in fury. "Out!"

The women continued to shout.

Japanese soldiers rushed in and began pushing the women out of the office with the points of their bayonets. They had a way of not breaking the skin unless they wanted to, but the message was delivered.

*We know our troops are on their way!*

*You'll be sorry then!*

JAN HOWARD HELL, AN EASYGOING, GREGARIOUS MAN KNOWN TO everyone as Pat, was a thirty-nine-year-old mining engineer from Arkansas. Hell had been working for a mining company in the mountains north of Manila, having left his pregnant wife stateside four months earlier with the promise that she could join him as soon as the baby was born. In his free time, he had set up a recreation center for children of the mine employees and also did volunteer soil analyses for local farmers, showing them ways of increasing their crop yields.

At first, when the Japanese invaded, he had no trouble hiding from them, and the villagers he had come to know well would have sheltered him for the duration of the war. But he saw a bulletin from the Japanese promising repatriation to any foreigner who surrendered, and he decided to come out of the mountains in the hope of returning home to his wife and baby. Instead he was taken to Santo Tomás, and he was one of the first eight hundred men sent to Los Baños.

He had been in charge of the camp garden, and with the help of volunteers had planted, carefully tended, and picked vegetables he delivered in a cart to the camp kitchen. Like hundreds of internees, Hell had ignored the committee's warnings about leaving camp during Freedom Week, and had learned that there was plenty of food outside the prison camp. Local Filipinos would happily trade food for much-needed clothing. He still had a few things he could trade, and even with the return of the Japanese guards, he decided to make another foraging trip out of camp. A friend was quite ill, and he thought some chicken soup and coconut milk would be good for her.

Dana Nance was working in the medical clinic on the afternoon of January 17 when he heard a rifle shot that sounded unusually close, followed quickly by several more. Although guards often took potshots into the woods for their own amusement, Nance was aware of the new warnings and tensions at the camp, and his first thought was that someone had been shot trying to escape.

A few minutes later, a Japanese soldier entered the clinic and requested Nance's help retrieving a body.

Nance was taken about thirty feet outside the northern boundary of the compound, close to a grove of trees, where he found Pat Hell. He had no pulse. Hell had been hit three times; one bullet entered the front of his head, one struck in the vicinity of the heart, and the third lodged in his abdomen. He had been killed instantly.

The doctor couldn't help noting that Hell was shot in the front and not in the back, as he would have if he were trying to escape.

He had obviously been trying to *return* to camp. Nance then saw that Hell had apparently been coming up an incline and was nearly at the outer fence when a guard must have spotted him and fired. His body had rolled back down the hill and landed on the bank of a small stream. A sack of coconuts and bananas was near his body. Nance reached into Hell's pockets and found a bag of uncooked rice, some coffee beans, and pieces of chocolate. In one hand, Hell still clutched a scrawny dead chicken.

The grave of Pat Hell. *U.S. Army Signal Corps.*

Ten days later, Nance heard another rifle crack in the early morning.

He quickly dressed and grabbed his medical bag. As he was preparing to leave, several internees rushed in to say that George Louis had been shot while crawling back under the outer fence with food.

Nance knew Louis well. He was twenty-seven years old and a native of Sacramento, California. He had been a mechanic for Pan America at its Cavite base when war broke out. He was one of the younger men who weren't intimidated by threats and would have been at the head of the line to enlist in the Army or Marines to fight the Japanese. A single, man-about-Manila during prewar days, Louis had entered camp with a nasty case of gonorrhea, which Nance had knocked back by scrounging from various sources enough doses of a new miracle drug called penicillin.

George Louis lay stranded in no-man's-land between the two fences at the northeastern end of the camp. He was bleeding and moaning from what appeared to be a shoulder wound.

Nance hurried forward but was stopped by soldiers.

"He's dead," said one of the Japanese.

"He's moving!" Nance shouted. "He needs medical attention!"

He argued more with the soldiers, but they would not let him come any closer, so Nance ran to the commandant's office along with committee member George Gray.

They were made to wait as Japanese soldiers hurriedly came and went. When they were finally shown into the commandant's office, he was at his desk with some other officers, including Konishi.

"As the camp medical director," Nance began, "I request that the wounded man be delivered to me at the hospital for medical treatment."

An interpreter translated Nance's request, which was followed by a lengthy discussion that the Americans could not understand. When the interpreter finally spoke, Nance and Gray were stunned by the message. The commandant decided that given his previous order that any internee caught escaping or found to be on the outside would be shot, the wounded man was to be executed.

Gray was the first to speak. "According to international law," he said, "a man cannot be executed if returning to camp but only when caught trying to escape."

The response came quickly: "He disregarded orders. Must be shot."

And with that, the Americans were taken from the building.

The Japanese soldiers had already brought Louis through the inner fence and laid him on the ground. He was awake and partially covered by a sheet. The guards let one of his fellow prisoners give him a cigarette, which he quietly smoked. Not long after he finished, another group of Japanese that included the commandant and Konishi arrived. Several guards rolled Louis onto a wood plank and carried him to the sentry post near the main gate.

From about seventy-five feet away, Paul Hennesen, a forty-one-year-old American employee of the U.S. State Department based in Manila when the war began, watched from a second-floor window of the chapel, where he'd gone earlier after hearing the gunfire. From this vantage point, he saw Konishi gesture to the soldiers, then draw a white-handled pistol from the holster on his belt and hand it to one of them.

A single shot rang out, echoing across the countryside.

When the soldiers delivered George Louis to the hospital, Nance and Dorothy Still were solemnly awaiting the body.

During the autopsy, Nance found what he'd suspected: the wound in the shoulder was not serious. It appeared to have been caused by a .30-caliber round, which was consistent with the Arisaka bolt-action infantry rifles the guards carried. Nance could easily have stitched it up had Louis been brought into the hospital earlier.

The second wound was made by a larger bullet, probably a .38 caliber, and was consistent with the sidearms carried by Japanese officers. Nance had seen many similar wounds while treating patients in Shanghai after the Japanese invasion. This execution-style shot had entered the forehead and exited at the rear of the skull.

Although the Japanese insisted that Nance write in his autopsy report that George Louis had been killed by a single bullet as he tried to reenter the camp, the doctor refused to do so. His official account stated: "The body has been pierced by two bullets. One bullet had a wound entrance above the outer border of the right clavicle and an exit wound along the upper border of the corresponding scapula. This missile grazed the scapula but struck no vital organs—did not even enter the chest cavity—and was in no sense a mortal wound. The other bullet entered the skull in the right frontal region and blew his brains out in the left occipital region. It would appear that this man was executed or given the coup de grace after having sustained minor injury."

Dorothy helped prepare the body for burial. When she was finished, she placed her hands under Louis's shattered head to assist other medical workers in moving the body into a sheet-lined coffin. When she withdrew her hands, they were covered with wet and slippery brain matter.

As a nurse, she was used to blood and gore, but this was too much. This was the destroyed brain of a man she had known so well she could tell he was nearby just by the sound of his big laugh.

Dorothy rushed to a basin and washed her hands. As she kept scrubbing, she recalled a story from the Bible about how Pontius Pilate had washed his hands before a crowd to prove he was innocent of spilling the blood of Jesus. Of course, she had had nothing to do with Louis's death and didn't feel this kind of guilt. Rather, it had to do with the horror of having held the part of him that had stored his intelligence, along with the wanton murder of a good man.

In all her time as a nurse, Dorothy had never had such a reaction. All day long, she could not stop washing her hands. She wondered if they would ever feel clean again.

That afternoon, the administration committee delivered a written protest to the commandant. It was signed by George Gray and accompanied by Nance's autopsy report.

*You, as commandant of the camp, have no power to order the imposition of the death penalty upon any internee here for any offense whatsoever. We call your attention to Articles 60 to 67 of the Geneva Convention of 1929, which soon after the outbreak of the present war your government agreed with the government of the United States to follow in the treatment of civilian internees. Under these articles, only a court may order the death penalty. The right of the prisoner to defend himself is safeguarded as well as his right to have counsel and to appeal. You have disregarded all these provisions in ordering the execution of Mr. George Louis this morning.*

*From no point of view was Mr. Louis guilty of any offense involving the death penalty. At the worst, he could only have been considered in the act of escaping when he was shot. The facts are to the contrary. He was actually returning to the camp and hence was not an escaping prisoner. There can be no doubt that the refusal to permit needed medical attention to be given Mr. Louis after he was first shot, and the order for his execution within an hour and a half thereafter without any court action whatever, constitutes a record unlawful, inhumane, and shocking.*

The grave of George Louis. *U.S. Army Signal Corps.*

NOT LONG AFTER THE KILLINGS, THE JAPANESE BROUGHT IN some local laborers who spent more than a week digging a trench that was ten feet deep and a few hundred feet long. It was located a short distance outside the main gate against the northeast corner of camp. Two other pits had been dug many months earlier to bury the camp's garbage, but they were not as large and there was still plenty of room in them.

Internees watched the digging with wonder—and worry.

As U.S. forces drew closer, were the Japanese so determined to prevent them from being liberated that they might kill them all?

# TEN

# "Do It Right, Joe"

T HE 11TH AIRBORNE RECONNAISSANCE PLATOON REACHED
Tagaytay Ridge ahead of the 511th paratroopers, who were
making their first regimental combat jump of the war.

Terry Santos and the other recon members climbed up from the
beach at Nasugbu, eastward to an elevation of more than two thousand feet, crossing through grasslands and forests and over rocky
outcrops. Near the top of a ridge, after a hike of more than twenty
miles deep behind enemy lines, they spotted a machine-gun pillbox
ideally situated to place deadly fire on troops advancing up the hill.

After making sure the others were in effective firing positions,
Santos edged forward silently. When he was within range, he unhooked a grenade from his web belt, pulled the safety pin, and let the
grenade fly. After the explosion, several Japanese tried to escape out
the back but were shot by recon as they ran away.

By the time the 511th jumped a few days later with the mission
to secure Tagaytay City at the top of the ridge, Filipino fighters had
cleared out many of the remaining Japanese, and enemy resistance
was light. A shortage of available planes meant the 511th had to
jump in waves, with the C-47 aircraft making three round trips from
Mindoro to load up and deliver all the paratroopers to the drop
zone. Despite some misdrops, the 511th quickly assembled atop the

ridge, from which they had unparalleled views in three directions. To the south was the Philippines' second-most-active volcano situated in the middle of picturesque Taal Lake. The Taal Volcano had a small crystalline lake of its own inside its crater. Thirty miles to the east lay the great inland lake Laguna de Bay, and an almost equal distance to the north—straight up Highway 17—was Manila. The men could see columns of dark smoke spiraling skyward from the city, an ominous sign that the "Pearl of the Orient" and its one million residents were facing death and destruction after more than three years of Japanese occupation.

11th Airborne paratroopers get into their jumping gear for the Tagaytay Ridge combat jump on February 3, 1945. *U.S. Army Signal Corps.*

Two days after the 511th reached Tagaytay, the Recon Platoon was sent on a nighttime reconnoiter up Highway 17 toward Manila. Henry Muller directed them to talk to any locals they came across and find out where enemy forces were located. Recon was "mounted" in jeeps so they could get out and back quickly. But it also meant they would be driving in the dark without headlights into possible ambushes, a precarious mission for a lightly armed unit. Recon was ordered not to enter Manila, but to return as quickly as possible with their findings.

George Skau had replaced the group's first leader, James Polka, and was its new lieutenant. On Leyte, Polka had made the cardinal mistake of telling General Swing that his men, who had just returned from a lengthy scouting mission, were "dog tired" and not in any condition to go back into the mountains without a hot meal and a day's rest. When Swing said that was out of the question, Polka had gone to the medics to plead his case. Recon had gotten its rest day, but Swing fired Polka soon afterward.

Skau was in many ways Polka's opposite. Polka was congenial and universally liked by his men, but Skau was gruff, demanding, and not well liked by the men of recon, with the exception of Santos, who appreciated his fighting ability and toughness. When Skau first took over recon, he asked Santos if he was the lead scout. Santos said he had been that under Polka, then added, "You can replace me if you want."

Skau replied, "Hell, no. You think I'm crazy?"

Santos soon came to appreciate that Skau, a muscular outdoorsman from the Hudson Valley in upstate New York, would not ask anyone to do something he wouldn't do himself.

Recon covered a lot of ground fast on the road to Manila. They were shot at several times but kept going at a fast pace unless they were forced to stop to remove obstacles placed in the road. Throughout the night they made contact with several bands of guerrillas; Santos's fluency in Tagalog was a bonus, as he questioned the Filipinos in great detail. They all reported that the road to Manila was open.

Recon members (left to right) Martin Squires, Terry Santos, Del Motteler, and an unidentified Filipino guerrilla. *Courtesy Margaret Squires.*

By 4 A.M., the recon team was not far from Manila when they came to a bridge over the Imus River that had been blown out. The Japanese had established a defensive line on the opposite bank, and they immediately began firing on recon with rifles and machine guns. Skau, Santos, and their men looked for another route and followed a dirt road that took them to another bridge, which, they discovered, had been mined. They defused the mines. Since they were under orders not to enter Manila, recon reported back to headquarters that Highway 17 was clear.*

When Swing heard this, he wanted to move his entire division into the capital. For months, he had campaigned to have the division

---

* Terry Santos, Martin Squires, George Skau, and the other members of the Reconnaissance Platoon on the jeep-mounted patrol up Highway 17 were each awarded the Silver Star for "gallantry in action . . . with utter disregard for his own safety" while moving through enemy lines.

jump into Luzon—including units of the 187th and 188th Glider Infantry Regiments that were also jump qualified—but had ended up with a compromise half-airborne (Tagaytay), half-amphibious (Nasugbu) operation. Now, instead of waiting at Tagaytay Ridge while the Sixth Army came down from the north to liberate Manila as MacArthur's planners envisioned—as well as the commander of the Sixth Army, Lieutenant General Walter Krueger—Swing proposed to his superior, Lieutenant General Robert Eichelberger, commander of the Eighth Army, which at the time consisted of only the 11th Airborne, that they head into Manila from the south.

Eichelberger and Krueger were MacArthur's two top generals, and they had long been antagonists, with wholly different styles of commanding an army. Krueger, who rose from the rank of private in World War I to four-star general in this one, was methodical and even plodding, preferring to move slowly with superior numbers and firepower that included armored tanks and heavy artillery. Eichelberger tried to catch the enemy by surprise with sudden and unexpected tactics, which he believed could compensate for less firepower.

Eichelberger and MacArthur had both gone to West Point and were longtime friends. In spite of Krueger's lobbying that only his army should undertake the Luzon campaign in order to retain "command unity" and avoid units in the same area reporting to different generals, Eichelberger convinced MacArthur to let him to take the 11th Airborne under his command and hold the high ground south of Manila, which would freeze the Imperial Japanese Army's Eighth Infantry Division, an estimated eight thousand to ten thousand men commanded by Major General Masatoshi Fujishige, in their positions in the hills and mountains south of Los Baños.

With the 11th Airborne on Fujishige's flank, Eichelberger had argued, the Japanese general would not want to move on Manila and place his division between the paratroopers and Krueger's army coming down from the north. Once MacArthur was convinced,

Krueger had no choice but to accept the plan. However, he had asked MacArthur to make it clear to Eichelberger that he should *not* enter Manila under any circumstances, and that the capital was to be liberated by Krueger's Sixth Army.

U.S. intelligence had picked up indications that in December, General Tomoyuki Yamashita, the overall Japanese commander in the Philippines, had given orders to start an evacuation of troops and supplies from Manila, which he decided not to defend because he wanted to avoid urban warfare; instead he wished to combine his more than two hundred thousand troops and make the U.S. Army come into the mountains to fight. Manila, as far as Yamashita was concerned, would be outside the combat zone. That meant U.S. troops should be able to clear the city quickly and without much damage. Reflecting such optimism, plans were laid for a great victory parade that MacArthur was to lead through the capital.

Eichelberger eagerly endorsed the idea of a "fast drive" up the open road to Manila. (Swing would write to his father-in-law, General March, "As you know there is no love lost between [Eichelberger] and Krueger. If [Eichelberger] isn't standing at the bar in the Army and Navy Club in Manila when Krueger walks in the door, then it won't be for lack of trying.") MacArthur gave his quick okay to approaching Manila from the south, no doubt fulfilling Krueger's biggest fear that after his army had fought its way down from Lingayen Gulf for a month, Eichelberger would waltz in from the south and liberate the city.

Swing immediately sent a battalion of the 511th northward by jeep, directing them to leave a holding force at the bridge that recon had found open, and for the rest of the convoy to head into Manila, stopping only when the enemy forced a fight. The 511th's other two battalions began marching at dawn up the open road to Manila. When the 187th and 188th Regiments, bringing two-and-a-half-ton trucks and other equipment, arrived at Tagaytay from the coast, they linked up with the 511th. Division headquarters was set up at the Manila Hotel Annex in Tagaytay City.

Muller thought the sudden change of plans for the division to move on Manila was a disaster because he had received no advance intelligence for such an action. At the staff level, it had been repeatedly beaten into their heads that the 11th Airborne was to remain at Tagaytay. The division didn't even have a map of Manila or its approaches. Muller radioed the Army engineers on Leyte and asked them to have maps delivered to him by air.

An Army Air Corps fighter plane soon dropped low over the hotel, and the pilot tossed out the open cockpit several trussed-up packets that practically landed on the hotel's front steps. Muller called for his driver and a jeep, and like harried tourist guides, they raced up Highway 17, handing out maps to the marching paratroopers so they would know where they were heading.

THE REASON THE MANILA ROAD WAS OPEN FROM THE SOUTH AND the paratroopers had made it so far without a major fight was that guerrilla coordinator Jay Vanderpool had planned things that way.

He had positioned thousands of guerrillas in the surrounding mountains and hills to neutralize enemy forces and provide security not only to the Tagaytay Ridge drop zone but also along the Highway 17 corridor. As the men of the 11th Airborne moved toward Manila, Vanderpool and his guerrillas were given the job of protecting their right flank, extending eastward to the shores of Laguna de Bay.

He rounded up his best guerrilla companies—nearly a thousand experienced fighters—and spread them out facing high ground where a reinforced Japanese battalion was dug in. The guerrillas had rifles but no machine guns, mortars, or artillery. A U.S. Army ammo truck had come up the night before and loaded up all the guerrillas with plenty of ammo. In the morning, Vanderpool set up his order of battle: the Hunters ROTC in the middle, the pro-Communist Hukbalahap (Huks) on one side, the Chinese National-ist guerrillas on the other side, and other guerrilla fighters scattered among them.

Vanderpool had decided to use one of the oldest infantry move-ments, known as marching fire: each soldier would place the butt of his rifle, which was held with both hands, against his right hip, and each time his left foot hit the ground, he would pull the trigger. When the time was right, Vanderpool gave the signal to advance, and everyone fired straight to the front, not aiming. *Step, fire, step, fire.* The amount of random fire that went into the target area—as well as ammo expended—was overwhelming, and the guerrillas routed the Japanese.

Later the next day, Vanderpool led the guerrillas into a bivouac for the night, settling into rows of abandoned nipa houses built on stilts along either side of a road. They posted lookouts and turned in. It was a cool night, good for sleeping, and the first sentries did not awaken to see the Japanese battalion—the same one they had fought the previous day—walking down the road in two columns with their rifles slung.

A guerrilla lookout finally spotted them about a half mile away and sent out an alert. When Vanderpool realized what was about to happen, he knew it would have been almost impossible to have set up such a perfect time and place for an ambush. It was a moonlit night with good visibility, his men had covered positions on either side of the road from thirty yards away with open fields of fire, and the enemy troops were strolling past them like a high school marching band missing only the drum major.

No one fired a shot until the center of the enemy column reached the middle of the rows of nipa houses. Then the guerrillas opened up with devastating fire. Not until daybreak, when he went outside, did Vanderpool realize the full extent of their success. He had never seen a bloodier mess, not even on Guadalcanal. They had badly chewed up the Japanese battalion. Some of the Japanese soldiers had escaped in the dark, but Vanderpool reckoned that the guerrillas had killed hundreds of the enemy. Guerrillas were going down the road with their machete-like bolo knives and killing any wounded Japanese they found still breathing.

Before Vanderpool could even send a message about what had happened, he was summoned to his field radio. On the line was Doug Quandt, the G-3 operations officer for the 11th Airborne. He said they had heard all the ruckus.

"What the hell is going on over there?" he asked.

"Oh, we had a firefight over here with a battalion of Japs," Vanderpool said. "So, we killed 'em."

"Boy, after all that ammo you used yesterday," Quandt said, "General Swing is going to eat your head off for wasting more today."

"Why don't you ask the general to come over and take a look?"

Swing showed up a short time later in a jeep caravan along with some of Eichelberger's staff officers. When they saw the bodies stacked up in the road for almost half a mile, a couple of the staff officers got sick.

Swing eyed the scene with his usual steely gaze, turned to his aide, and said, "Give Vanderpool all the goddamn ammunition he wants."

Any hope that Manila could be liberated with few casualties and little damage vanished when elements of Krueger's Sixth Army reached the capital on February 3, captured a bridge leading into the northern part of the city, and were unexpectedly hit by Japanese troops that had been waiting to defend their positions.

An estimated twenty thousand Japanese—mostly naval personnel stranded in Manila after their ships were sunk, as well as several thousand soldiers—under the command of Imperial Japanese Navy Rear Admiral Sanji Iwabuchi, who had defied Yamashita's order to leave Manila, were manning defensive strongholds throughout Manila. Iwabuchi, who had lost a battleship under his command at Guadalcanal, and his troops were prepared for a suicidal fight to the death. His diverse force of shipwrecked sailors and soldiers was armed with rifles, automatic weapons, and machine guns. His ordnance men had removed large naval guns from sunken ships in the bay and adapted them for use against ground forces—fifty of these weapons were placed around the city; they had also taken machine guns from destroyed or damaged aircraft and antiaircraft weapons. The collection of weaponry also included heavy artillery pieces and antitank guns.

Most of this arsenal had been hidden behind concrete walls and in bunkers that would be difficult for the Americans to breach. Moreover, every house, tall building, and municipal and civic structure could be an enemy stronghold, and the Japanese could be hiding at every crossroads, roadblock, and bridge. The Americans would have to root out the enemy street by street in what would become one of the bloodiest battles of World War II.

Iwabuchi's plan involved extensive demolitions of buildings and supplies to prevent the Americans from being able to use them. The destruction of the port area, bridges, transportation facilities, and electrical and water supply systems was well under way. Fires set off by explosions from Japanese detonations—as well as from U.S. strikes on military targets—rapidly spread to nearby structures, and soon entire blocks were on fire. As Filipinos fled their burning homes and shops, thousands of men, women, and children were cut down in the streets by Japanese troops who had no hope of escape and knew that most Filipinos were fervently pro-American and had long been against them.

For the paratroopers of the 11th Airborne, the journey up Highway 17 had been uneventful until their arrival in Bacoor City, south of the Parañaque River about ten miles from Manila, where they received a tumultuous welcome reminiscent of those given Allied forces as they liberated towns in France following the D-Day land-ings at Normandy. Thousands of Filipinos turned out in the streets, waving U.S. and Philippine flags, handing out bananas and fried chicken, all while a seventeen-piece band played "The Star-Spangled Banner" and a selection of John Philip Sousa marches. As the para-troopers worked their way through the jubilant crowds and entered the suburbs of Manila, however, they came under increasing hostile fire, and the celebrations soon stopped.

On February 4, the paratroopers came to a bridge over the Parañaque River that was damaged but not completely destroyed. As they started to cross it, they discovered that the Japanese were waiting for them. From emplacements and pillboxes on the opposite bank, they unleashed mortar and machine-gun fire on the Ameri-cans. Booming, earthshaking artillery rounds from miles away poured in on their positions. As night fell, the furious firefight con-tinued. The 511th, one of the top U.S. combat units in the Pacific, which had achieved a historic 45–1 kill ratio in the mountains of Leyte, was stopped cold.

It took the 511th two days to make its way across the bridge and to move a couple of miles. These seasoned jungle fighters were now engaged in a wholly different kind of warfare: street by street and house by house. The paratroopers had to rely only on the weapons they carried—rifles, grenades, machine guns, mortars, flamethrowers, and demolitions. Entering the suburbs of Manila, they found the houses and shops destroyed. Neighborhoods that had been among the city's most expensive before the war were not spared, as once-stately mansions had been reduced to smoking piles of rubble.

The 11th Airborne was up against the enemy's main fortified defenses in southern Manila. It had taken the paratroopers less than a week to roll more than 150 miles from Nasugbu through Tagaytay to the outskirts of Manila; it would take them nearly three weeks to go the next three miles.

Five thousand men of the Imperial Japanese Southern Force's Third Naval Battalion, reinforced by a company of the First Naval Battalion and artillery units, were hunkered down in entrenched positions known as the Genko Line, a series of hundreds of concrete pillboxes and bunkers with connecting tunnels that wound for several miles across Nichols Field, a prewar U.S. military airfield, to Fort McKinley, established by the United States in 1901 and named after president William McKinley. Many of these machine-gun pillboxes had been covered with dirt long enough for grass to grow over them and others were hidden under thick foliage.

Japanese commanders had long believed—erroneously, it turned out—that the main U.S. landings in Luzon would come in the south and had built up their defenses accordingly.

Short distances in ground warfare are won against fortified defenses not only by infantry but by tank units and heavy artillery that can knock down fortifications. The 11th Airborne had the will and experience to prevail against their enemy, but being "light infantry," the paratroopers did not have the tanks and artillery to batter the fortresslike defenses.

After the 511th was reinforced by the 187th and 188th Regiments, the 11th Airborne was told to capture Nichols Field and Fort McKinley—two miles separated the airfield and the old fort—where Japanese were entrenched behind concrete walls and bunkers. Most of the big naval guns the Japanese had lifted from the bay were now behind the thick concrete walls of Fort McKinley. To dislodge an enemy with such firepower in well-defended, fortified positions would require acts of bravery and sacrifice from the troopers of the 11th Airborne.

Early in the battle for Manila, MacArthur decided to attach the 11th Airborne to Krueger's Sixth Army. Given the close-quarters fight taking place, having Krueger's and Eichelberger's two armies operating in the same streets would have been a threat to the command structure, as well as to efficient communications and coordination.

With no troops left to command after MacArthur took away the 11th Airborne from his Eighth Army, Eichelberger left Luzon on an Army transport plane.

Meanwhile, MacArthur quietly canceled the downtown Manila victory parade and was now accompanying Krueger's Sixth Army on its push into the city against a dug-in force of diehards who would sooner die for their emperor than surrender.

FOR MONTHS, MACARTHUR HAD BEEN RECEIVING GRAPHIC REports about how horribly the Japanese were treating their prisoners of war, particularly in the biggest camps in the Philippines on the island of Luzon.

In mid-December 1944, the Japanese guards at a POW camp on Palawan, an island off the western coast of the Philippines chain, mistakenly thought a U.S. invasion fleet sailing from Leyte was headed for them. Instead of taking the chance that their 150 U.S. military prisoners would be rescued, the guards pushed them into wood-covered trenches, poured in gasoline, and set them afire with flaming torches. Those trying to escape the fire were machine-gunned. Only a handful of POWs survived by jumping over a cliff and hiding in the rocks along the beach or swimming to a nearby island.

After the U.S. landings in Luzon in January, new intelligence suggested that many more prisoners would die unless they were rescued soon. MacArthur was convinced that the Japanese became more sadistic in the treatment of their prisoners with every step the U.S. troops drew closer to the camps.

With his forces now on Luzon, MacArthur directed his commanders to make every effort to liberate the POW camps as soon as possible. The first prison-camp liberation came sixty miles north-east of Manila at Cabanatuan on January 30, 1945, when U.S. Army Rangers, Alamo Scouts, and Filipino guerrillas freed five hundred Americans and Allied military prisoners, many of them survivors of the Bataan Death March. These freed POWs were able to describe the atrocities the Japanese had subjected them to, which heightened the urgency to free other prisoners.*

Heartened with the success of the Cabanatuan raid but shocked at the condition of the POWs, MacArthur personally ordered Lieutenant Colonel Haskett "Hack" Conner Jr., commander of a leading unit of the Sixth Army's First Cavalry Division then approaching Manila from the north, to take seven hundred men with a tank company and a battalion of 105-mm howitzers on a race into the city through enemy lines.

"Don't stop to engage enemy units en route but bounce off them and get to Santo Tomás as fast as you can to liberate the internees," MacArthur said.

After sunset on February 3, armored tanks smashed through the gates of Santo Tomás. Panicked Japanese guards took two hundred hostages and sought refuge in a three-story building. After the internees were warned by U.S. forces to take cover, the tanks fired on the building, trying to convince the Japanese to surrender, but they would not give in. The next day, the American commander negotiated an agreement in which the Japanese were given safe passage to a location in Manila in exchange for releasing the hostages

---

* Confirmation that Japan had an official policy to mistreat and humiliate U.S. and Allied prisoners, then to kill them before they could be liberated, was uncovered in Japanese files by a U.S. investigating team in Formosa six months after the war. An August 1944 document signed by the vice minister of war in Tokyo ordered all POW-camp commandants who believed their camps might fall into the hands of Americans to kill all military prisoners and civilian internees. "Whether they are destroyed individually or in groups . . . with mass bombing, poisons, decapitation . . . dispose of them as the situation dictates . . . It is the aim not to allow the escape of a single one, to annihilate them all, and not to leave any traces."

unharmed. The same U.S. force freed eight hundred military POWs being held at Bilibid Prison ten blocks away. U.S. troops and tanks took up positions to protect the liberated prisoners at both camps until trucks could safely get through the streets to evacuate them from the city.

On February 7, before the prisoners could be evacuated to safety behind U.S. lines and while fighting was still going on in the streets of Manila, MacArthur visited Santo Tomás. As he entered the first building, he was pressed back against the wall by hundreds of joyous men and women of all ages in ragged clothing, with tears streaming down their faces. One man threw his arms around MacArthur, put his head on the general's chest, and cried.

As they wept and laughed and cheered, they all delivered the same message: *Thank you.*

One prison camp on Luzon still needed to be liberated, but freeing the internees at Los Baños, located forty miles farther south and that much deeper into enemy territory, would be more complicated than any of the previous operations. MacArthur knew the Sixth Army needed a number of weeks to finish the fight in Manila before they could make their way to Los Baños. By the time they reached the camp, it could be too late for many of the imprisoned men, women, and children. An audacious plan that combined stealth, mobility, and rapid response was necessary to liberate the more than two thousand people in the camp.

"I knew that many of these half-starved and ill-treated people would die unless we rescued them promptly," MacArthur explained later. "The thought of their destruction with deliverance so near was deeply repellent to me."

THE 11TH AIRBORNE MOVED ITS HEADQUARTERS NORTHWARD from Tagaytay City to Parañaque, a town that had supplied the guerrilla movement throughout the war with many fighters and leaders as well as much food and arms, and was the first major Luzon municipality to be liberated by U.S. forces.

General Swing and his staff, including Henry Muller and Doug Quandt, set up their offices in an old Spanish villa that had French doors opening onto a wide veranda with wrought-iron railings and the weedy remains of a once-formal garden that had been the setting for prewar afternoon teas and evening cocktail parties. The villa's large, tiled swimming pool was empty, and was now used only as a shelter during enemy artillery shelling.

Within hours after the 11th Airborne captured a portion of the expansive Nichols Field—and while the fight at Fort McKinley continued unabated—its engineers went to work with bulldozers filling up bomb craters so one runway could be opened. A light spotter plane carrying MacArthur was one of the first to land on the bumpy surface as he arrived to meet with Joe Swing.

They met out in the open even though enemy snipers were still taking potshots whenever they had a chance. Befitting their personalities, both generals were oblivious to the risk of sporadic gunfire; each had made it a practice to lead from the front. During World War I's trench warfare, MacArthur, then a brigadier general, moved in the front lines of his advancing infantry so often that he was gassed on several occasions and wounded while verifying a gap in the enemy's defense.

Each general had brought along a single aide, and Swing had with him his G-3 Doug Quandt, who was responsible for planning all operations. The thirty-year-old Quandt, of Benicia, California, was a 1937 graduate of West Point. He had become an aide to Swing shortly after graduating, and had served under him in various positions ever since. Brilliant and soft-spoken, Quandt was a former Army polo player (like Swing) and member of what was known around headquarters as the "Royal Family," those honored few invited to have nightly cocktails with Swing, not so much an occasion for frivolity as for strategic and tactical planning.

After the men spoke briefly about the battle raging in Manila, MacArthur said he was surprised by the stiff opposition the airborne division had come up against at Nichols Field and Fort McKinley.

"Your boys have done a grand job," he said, suggesting that Swing write his father-in-law, General March, who as a young officer served as aide to MacArthur's late father, General Arthur MacArthur Jr., and "tell him I said so."

MacArthur then came to the subject that had brought him this far for a face-to-face with Swing. "Joe, I want you to liberate Los Baños as soon as you can. Start making your plans. You'll be working for me on this one."

The supreme commander was making it clear that the 11th Airborne would not come under the jurisdiction of Krueger's Sixth Army. It was rare for a division to operate on its own in wartime, and rarer still for MacArthur to assign a mission personally to a division's commanding general. He usually assigned missions to armies and corps whose generals decided how to deploy their units.

"And if you're going to do this, do it *right*, Joe."

After MacArthur left, Swing and Quandt returned to the villa.

Quandt went to see Muller right away to tell him they had a go to liberate the Los Baños prison camp. He mentioned MacArthur's do-it-right comment. They both agreed that MacArthur wasn't worried that they would flub the assignment, but rather that he was giving his okay for them to divert enough men and equipment to get the job done. That meant pulling troops out of the battle at Fort McKinley at a time when the division—half the strength of a regular infantry division to start with—had already been depleted by one-third due to casualties, illnesses, and diseases such as malaria.

Quandt and Muller, as G-3 and G-2, worked closely together. As they had been taught at Command and Staff School, their desks were situated near each other in the villa. Quandt would draw up the operational plan for the rescue, based on intelligence Muller gathered from all sources about the enemy, the camp, and its prisoners.

Given how well they meshed professionally and personally, Muller had entrusted Quandt with everything he learned so far about Los Baños. He had done this even when Swing had still considered it a waste of staff time because the camp was too far removed from their area of operations.

As Muller started to pull out the maps, eyewitness accounts, and guerrilla reports he had been quietly accumulating since he first heard about Los Baños from the Filipino grower in Leyte more than a month earlier, he thought, *Thank God for bootleg intelligence.*

# ELEVEN

# The Escapes

BEN EDWARDS AND GEORGE LOUIS HAD MET WHILE WORKING
as aircraft mechanics in Cavite and were among thirty-four Pan
Am employees captured by the Japanese.

On January 27, 1945, Louis was one of several men who slipped
out of camp in search of food. The others had made it back safely
in the dark, but Louis waited too long. When the sun came up, the
Japanese, suspicious about departures during the night, doubled the
guards inside camp and increased the number of soldiers on patrol
outside the compound.

Ben, along with George Gray of the administration committee,
went to the east end of Barracks 12, which was only about thirty feet
from the perimeter fences. They knew this was where foragers had
recently been leaving and returning to camp. They got as close to
the fence as they dared and pretended to have a normal conversation
while talking loudly enough for someone outside the fence to hear.
As they chatted, they interspersed words of warning. Louis, whom
Ben knew to be independent and somewhat impatient, had either
ignored the warnings or not heard them because Ben was shocked
to see his friend appear from under the sawali-covered barrier and
hurry toward the inner fence almost under the nose of a Japanese
sentry who raised his rifle and shot him without warning.

Louis lay on the ground while George Gray and Dana Nance

rushed off to speak to the commandant. About the time the commandant and Konishi arrived at the scene, a flight of U.S. bombers passed over at about twenty thousand feet, headed north toward Manila. All the internees milling about were ordered to return to their barracks, which had become standard protocol during flyovers, and the guards ran for the nearest cover. Looking back over his shoulder, Ben saw Konishi crawl under a shrub and pull down a leafy branch to hide his face.

When the planes were gone, the Japanese came back out, but they made it clear they were not going to allow Louis to get medical treatment. George Gray asked that a priest be allowed to see him, and that request was denied. After Konishi and the guards took Louis inside the guardhouse, Ben heard the crack of the single shot and knew what had happened. *Cold-blooded murder.*

Since his earlier escape at Santo Tomás and unsuccessful attempt to cross the bay to Corregidor to join the fight against the Japanese—as well as the executions of the three Britishers after their futile escape—Edwards hadn't even considered escaping. When he got to Los Baños, he had quickly realized that the hard part wasn't getting out but figuring where to go afterward. From his work on the wood-gathering detail, he learned that enemy troops were operating throughout the area. Even though U.S. forces were back on Luzon, it could be a perilous journey to reach their lines. Yet with all the deaths due to starvation and illness, the killing of Pat Hell and the execution of George Louis, and the long trench the Japanese had recently dug, Ben started thinking about getting out of Los Baños.

One of his friends in camp, twenty-year-old Alfred "Freddy" Zervoulakos, was already leaving camp regularly, although each time he came back. Freddy was Filipino by birth and one of nine children. His father, Angel, was the scion of a prosperous Greek family who emigrated to the United States, where he enlisted in the cavalry. Sent to the Philippines to fight insurgents, Angel never left. After the Army, he served as an aide to the U.S. high commissioner in Manila, knew MacArthur socially, and had played poker with Dwight Eisenhower when he was an Army major assigned to MacArthur's staff.

After war came, the Japanese called Angel in for an interview, and sixteen-year-old Freddy came with his father. Angel was arrested as an enemy alien, and Freddy was taken into custody with him. They ended up in Santo Tomás, where Angel soon suffered a near-fatal heart attack. He was released to the care of his family in Manila—he died before he could see MacArthur's return to the Philippines—while Freddy was among the first group of men sent to Los Baños.

Freddy was taller than most Filipinos, and quick and agile on his feet, attributes that had helped him become a school basketball star. His athleticism would also have served him well had he chosen to join his brother, Tony, a captain in the Hunters ROTC guerrillas. But instead Freddy relished his role as self-appointed "official camp spy," reporting to the local guerrillas about the routines of the Japanese guards and worsening conditions inside the prison camp.

Alfred "Freddy" Zervoulakos. *Courtesy Olga Zervoulakos and Liz Owens.*

In the early hours of February 13, Freddy slipped back into camp after a late meeting with a guerrilla leader at the home of Romeo and Helen Espino about a mile from camp. As usual, Romeo had not been home. He was a local commander of the PQOG—President Quezon's Own Guerrillas—and went by his nom de guerre, Colonel Price. Romeo, whose father had been educated at Johns Hopkins and was a member of the prewar faculty of the agricultural college, had joined the Philippine Army in 1937 after graduating college. He survived the battle in Bataan and escaped the Death March. When he made it back to Los Baños, he joined the guerrilla movement. Helen had remained at home on Faculty Hill, a forested, hilly neighborhood of faculty residences, and functioned as a facilitator for guerrillas; the Espino home was often the site of clandestine rendezvous.

Ben knew about the Espinos and had met Colonel Price when he brazenly waltzed into camp with seventy of his armed fighters shortly after the Japanese departed in early January. The guerrilla leader had introduced himself to the prisoners and made arrangements for locals to bring food into camp. After the Japanese returned, the guerrillas stayed nearby in the woods, keeping watch on the camp.

After morning roll call, Freddy found Ben, who was with his friend Pete Miles. He excitedly told them both about his meeting with a Hunters ROTC officer named Gustavo "Tabo" Ingles, whom he had met through his brother. He showed a fresh pack of Lucky Strike cigarettes Ingles had given him, irrefutable proof—as far as the internees were concerned—that Ingles had been with U.S. Army units. Freddy pulled out a typed letter Ingles had given to him directing Ingles to contact local guerrillas in the Los Baños area to determine their strength, as well as the size and location of enemy troop concentrations, in preparation for the liberation of the prison camp. The letter asked Ingles to determine the number of internees at Los Baños, and their physical conditions; specifically, how many could walk any distance and how many required transportation. It was signed by Major Jay Vanderpool, U.S. Army.

Freddy explained that Ingles wanted to meet a camp leater. "Tonight."

By now, Ben and Pete were as excited as young Freddy.

Prentice "Pete" Miles was a rough-and-tumble Texan in his early thirties. A mining engineer–cum–adventurer, he had been sent to Sumatra before the war by the St. Louis Zoo to collect wild exotic animals. After completing that assignment, he found he enjoyed the Manila nightlife so much that he took a job as a bouncer at a nightclub. In the opening days of the war, Miles was hired by the U.S. Army to do demolition work in and around Manila. He used dynamite to blow up a long railroad bridge as the Americans retreated in front of the advancing Japanese. Injured in a skirmish, he returned to Manila, where he hid out for a few months before being picked up and sent to Santo Tomás.

While Freddy, who had been awake all night, went to get some sleep, Ben and Pete found George Gray and told him about Freddie's meeting with the guerrilla. Gray gathered the other members of the administration committee. He was surprised and disappointed to discover that they were apprehensive about having contact with the guerrillas. They feared that if the Japanese found out, it would be detrimental to the entire camp.

By this time, Gray had convinced himself that doing nothing when so many of his fellow prisoners were suffering and dying was not the right course to take. He decided on his own to meet with Tabo Ingles at the Espino home. Late that night, he crawled under the double fences with Freddy as his guide.

TABO INGLES, WHO WAS THE INSPECTOR GENERAL OF THE HUNTers ROTC and a member of Major Vanderpool's guerrilla liaison staff, had been busy the past few days helping to link up various guerrilla groups.

Since Henry Muller and the 11th Airborne arrived in Luzon and asked for updated intelligence on Los Baños, Vanderpool and Hunters ROTC commander Terry Adevoso had put Ingles in charge of gathering information about the camp.

Although only twenty-three years old, Ingles, from Mauban, Quezon, was already a hardened war veteran. He had been a nineteen-year-old plebe at the Philippine Military Academy (PMA) in Baguio when the war started, and along with other classmates had been trucked to Manila, where they underwent a quick training course for deployment in Philippine Army infantry divisions being sent to Bataan.

A week before Christmas 1941, the academy announced that it was disbanding the lower two classes, and the cadets were ordered to exchange their uniforms for civilian attire and return home. On April 6, 1942, only days before the U.S. surrendered at Bataan, Ingles and a few dozen other young men barely out of their teens—led by fellow PMA cadet Terry Adevoso—walked into the foothills of the Sierra Madres with Springfield and Enfield rifles, shotguns and revolvers, to continue the fight against their country's occupiers.

Hunters ROTC officer Gustavo Ingles.
*Courtesy Ingles family.*

That summer, they succeeded in their first ambush of a sizable enemy force. By the end of 1942, Ingles was operating an intelligence network in Manila while working as a janitor in a municipal building that housed the offices of Japanese officials. Everything went well in terms of passing along information about enemy plans and movements until June 23, 1943, when Ingles was betrayed by a new recruit and arrested by Japanese soldiers while sitting at an outside café.

Ingles's extended journey

of punishment and torture began in a dank basement with a burly Japanese guard asking: *"Geriray ka?"* (Are you a guerrilla?)

"No," Ingles answered.

When a hard slap landed on his cheek, Ingles lost his balance. Falling to the floor, he bowled the guard over with him. The soldier jumped up and landed fists and kicks on the sprawled Ingles. In between blows to his face and other parts of his body, Ingles denied being a guerrilla.

Ordered to strip, he was subjected to the dreaded "water cure." While bound in a prone position, water was forced through his mouth and nostrils into his lungs and stomach. Feeling as if he were drowning, he soon lost consciousness. He was revived, and the process was repeated. Then came the beatings with mangrove firewood and being strung up by the thumbs with his feet barely touching the floor until he passed out.

After several days of torture and interrogation, Ingles admitted only to being an "errand boy" for the guerrillas. Then came field trips to several locations, during which he was ordered to identify people and places connected to the guerrillas. When he had nothing to say for two weeks, he was taken to Fort Santiago, a sixteenth-century bastion built by Spanish conquistadors that had been turned into a torture prison run by the Kempei, the feared military police arm of the Japanese Army.

More questioning and torture followed—electric shocks that caused his body to lift off the ground and bamboo slivers inserted beneath his fingernails. Finally the Japanese gave up on prying anything useful from him and transferred him to New Bilibid Prison, twenty miles south of Manila, to serve a thirteen-year sentence.

On June 24, 1944, after a year in captivity, Ingles and fifty other guerrillas were broken out of prison during a nighttime raid by Hunters ROTC. Tabo's resolve had not been weakened; his determination stronger than ever, he rejoined the effort to drive the Japanese from his homeland.

Now, after leaving 11th Airborne headquarters at Parañaque, Ingles had reached Binan, on the western shore of Laguna de Bay, where a small boat and crew waited to take him across the lake. Upon landing at Nanghaya, a small barrio on the southern shore, he was met by a local guerrilla leader who took them to his camp. Runners were sent out inviting the commanders of different guerrilla units operating in the area to an informal conference. The Huks, Chinese Nationalists, Markings Fil-Americans, and the Hunters ROTC all sent representatives.

Everyone was in favor of attacking the Japanese guards at Los Baños and freeing the prisoners. But having adequate arms and ammunition for a major operation was always a challenge for many of the groups. Also, with the camp being so far behind enemy lines, it could not be held for long if the Japanese launched a strong counterattack. They had also not devised a way to evacuate the internees to a safe location. After discussing various scenarios, Ingles agreed to another meeting with the guerrilla commanders on his way back from Los Baños.

The next day, he was taken by guide to the PQOG headquarters in Tranca, three miles south of the internment camp. There he met Romeo Espino, aka Colonel Price. The Hunters ROTC and the PQOC did not have a long record of working together; over the years some of their commanders had developed a distrust for one another. Espino quickly concluded that what was being planned was solely a Hunters ROTC operation, and he loudly protested that no guerrilla operation would be permitted within his area without his approval.

Ingles said he was not representing the Hunters alone, but was gathering information for Major Vanderpool, who, as the personal representative of MacArthur on Luzon, was coordinating guerrillas in the area and had been attached to 11th Airborne Division, now headquartered at Parañaque. He showed Vanderpool's letter.

Espino realized he had overreacted and offered to cooperate in a joint operation to free the internees. When Ingles asked if it would be possible for him to get firsthand information about enemy strength in the camp, as well as the condition of the internees, Espino offered to set up a meeting with an internee who slipped in and out of camp regularly. The next day, Ingles went to the Espino home with an escort of local PQOC fighters.

The night after Ingles's first meeting with Freddy Zervoulakos, the young Filipino internee reappeared at the Espino home with a tall, lanky American. The men shook hands, and Ingles said he had come from 11th Airborne headquarters in Parañaque. George Gray began describing for Ingles the condition of the internees, their numbers, how many were aged or sick, how many women and children. Ingles interrupted several times with questions that Gray answered.

Ingles said he was expecting a shipment of U.S. Army arms and ammunition to be delivered by boat at Nanghaya, and he would be distributing them to the guerrilla units participating in the operation. Possibly some of these arms, he offered, could be smuggled into camp so the people there could defend themselves?

Gray stopped him right there. "Under international law, we are a civilian internment facility, and as such we are forbidden to take part in any military action," he said.

Ingles was taken aback. Didn't Gray realize what the Japanese had been doing to noncombatant Filipinos in Manila and elsewhere? Had the Japanese followed international law by starving and shooting civilians at Los Baños?

Gray was adamant: the internees would do everything possible to assist in their liberation, but they would *not* take up arms against trained soldiers. Furthermore, Gray was scared that prisoners might be caught in the crossfire of an extended gun battle if the guerrillas attacked the camp. In such a situation, "we could be subject to retaliation by the guards who might turn their guns on us."

A final question Gray asked—by now it was getting late and time for him and Freddy to return to camp before sunup—concerned what would happen to the internees should the guerrillas' attack on the garrison be successful.

"Do you have any way to transport more than two thousand people, some sick and feeble, out of enemy territory to U.S. lines?"

Ingles admitted those logistics had not yet been worked out.

As Gray stood to leave, Ingles asked if he would come out and meet him again in four nights. Gray made no commitment and issued a final caution. He wanted Ingles to make sure everyone involved in planning the rescue knew that the health of the people in the camp was very poor, and to ask the guerrillas not to liberate the camp without the "consent, approval and assistance" of U.S. Army authorities.

Gray and Freddy hurried out the door and made it through the pitch-black woods and under the fences into camp just before dawn.

Gray reported to the committee later that morning. He expressed his own concerns about what sounded like a half-baked plan by the guerrillas to liberate the camp. While everyone appreciated the Filipinos' willingness to try to rescue them, they all believed their safety should be left in the hands of the U.S. Army, with whom they felt they should be in direct communication at this point. But whom should they send on the treacherous journey through Japanese-occupied territory to try to reach the 11th Airborne at Parañaque?

Leaving the meeting, Gray called together Ben, Pete, and Freddy. After discussing the matter, all agreed that involving the U.S. Army in the camp's rescue was paramount, as was getting information to them not only about the internees but the Japanese soldiers guarding the camp, including the location of sentry towers, machine-gun nests, pillboxes, and other defenses. All three men volunteered for the job.

Gray knew and trusted each one of them. Each possessed unique qualities. Ben, feisty and enterprising, knew the surrounding area from his work on the wood-gathering detail. Pete had an engineer's grasp of details and a photographic memory. The irrepressible Freddy knew how to get out of camp safely, spoke Tagalog, and had valuable contacts among the guerrillas. All three, despite having lost tens of pounds, were still relatively fit and unweakened by illnesses.

Gray wanted to be sure they understood that they could not return to camp. Furthermore, if they were caught by the Japanese—either escaping or roaming the countryside—they would likely be killed.

The three men said they would take that chance.

As the men were planning this mission, the Japanese made getting out of the camp more dangerous than it had been. As a way to halt the nighttime exoduses in search of food, the guards instituted a curfew that prohibited internees from leaving their barracks after 7 P.M. The new restrictions prevented even the crossing of roads between buildings, putting an end to evening visits by friends and families between barracks. Anyone caught breaking the curfew would be shot on sight.

At 9 P.M., on February 18, the three men, who lived in the same barracks, walked out the door with a lantern. Pretending to be ill, Miles, limping and groaning, was in the middle, with an arm draped over the shoulders of each of the other men. They headed for the hospital in the northeastern corner of the camp and reached it without being challenged. Behind the hospital was a ravine that headed away from the camp into the woods. A barbed-wire fence stretched over the ravine, but there was a gap underneath it large enough for a man to crawl through. A manned sentry post was located not more than forty feet away.

Inside the hospital, the three men made their final preparations. Abandoning the lantern and saying goodbye to the nurses on duty—hugs were exchanged as the men were wished Godspeed—they slipped out the back and crawled into the ravine and under the fence.

The ravine emptied into a gulley about forty feet deep. As they moved in single file, Ben inadvertently kicked an empty tin can. The noise was deafening. As they were still within hearing distance of the guardhouse, they froze and remained motionless for several minutes. When they were sure that no one had heard anything, they continued down the gulley, crossing under the bridge at the northern end of the camp near the main gate.

When they reached the woods where Freddy always met with guerrillas on his forays from camp, they found several armed men in the bushes. The men spoke to Freddy in muted voices, and he then passed the word to Ben and Pete that they were being taken to the PQOG camp at Tranca.

When they arrived at the guerrilla camp close to midnight, Romeo Espino greeted them. The former Philippine military officer understood the importance of their reaching U.S. forces with their firsthand knowledge of the camp. He told them the journey to Parañaque would be by foot and boat for some thirty-five miles through enemy territory.

After a long discussion, it was decided that the three internees would be escorted to Nanghaya on the shore of Laguna de Bay. From there, Pete would leave for Parañaque. Ben and Freddy would stay in a guerrilla camp at Nanghaya and wait for a message that Pete had arrived. If Pete didn't make it or they didn't hear from him in a few days, Ben would go next. To reach the great lake by dawn, they left Espino's camp at 1:30 A.M., accompanied by eight young guerrillas.

The moon that had lit their way through the woods to Espino's camp was now gone, obscured by clouds. As they headed into the darkness, Ben remembered what the Midwestern farmers of his youth used to say about a night like this: *As black as the inside of a cow.*

# TWELVE

# The Los Baños Force

HENRY MULLER KNEW EARLY ON THAT RESCUING MORE THAN two thousand people from the Los Baños camp would require coordinating many different units. That was why he made sure that Doug Quandt, a strategic planner with great common sense and an encyclopedic knowledge of the 11th Airborne's capabilities, knew as much as he did about Los Baños from the Filipino grower six weeks earlier.

Once MacArthur had assigned the liberation of Los Baños to the division, Muller was able to expand his intelligence-gathering efforts. His first action was to order Army Air Corps photo reconnaissance to fly over the camp and surrounding areas. Muller then put his photo interpretation team to work on the photos, having them piece together the images into a large mosaic that showed every building in the prison camp along with the perimeter fences. They were also able to produce large-scale military maps of the area with precise locations of roads, bridges, and topographical features.

Soon a picture of Los Baños came into sharp focus for Muller.

The camp was forty miles south of Manila and two miles south of the southernmost shore of Laguna de Bay. National Highway 1 ran south out of Manila following the western shore of the lake, and at the town of Calamba, it intersected with National Highway that headed ten miles east to the town of Los Baños, which was two miles north of the camp.

Railroad tracks ran through the town, then curved to the southeast, passing to the north and east of the prison camp. A paved road went from the town into the camp, which was some fifty acres in size, bordered on three sides by mostly open terrain, sagebrush, and grasslands. A thickly wooded area lay to the west, where tree-studded foothills extended to the eastern slope of the dormant volcano Mount Makiling, which, at more than three thousand feet, was the highest peak for miles around. The camp was enclosed with double barbed-wire fences. The compound had two vehicle entrances, each with a guarded gate.

11th Airborne's planners of the Los Baños raid: Henry Muller (G-2), second from right, and Douglass Quandt (G-3), far right. The other officers are, left to right, Glenn McGowan (G-1) and Roy Stout (G-4). *U.S. Army Signal Corps.*

The camp was encircled with numerous guard posts and gun towers, and Muller estimated that a hundred and fifty to two hundred Japanese soldiers were at the camp. He suspected most were combat veterans. Some may have been placed on the lighter duty of guarding prisoners because they'd been wounded or incapacitated by illness, but battle-experienced troops would be disciplined and well-trained, and could be expected to put up a fight if necessary.

Muller, like every G-2 in the Army, had been taught that raids behind enemy lines required an abundance of accurate information. As he continued to gather intelligence, he also relied on his recon scouts and guerrilla reports relayed through Jay Vanderpool, whose General Guerrilla Command was now working out of division headquarters, providing Muller with a daily briefing about Los Baños and guerrilla operations. Muller was soon able to identify all the enemy forces nearby that were capable of interfering with the raid:

- A Japanese infantry company of about two hundred men, two 105-mm artillery weapons, and four machine guns that was stationed at a rock quarry two miles west of the camp.

- Twenty Japanese soldiers and a machine gun located two miles to the north at Mayondon Point who could watch activities on Laguna de Bay.

- Two artillery guns on the Los Baños wharf, overlooking the shoreline and approaches from the lake.

- An infantry company of about eighty Japanese soldiers at San Juan River west of Calamba.

- Two 77-mm artillery weapons aimed up Highway 1 to the north, toward Manila. They were to the west of the camp on the Lecheria Hills, and the several dozen soldiers manning them could detect any troop movements south from Manila.

Looming as the largest threat to the mission were the infantrymen, mixed artillery, and combat engineers from the Imperial Japanese Army's Eighth Infantry Division under General Fujishige that had caused MacArthur to position the 11th Airborne on the high ground south of Manila to keep them from entering the fight in that city. Fujishige had divided his eight thousand to ten thousand men in two strategic areas. The majority were astride Highway 1, ten to twelve miles south of Los Baños. The others were in a heavily fortified position on Mount Macolod, south of Lake Taal.

Muller was sure that Fujishige would never abandon his primary mission of keeping the United States from advancing south and taking all of Luzon, but that didn't mean he couldn't still react to the raid by sending an infantry battalion of about eighteen hundred men to Los Baños and catch the operation while it was in the middle of evacuating the internees. A fight at that point would surely result in heavy casualties.

Quandt and Muller needed to determine the best way to approach the camp, and they quickly eliminated some they knew would not work. A ground assault—like the one that had liberated Santo Tomás in downtown Manila—would involve travel over too great a distance through enemy territory. Having such forces moving on the ground toward Los Baños would present the Japanese with time to move the internees in a forced march, if not more extreme measures. Another option was waiting until U.S. forces had secured more territory south of Manila before attempting to free the prison camp. But that could push the operation

Japanese Imperial Army Major General Masatoshi Fujishige. *National Archives, NARA.*

back as many as ten days to two weeks. According to all reports, such a delay would result in the deaths of more internees.

Also, they knew the Japanese had blown bridges, which would slow down any U.S. advance from Manila. Even if the bridges could be rebuilt in time, such a long convoy through enemy territory might well result in the loss of the element of surprise at Los Baños.

Muller knew there needed to be an element of surprise to the raid. A *little* surprise would not be enough, because if the Japanese soldiers had any warning that a rescue was being attempted, they might turn their guns on the civilian internees before they could be liberated.

This operation called for a *big* surprise, and the best way to do that was with parachute troops. Reconnaissance showed open ground nine hundred yards east of the camp that could be used as a drop zone, although based on its size there was a limit to the number of paratroopers who could land there. But Muller knew a parachute assault alone was insufficient because even the best paratroopers in the world—and those of the 11th Airborne were crack, battle-tested sky soldiers—would take at least fifteen to twenty minutes to reach the camp's perimeter from the time they stepped out the open doors of the C-47s, floated to the ground, unhooked their chutes, gathered their equipment, and went at a full run for half a mile. Twenty minutes was too long. Even ten minutes was too long.

Only instant and complete surprise would work. A way to achieve that, Muller decided, was to use the Recon Platoon, which had served so well in both Leyte and Luzon as the division's eyes and ears. But now Muller and Quandt saw a different type of mission for the scouts. They would leave a couple of days before the raid, make their way across Laguna de Bay, through the woods, rice paddies, and coconut plantations at night, and get into position close to the camp, then hit critical guard posts simultaneously on the morning of the raid.

Recon's attack would start the moment the first paratrooper stepped from a plane overhead, which meant that for a short time members of recon would be on their own to engage, pin down, or put to flight the guards on duty and get into camp quickly to protect the internees. It was a lot to ask of a small force, which, due to injuries, illnesses, and transfers, was down to only twenty-two of its more than thirty members. Even so, Muller considered them the elite of the elite and thought they were up to the task.

Jay Vanderpool proposed augmenting recon with guerrilla fighters, assuring Muller and Quandt that some of his best guerrilla groups were ready and willing to participate in a raid to liberate the camp. They could also act as guides to the camp.

A group of guerrillas had already started out once to attack the Los Baños camp. Vanderpool stopped the mission with an urgent radio message stating that liberation of Los Baños was now an 11th Airborne mission and assuring the guerrillas that plans were already in the works. The guerrillas had reluctantly returned to their camps.

Everyone at 11th Airborne headquarters did agree that the guerrillas should continue to watch the camp, and launch their own attack if they saw the guards starting mass executions, something everyone feared might happen given how brutal the Japanese had been with other U.S. and Allied prisoners. Since it wasn't likely they could execute more than two thousand people all at once, those keeping an eye on the camp would presumably see some sign of preparation for such a horrific undertaking.

By the time Quandt and Muller jointly briefed Swing, they had a tactical plan involving air, land, and sea components that they believed would work, although it violated an accepted principle of war: simplicity. A simpler plan was usually preferred because it meant fewer things could go wrong. That was combined with another rule often cited by military planners. Murphy's Law: *Anything that can go wrong will go wrong.* Muller and Quandt realized that everything had to go right for this complex attack plan to succeed.

Their plan for preventing Fujishige from sending reinforcements to the camp was to deploy the 188th Glider Infantry Regiment, reinforced with the 637th Tank Destroyer Battalion and two field artillery battalions, down Highway 1 in order to deceive the Japanese commander into believing the Americans had begun a major advance southward. Based on reconnaissance, it was thought they would make it as far as the San Juan River, where the Japanese had blown the bridge and were waiting on the opposite bank. It was hoped the fight at the river would be loud and long enough to keep the rest of Fujishige's force hunkered down in the hills. If things went badly for the raiding party at the prison camp, this force would have to fight eastward seven or eight miles to reinforce the besieged camp.

Swing listened intently as Quandt and Muller outlined the plan, asked a few questions, but made no changes. He gave the men his approval to form what became known as the Los Baños Force.

THE NEXT DAY, AN EXHAUSTED PETE MILES WALKED INTO 11TH Airborne headquarters.

Muller saw a once-strapping man who was now quite thin and spent from his long journey, which had been by jeep for only the last few miles after he made contact with U.S. forces south of Manila. Miles hadn't slept since leaving Ben Edwards and Freddie Zervoulakas, and he had dark circles under his eyes. He seemed to perk up when Muller told him that in five days the 11th Airborne was launching an operation to liberate the Los Baños camp.

Miles took out a crumbled map he and Edwards had hastily drawn at Nanghaya and pointed out important details. He also described the dire conditions in the camp, explaining how many prisoners were sick and wasting away with little to eat. He then told about the two Americans recently shot and killed while trying to bring food back into camp.

Muller and Miles together reviewed photos and a large map of the camp, and right away Miles began identifying the various buildings, such as the Japanese barracks and commandant's office, as well as the positions of guard posts and the routes the sentries patrolled. Miles also told them where to find several camouflaged machine-gun positions. He and Edwards had paced off distances in the camp, and even without notes, Miles was able to recall them.

**Los Baños Internment Camp**

Road to Los Baños

Baker Memorial Hall

Athletic Fields

Faculty Hill

Main Gate

Guard Post

Bamboo Groves and Grass, Six Feet High

N

Guard's Storehouse

Guard Post

Barracks

Hospital

Deep Ravine

YMCA

4 Guards

Cemetery

Kitchen

Commandant Headquarters

6 Guards
2 Dirt Pillboxes

Trail

Guard Post

Guard's Gun Rack

Guard Barracks

Double Barbed Wire Fence

Office

5 Guards

4 Guards
2 Dirt Pillboxes

Chapel

Two Japanese on Outpost

Guard Post

Tree

Ditch

Mt. Makiling

Thick Foliage

Boot Creek

4 Guards
2 Dirt Pillboxes

✛ = Barbed Wire

Muller suggested they go over the camp's daily routine.

"Start from the time you get up in the morning," he said.

Miles started with the morning roll call. Then he described where and how the guards spent their days, and how and when the sentries were changed.

Muller grilled Miles without letup for an hour. Even though Miles clearly needed food and sleep, he showed no interest in cutting short his debriefing after he'd risked his life to get to headquarters and tell what he knew.

At some point, Miles mentioned something in passing about how every morning the soldiers not on guard duty had to report for outdoor calisthenics.

"*Every* morning?" Muller asked.

"Yes, and always at the same time."

"What time?"

"They start exercising at quarter to seven."

Muller pulled out more details. Every morning the soldiers not on duty had to report to an open field about fifty yards from their barracks for ritualistic exercises that started at 6:45 A.M. and ended at 7:15 A.M. Only a couple of dozen guards remained on duty at their posts while the rest of the garrison—their guns stacked and locked in a connecting room between the Japanese barracks inside the north gate of the camp—went into the field wearing only sandals and traditional *fundoshi* undergarments. Miles described it as a "saber-dancing ritual" complete with guttural sounds and yells in unison that were terrifying for many of the internees to hear every morning: *"Tenno Heika Banzai!"* ("Long live the Emperor!")

To Muller, this was almost too good to be true. It didn't require the military mind of Napoleon to see its importance. He rushed into Quandt's office and said they had to change the time of the attack from 8 A.M. to 7 A.M. in order to catch most of the enemy in the open field, unarmed and practically naked. The initial time had been chosen so that the heavily laden C-47 transports carrying paratroopers didn't have to take off from Nichols Field in the dark, as the field still had no operating runway lights. Quandt immediately agreed to change the time of the attack and the entire operation would now be keyed to 7 A.M.

Muller and Quandt continued to worry about how they would get the internees out of the camp safely because so many were said to be weak and sickly. The plan was first to secure the camp from the Japanese, then bring in a convoy of two-and-a-half-ton Army trucks, an iconic military vehicle known as a "deuce-and-a-half," which could carry twenty-two soldiers with full packs, down Highway 1 and roll into Los Baños to pick up the prisoners. However, the engineers had reported that their feverish repairs on the blown bridges might not be finished in time. Also, there was a possibility the Japanese would try to destroy any rebuilt bridges. If even only one remained impassable to vehicles, it could thwart the entire rescue mission.

Reviewing a list of available units in the area, Quandt came across the 672nd Amphibian Tractor Battalion, equipped with new LVTs (Landing Vehicle Tracked). Known as amtracs, these noisy, sixteen-ton amphibious vehicles were operated by a crew of three and could carry up to thirty passengers. The battalion had recently arrived in the Manila area, and its amtracs were now being used to carry cargo across rivers.

Quandt and Muller discussed how the evacuation would work using the 672nd Amphibian Tractor Battalion and its LVTs. The amtracs could "swim" across the Laguna de Bay to its southern shore, rise out of the water, drive the two miles down the road to the camp, load up the internees, drive back to the lake, and swim to Mamatid, where trucks and medical vans would carry the internees to a fully staffed medical facilty that was being set up for them in the New Bilibid Prison fifteen miles to the north along a coastal road in U.S.-held territory.

Sixteen-ton amphibious vehicle known as an amtrac. *U.S. Army Signal Corps.*

Quandt and Muller now completed the plan. Amtracs would carry two companies of paratroopers across the lake. Another company of paratroopers would jump next to the camp. The drop would have a dramatic effect because an airborne operation always looks twice its actual size, as billowing parachutes fill up a lot of sky. The paratroopers landing next to the camp would move quickly to reinforce recon and the guerrillas. The amtracs bringing the additional troopers would roll into camp and start loading the internees for evacuation.

Airborne headquarters began pulling out of action the units that would be required for the raid. Most of the 11th Airborne's units needed were still involved in the heavy fighting at Fort McKinley. Hot, tired, and hungry for a hot meal, they were told only that they were being withdrawn for a few days' rest.

AFTER MULLER COMPLETED HIS DEBRIEFING OF PETE MILES, HE sent recon scouts George Skau and Terry Santos to Los Baños. Skau initially thought he would take the entire platoon, but Santos—by then an acting sergeant—pointed out that the two of them could do the job quicker and quieter.

They crossed Laguna de Bay by *banca,* a trip that took five hours because they had to steer a circuitous route to avoid a Japanese patrol-boat base located on an island in the middle of the lake. When they arrived at the barrio of Nanghaya, ten miles up the southeastern shore from Los Baños, they were greeted by guerrillas who took them to their nearby camp. There they met Ben Edwards and Freddy Zervoulakos, who were happy to hear that Pete Miles had arrived safely at 11th Airborne headquarters.

After their nightlong trek from the PQOG camp at Tranca, Ben, Pete, and Freddy and their guides had arrived at the shore of Laguna de Bay about dawn. The guerrillas commandeered two sailing *bancas* that were loaned to them not at all reluctantly by their owners when they saw the Americans in the group. Pete and his guides had left in one *banca* heading northward, and Ben, Freddy, and their companions had sailed to Nanghaya, where they landed about noontime. They were taken to a guerrilla camp where the leader assured them he would pass along any messages from or about Pete. Soon a parade of villagers arrived bearing culinary offerings. Fried duck eggs, boiled rice that had been warmed in a skillet with coconut oil, fried freshwater fish, strips of pork loin, and additional delicacies were laid out on banana leaves. Everything looked and smelled as delicious as it tasted. For Ben, no meal in his life had been more welcome.

Skau, with his characteristic hard edge, told Ben and Freddy he had orders for them to accompany him and Santos to the internment camp and show them the lay of the land on the way. Until that moment, Ben had given no thought to going back to Los Baños and assumed he never would. It would be much safer to stay where he was in the guerrilla camp. He knew if he went back and was captured, the Japanese would kill him. As a civilian, he could defy

Skau's orders, but Ben was willing to do anything to help the rescue of his friends and fellow internees.

They left Nanghaya in two sailing *bancas,* reached the shore near the town of Los Baños, and set off inland. Arriving in the predawn twilight, they first checked out the field being considered for the drop zone, which turned out to be old rice and corn fields. There were railroad tracks bordering the field that could cause some broken ankles, and the high-voltage lines could electrocute anyone who got caught in them, but Skau and Santos verified there was enough room for a company of paratroopers to land.

"This should work," Skau told Santos as he wrote with the stub of a pencil in a sweat-stained notebook he carried in his shirt pocket. "It's not far from the camp but not close enough to panic the Japs into opening fire on the internees."

As they explored the northeast side of the camp, Ben took them to a stand of bamboo that abutted the perimeter. It had been chopped down at one time but had grown back to six to eight feet in height. The thick reeds could provide good cover for anyone approaching from that direction. To the southeast of the camp, Ben showed the best route for the paratroopers to take from the drop zone to the nearest guardhouse. He also identified two hidden machine-gun pillboxes, which, Santos noted, were made out of dirt, not concrete. That would make them easier to take out with grenades.

At one point, they went so close to the fence they could hear sounds from one of the barracks. With the sun rising over the jungle canopy, they found a place to hide on a hillside overlooking the camp.

By 6:45 A.M. sharp, a large group of unarmed and nearly naked Japanese lined up in an open field just outside the north gate. They bowed in unison to their emperor, then began their morning drills.

Santos carefully observed his enemies. Even though they were wearing less clothing than he was used to seeing them in, they were making the same guttural and unearthly sounds they did in the heat of battle. It was a sound that always terrified American soldiers when they heard it for the first time.

But Santos had killed enough of them in the war to know they weren't supermen. The closest they had come to killing him was when one of them tried to stick a bayonet in his back and paid for it when Santos whirled around and thrust his razor-sharp Bowie knife into the man's groin. His attacker dropped his rifle and ran off screaming into the jungle. Santos hadn't even bothered to shoot him because he knew he wouldn't go far with that wound. *No, not supermen.* All the yelling, Santos had learned from fighting them, was as much to jack themselves up with bravado as it was to scare their enemies.

It wasn't long before the internees began pouring out of the barracks and milling about. Ben explained that they were preparing for the barracks monitors to take morning roll call, which lasted from 7 A.M. to about 7:30 A.M.

That was *very* bad luck. The recon scouts would have preferred to hear that the internees would be in their barracks at the time of the attack, not out in the open. They were sure a gunfight would break out with the guards, and this timing would put the internees right in the crossfire.

When the four men made their way back to the lake, there was only one small *banca* without a sail, instead of the two sailing boats they had brought down from Nanghaya. Locals had obviously stolen the other *banca*. It was imperative that Skau and Santos return to headquarters with their information, so they took off paddling, leaving Ben and Freddy and their guerrilla escorts to find another boat.

Within days, the two escaped internees would again return to the prison camp. Only next time, they would be armed for a fight.

# THIRTEEN

# "Rescue Must Come Soon!"

MARGIE WHITAKER HAD BEEN WATCHING HER PARENTS GO downhill since they arrived at Los Baños in December 1944. They were in their fifties but looked like they were in their seventies now. Her smart, capable, and once-sturdy father was getting weaker by the day. She worried that he would not live to see the end of the war.

The secret diary she kept was filled with hope and despair.

*February 4, 1945*

*And we're still here. It's hard to keep from feeling depressed, and we're so hungry. Konishi has cut us down twice since I last wrote, and we're getting absolutely no meat from outside. Yet they kill [carabaos] and eat them all up themselves, then say they can't find any meat for us. No sweet potatoes, either, or coconuts. Bananas are a memory, too . . . I haven't seen a Jap plane overhead for days. Our planes sail around masters of the skies . . . I wonder if Santo Tomás is free.*

*February 8, 1945*

*The Marines aren't here yet. It's been said that the first hundred
years are the hardest, but I heartily disagree. I agree with the saying
that "the last half hour is always the longest." I know it's the last
"half hour" but it's dragging so slowly! Dad is dreadfully thin, and
so is Mother.*

Margie waved at low-flying U.S. planes every chance she got
and daydreamed of being rescued by big, handsome U.S. Marines—
all while watching helplessly as people around her died needlessly.
Every day now, someone who didn't come outside for morning roll
call would be discovered to have died in their sleep. On some days,
two or three people expired during the night.

Margie had seen George Louis lying on the ground after the Japanese shot him in the shoulder. The bananas and coconuts he was bringing into camp had spilled out. After he was dragged away—the guards
gathered up the fruit and took it away with them—she heard the fatal
shot, though she didn't see what happened. She knew George had gone
out of the camp and back a few times, always bringing in food that he
shared or traded. Margie had a difficult time understanding how a
decent man could be killed because he'd gone to get a few pieces of fruit
that grew bountifully just on the other side of the barbed wire.

Like other internees, Margie watched the big ditch being dug.
*Was it going to be their mass grave?* She also saw the machine gun that
had recently been placed on a slope above the ditch. *Were they all going
to be executed like poor George?* People talked about the Japanese having
a long history of not freeing their prisoners. Some internees who had
spoken with guerrillas were even more convinced, based on what the
Filipinos reported, that the guards might be planning to kill them
all. Whether or not these execution rumors were true, Margie had
learned firsthand that there was another way to kill large numbers
of people: just stop feeding them.

*February 15, 1945*

*Conditions here are very bad . . . A man died last night of starvation in his sleep.*

*February 17, 1945*

*The camp rice supply will be gone by Monday. Then we'll really starve. We're starving now but it's sort of a chronic ailment. I weigh 83 lbs. Another man died this a.m., two yesterday. One went completely off his nut and began to chew on his trousers and belt. I heard he finished his trousers. The gravediggers work overtime. Rescue must come soon!*

IN MID-FEBRUARY, DANA NANCE PERFORMED A DIFFICULT SURGI-cal repair, with his only light coming from a kerosene lamp held by a nurse. A loop of the patient's bowel had become confined in an inguinal hernia and the bowel was at risk of strangulation. Once the bowel lost its blood supply, it would no longer function. When Nance cut into the patient, he found the bowel still viable, and he gently pushed it back into the abdominal cavity and repaired the hernia.

Without electrical power, he could never be sure his surgical tools were properly sterilized. He had been working without power for most of the past month, apparently due to bomb damage at the local power plant. Also, without refrigeration, the hospital's serums had spoiled. No electrical power meant the hospital and barracks went dark from sunset to sunrise. And without electricity to power the well's pump, everyone had put jugs out to collect rainfall.

The health of the people in the camp had descended to depths unlike anything Nance had seen in all his years practicing wartime medicine, going back to his days in Japanese-occupied China. Virtually every internee suffered from beriberi, either the wet or dry kind, both of which were caused by a lack of protein. With dry beriberi, people shriveled up as they seemingly wasted away. The wet kind was deadlier, and more men than women got this type because their bodies required additional protein.

The disease manifested itself in both men and women with grotesquely swollen legs, faces, and stomachs; some people's ankles were the same size as their thighs and were full of water. They looked like aspic, all pale and wobbly; many of the internees were too weak to stand in line for food. They could die very quickly, particularly the older patients. Overnight, their faces, hands, and legs would bloat to several times their normal size. This was a sign for Nance that the person didn't have long to live because the heart would also be greatly enlarged, which would result in pulmonary edema and congestive heart failure.

Nance kept a list of the death toll, although every time he wrote "beriberi" as the cause of death, he knew starvation was the true cause.

W. R. Shaw, age 59, American, died Feb. 14 of beriberi.

George Whitmoyer, age 49, American, died Feb. 17 of tuberculosis.

Guilford Campbell, age 77, American, died Feb. 18 of beriberi.

Charles Magill, age 68, American, died Feb. 19 of beriberi.

Herbert Blair, age 65, American, died Feb. 20 of beriberi.

H. E. Burton, age 68, American, died Feb. 22 of beriberi.

The camp's gravediggers were now working on double shifts, digging graves in advance of deaths because it was vital that unembalmed remains be buried quickly due to the tropical heat and humidity. The construction of coffins by carpenters suddenly halted, however, when the Japanese stopped supplying lumber. Bodies were now being placed directly into shallow earthen graves.

In mid-February, just when Nance and everyone else thought the food situation could get no worse, Konishi stopped supplying the camp kitchen with white rice. He did so even though plenty of rice remained in the warehouse. Instead, he had sacks of unhusked rice known as palay distributed to the internees. The internees lacked any way to separate the rice from the indigestible hulls. Since the late 1800s, most of the world's unhusked rice had been milled with modern rice-hulling machines that removed the hulls from the raw grain to reveal whole brown rice, which could be milled further to remove the bran layer, resulting in white (or polished) rice. Societies in undeveloped areas that unhusked rice manually did so in a labor-intense process that utilized vat-sized pestles and rice pounders as tall as a man.

On February 19, the Japanese issued four days' worth of palay, and even though more than forty people worked in the camp kitchen, they were unable to husk enough rice that day for the evening meal. In desperation, the committee decided the next day to give the palay directly to internees—about two cups per person—and let individuals husk and cook it themselves.

Hungry people tried lots of different methods to husk the rice. Some rubbed it between two boards; others put it in a container and pounded on it with the end of a stick. There were those who tried striking each kernel with a rock until its hard hull cracked. Grain by grain, slowly and methodically, an entire day's effort by a family might result in only a cupful of rice. Many were left exhausted from the effort, which burned more calories than the rice provided. Those who were too weak or too hungry to go through the lengthy process tried boiling the palay without removing the husks, leaving many with internal lacerations and bleeding.

The administration committee protested strenuously that they were no longer being given their supply of rice while they watched the soldiers still receive their regular thrice-daily rations. In a meeting with Konishi on February 21, the committee urgently requested additional rice supplies at least until the camp kitchen could find a more efficient way to unhusk the palay.

"No," Konishi said flatly.

"Can we bring in Filipino laborers to thresh the *palay*?"

"No."

"Can we send it out to be threshed?"

"No."

George Gray pointed out that the kitchen did not have the machinery needed to process the palay and had managed to provide only a small meal that morning and no grain for the evening meal.

"What is the camp going to eat tonight?" Gray asked.

Konishi called the question ridiculous. He said the camp kitchen obviously could not hull enough of the palay for the whole camp. "Everyone must hull their own," he said, shrugging.

"We have people who are too weak, old, or infirm," Gray argued. "It is hopeless to expect individuals to be able to do this in most cases."

Another committee member said he did not understand how the Japanese could treat innocent men, women, children—old and sick people as well—in such an uncivilized manner.

"You are keeping us here. It is your responsibility to feed us."

Konishi made no response, so the committee member asked what they could expect for future rice or grain distributions.

"Nothing," Konishi said. "Only *palay*."

"In that case," Gray said, trying to stay patient, "what can we bring in from the outside? We know the local Filipinos are willing—"

"I cannot permit such questions!" Konishi exploded, his face reddening. "No good to talk about. Meeting over!"

It was the committee's last meeting with Sadaaki Konishi.


WHEN MARGARET SHERK EMERGED AFTER TWO WEEKS IN THE dysentery ward at the camp hospital, she was amazed she could still nurse Gerry Ann, though she knew the quantity and quality of her milk had diminished. While she had been in the ward, Jerry had brought their baby to her every four hours during the day to nurse.

They had worried constantly that the baby would catch the infectious disease. Gerry Ann did not, but Jerry did.

He went into the hospital for the same treatment soon after Margaret was released. Sulfa drugs to kill the bad bugs in the digestive tract and a daily glass of castor oil to act as a purgatory: a classic case, they agreed, of the cure being as bad as the bite.

They both lost a great deal of weight during their illnesses, and grew hungrier and weaker with each passing day. Jerry weighed less than a hundred pounds, and his usual weight was 180 pounds. David, now seven years old, was so undernourished it had stunted his height. Gerry Ann, at thirteen months, was showing signs of malnutrition since they opened the last little can of her oatmeal at Christmas. Margaret could not bear looking at the young babies in the camp. They looked like the photos of starving babies she had seen in magazines that resembled tiny rats: all head, big eyes, and bloated stomachs. Gerry Ann, *her baby,* would soon look like those pictures.

Before they had been taken ill, Margaret and Jerry had talked about escaping if conditions in camp did not get any better. Jerry, whom she considered the bravest man of them all, was confident that once in the jungle, they could make contact with Filipino guerrillas who would help them reach U.S. forces. After they both came out of the hospital, they talked again about leaving. If they were ever going to do it, they agreed it had to be while they still had the strength to walk. They feared that even in another week, they wouldn't be able to.

In the end, it came down to the children. Up and down the family barracks, children were crying day and night from hunger pains. David had not yet started crying from hunger, but Gerry Ann cried a lot, no doubt because she was never able to fully satisfy her appetite. Margaret decided she would rather be shot dead escaping, even if it meant her children would die quickly, too, than watch them slowly starve to death.

And so, Jerry and Margaret made plans to escape.

First they wrote out a will. In the event they died and the children lived, the baby was to go to a missionary couple who adored her and always wanted a little girl of their own. David was to return to the United States and live with his grandmother; and one day perhaps he would be reunited with his father.

Margaret and Jerry had become friends with Dana Nance, and the physician tried to talk them out of their escape plan. When reasoning failed, Nance offered to give the baby a shot on the night they left so she wouldn't cry as they went under the fence. As for David, Margaret thought she could impress upon him the seriousness of the situation so he would stay quiet.

They would travel light, with a few extra clothes, a blanket, and a mosquito net. On the day they had chosen for their escape—February 21—Margaret gave away their remaining possessions to other families. Jerry intended to take his radio so he could keep hearing the war news.

That evening, they put the children to bed early so they would be sleepy when they were awakened a little later. Margaret and Jerry did not get much sleep. Then it was time. They woke up the children, gathered their few things, and stepped into a moonlit night.

By the time they reached the hospital, Margaret was panting from the exertion and shaking with fear. Nance greeted them quietly in the shadows of the hospital. He made one more attempt to persuade them to stay, even for just a few days more. They knew the U.S. Army was fighting in Manila and would then be heading this way. Nance tried to convince them that it would be soon. Why take the chance now? he said. When he saw that Jerry and Margaret were committed to their plan, Nance handed them thirty Philippine pesos and gave the injection to Gerry Ann, who let out a wailing scream.

The baby continued to scream as they all waited for the shot to take effect and for her to go to sleep. Two hours later, she was still crying.

It was obvious to everyone that they couldn't sneak under the camp fence behind the hospital with a crying baby.

"I'll try giving her something different next time," Nance promised, "that will really put her to sleep."

With that, they returned to the barracks.

The baby cried all night, and so did Margaret. Every minute of it.

FOURTEEN

# "The World Will Be Watching"

T HE MESSAGE FROM GENERAL SWING AT 11TH AIRBORNE
Division headquarters was hand-delivered to the front lines at
Fort McKinley: the commander of the 511th Parachute Infantry
Regiment was to select one of his companies for a parachute opera-
tion behind enemy lines.

Lieutenant Colonel Edward Lahti, a thirty-one-year-old, 1938
graduate of West Point, from Portland, Oregon, had been regimental commander for a scant ten days following the death of Orin
"Hard Rock" Haugen, the regiment's first and only commanding
officer since its activation at Camp Mackall in 1943. Haugen had
been mortally wounded on the outskirts of Manila by an artillery
shell that came through a window and exploded in a room where
he was conferring with General Swing and other officers. Haugen
was the only one wounded by the blast, and he received a sucking
chest wound. He died several days after emergency surgery while
en route to Hollandia, New Guinea, aboard a medical evacuation
flight.

Lahti had been Haugen's second-in-command, and knew the
511th well. He believed every one of his battle-tested companies
could handle any assigned task. He turned to the regiment's personnel officer and asked which company had the greatest strength at
that moment. The ongoing battle for Manila had resulted in heavy

casualties, and none of the companies was at full strength, which was generally about 120 men per company with four companies per battalion. He was told B Company of the First Battalion was closest to full strength.

Lahti knew B Company's commander, First Lieutenant John Ringler, was an experienced combat leader who had taken over his company in time to make the Tagaytay Ridge jump. Lahti was confident that Ringler could lead whatever mission they had in mind. He told Ringler his company had been selected for a special mission and ordered them to disengage from combat immediately so they could be pulled off the line and sent to the rear.

"John, you are to report right away to the division commanding general," Lahti said, "and I'll take you there now. My jeep is out front."

Ringler was twenty-seven years old, with an open, cherubic face. He looked only slightly older than the farm boy he had been growing up outside Buffalo, New York. He joined the Army as an enlisted man in 1940, and after Officer Candidate School in 1942, he was an early volunteer for parachute training and had been with the 511th since jump school. Like a number of his men, he had a wife at home who had given birth to a baby he had not seen: a daughter born in 1944.

An apprehensive Ringler asked on the way if Lahti had any details about the special mission. Lahti said he did not, and his tone made it clear he had nothing else to add. When they reached headquarters, they were ushered into General Swing's office. Ringler had never met the general, though he had seen him from a distance. When the two-star general with the piercing sky-blue eyes stood up from his desk, Ringler couldn't help but wonder, *Why me?*

"Is this the commander of the company making the jump?"

"Yes, sir," Lahti said. "Lieutenant Ringler, B Company."

Swing focused his gaze on Ringler. "Lieutenant, your company has been selected to jump outside Los Baños Internment Camp."

*Los Baños?* Ringler had never heard of the place.

"You will kill the guards and organize the prisoners for evacuation," Swing continued. "You'll be right outside a main enemy force. If things go wrong, you and your men may not get out alive. Do you have any questions?"

"No questions, sir," Ringler said.

Swing nodded. "You'll be briefed by my G-2 and G-3. Good luck."

As Ringler marched from the office, he wondered if a major general in the entire history of the United States Army had ever met with a lowly company lieutenant to personally give him a mission.

Ringler doubted it.

Next he was hustled into a briefing with Doug Quandt and Henry Muller, from whom he learned the details of his company's mission as well as the roles given to other units.

Lahti had selected the other companies of the First Battalion to cross Laguna de Bay in the amtracs. Once they landed, they were to set up a protected beachhead and assist in evacuating the internees. Again Lahti felt that any of his three battalions could accomplish the mission, and only selected First Battalion to avoid any confusion caused by having too many commanders from diverse units involved in the same operation. Ringler's direct superior on the ground would be his battalion commander, Major Henry Burgess, who would be in command of the amphibious assault.

Ringler was impressed with the amount of intelligence that had been gathered about the prison camp, the internees, the Japanese garrison and its defenses, as well as other enemy units in the area. The intelligence was so precise he would be able to give his individual platoons specific assignments to carry out in the attack on the camp. It was sobering news, however, to learn about the Japanese infantry division only miles away. If they reacted quickly with reinforcements, Ringler knew the mission could be at risk, along with his men and the internees.

Ringler was shown maps and aerial photographs. He agreed that the open field to the east of the camp appeared to be the best drop zone, even though it looked barely big enough to play a decent game of football. To be sure that everyone landed in the right place and did not drift far afield, he decided the jump could not be made from the usual one to two thousand feet.

Also, a lower-altitude jump would limit their exposure to enemy fire while descending under their parachute canopies, always a paratrooper's most vulnerable time. The lower the altitude, the faster the landing. As the company commander, Ringler would be the jump-master and the first out the door of the first plane. That was an airborne tradition. He would also decide the jump altitude.

"What are you thinking, Lieutenant?" one of the planners asked.

"Four hundred feet," Ringler said without hesitation.

Jumping from such a low altitude meant that after their main chutes opened, the troopers would swing only once or twice under the canopy before striking the ground hard. Ankle and leg injuries, including broken bones, could result because the chutes wouldn't have much time to slow their descent.

Noting the railroad tracks on the north end of the field—the direction from which the planes would fly in over Laguna de Bay—he decided they would serve as the "go" point for the paratroopers to start jumping. They were easy to see and recognizable from the air.

Ringler had already requested extra firepower for this mission: his eighty-eight men of B Company would be joined by twenty-two of the headquarters machine-gun platoon who would bring six .50-caliber machine guns. Together they were to free a prison camp with twice that many guards and defensive fortifications. His thoughts kept returning to the large enemy force sitting in the hills just a few miles away.

In operations in North Africa, Sicily, Normandy, and Holland, every drop of U.S. paratroopers behind enemy lines had resulted in heavy losses from landing in the wrong places—"misdrops" in airborne vernacular—and finding themselves surrounded by superior forces.

Ringler had one remaining, unasked question. *Why us?*


ONLY HOURS AFTER SKAU AND SANTOS RETURNED TO HEADQUARters from their reconnaissance of Los Baños, they stood before the Recon Platoon at their bivouac and briefed the other scouts on the upcoming mission. They would be leaving after dark that night— some forty hours before they were to launch the attack on the camp.

When the briefing was over, Saku told his men to get some hot chow and shut-eye. It could be days before they would get either again.

The platoon reassembled at 9 P.M. and climbed into trucks for the drive to the lakeside barrio of Wulilyos, where three sailing *bancas* and their Filipino crews awaited. The crews assured the Americans they would make it across in two or three hours, arriving at Nanghaya in the middle of the night as planned. Skau divided the group into three teams, which were to leave at intervals. Santos, Martin Squires, and three other scouts departed in the first *banca*. Fifteen minutes later, Skau and his small team followed. The largest of the *bancas,* which was carrying a dozen recon members, would follow with the platoon's extra weapons and ammunition, rations, and other supplies.

Santos told their Filipino helmsman that if a Japanese patrol vessel stopped them on Laguna de Bay, he should say they had been out fishing, the catch had been good, and they were late returning home.

"If they want to approach or board us, let them come closer," Santos said. "Then we'll blow them out of the water."

Santos hoped that would not be necessary because a gunfight in the middle of the lake was sure to bring out other enemy patrol boats.

Santos had already crossed Laguna de Bay twice without being challenged, but this time he heard an approaching engine when they were in the middle of the lake. Soon a spotlight caught them in its beam, and a voice demanded to know their business.

The other scouts had flattened themselves at the bottom of the *banca*, with their weapons at the ready. Santos remained seated upright in the bow, with a BAR light machine gun on his lap.

Santos knew the small patrol craft was sinkable with the firepower he and the scouts possessed. If the Japanese wanted to search the *banca*, he would wait until the last possible moment to open fire.

After a few more exchanges, the patrol boat's spotlight was switched off, and it motored away.

The next challenge came from the wind, which had been light when they started out, then completely disappeared from their sails when they were in the middle of the big lake. As the hours passed, they went nowhere.

Santos and Squires searched for paddles but found none. All they could do was wait. As the rising sun lit the morning sky, they knew they were visible from the shore. All the scouts except Santos again ducked out of sight. The journey across the lake to Nanghaya was supposed to take only a few hours but ended up taking ten.

Santos's team was met by guerrillas at the shore and taken to the village's one-room schoolhouse, where they reunited with Skau and his men, who had arrived only two hours earlier. They stayed out of sight the rest of the day awaiting the third *banca*.

More than one hundred members of guerrilla groups drifted in and received their own assignments. The Hunters ROTC would provide the bulk of the fighting force joining recon, helping to attack the sentries and rushing into the camp to protect the internees. The local contingent of PQOC would be guides and warn nearby residents to leave the area. The Hukbalahaps would secure the jump site and act as reserves. The Chinese guerrillas—kept out of the fight at the camp for fear they could be mistaken for Japanese—would guard the highway north and west of Los Baños. The Makings and Fil-Americans would secure the beach for the amtracs and protect the evacuation route.

Ben Edwards and Freddy Zervoulakos, who had remained at Nanghaya after their reconnaissance of the camp with Skau and Santos, joined recon in the schoolhouse. When they said they intended to join the raiding party to liberate the prison camp, nobody tried to dissuade them because their firsthand knowledge would be valuable to the raiders.

Skau asked Ben and Freddy to address the group about what they could expect to face. Standing in front of a school blackboard, Ben used a piece of chalk to sketch the camp, its terrain on all sides as well as the roads and trails leading into it. He and Freddy pointed out the main guardhouse and the other guard posts that were manned twenty-four hours a day. They described the terrain and pinpointed access roads and trails that led to the camp.

After more briefings and discussions, Skau and the guerrilla leaders began making assignments. They would split into six groups composed of both recon scouts and guerrillas: four to hit the guard posts at various locations, one to cover the drop zone, and one to cover the amtrac's landing area.

When the third *banca* still hadn't arrived by early evening, Skau had to draw up Plan B. The largest *banca* was carrying not only the extra ammunition and supplies—much of it meant for the guerrillas—but more than half of the recon scouts. Instead of three or four of them on each team, they would be down to one recon member leading all-guerrilla teams. Skau did not like it, but there was nothing he could do.

As it got dark and they were preparing to leave, the last *banca* arrived. They had been delayed by a broken rudder that had to be replaced, and they, too, had found no wind in the middle of the lake. Their journey had taken twenty hours, most of them during daylight, which meant the Americans had to stay low and out of sight.

The large *banca*'s extra weapons and ammunition were passed out to the guerrillas: seventy rounds per man, a luxury for units that often fought with only a few rounds for each gun.

During a final briefing session in the schoolhouse, Skau cautioned everyone not to give away their positions during the night. "Let them think they hear animals in the woods," he said. "If they think a rescue force is heading for Los Baños, they could start slaughtering the internees before we get there."

To his recon members, he said: "If anyone is hit during the night, carry them with you. Leave no evidence of American troops in the area."

Skau ended the briefing with a terse "Good luck."

Freddy joined a group that included Staff Sergeant John "Jack" Fulton, a twenty-three-year-old radioman with the 511th Signal Company who was from Clifton, New Jersey. He had been living with guerrillas for two weeks—mostly at their Tranca camp south of Los Baños. Fulton relayed messages by shortwave radio to and from 11th Airborne headquarters. His latest coded message to headquarters, sent two days ago from guerrilla leader Romeo Espino (aka Colonel Price), said: "URGENT: Espino to Vanderpool. Have received reliable information that Japs have Los Baños scheduled for massacres."

This information was based on guerrillas' seeing the trench the Japanese had dug. A new urgency to liberate the camp swept the guerrilla ranks, and Fulton had been on the move with them since then, ending up in Nanghaya with the guerrillas who were to take part in the raid.

Fulton saw in Freddy a "gangly kid full of beans" who was serious about doing his part to free his friends. Somehow Freddy had gotten hold of an old pistol that was too big for him but he couldn't wait to use it. Feeling protective of the teen, Fulton decided to stay close to Freddy during the raid and keep an eye on him.

Ben was assigned to a group led by Martin Squires, whom

Santos had earlier dubbed "Martin the thinker." Squires was now an acting sergeant in the unit he had had to spend months trying to join because he wore glasses. Squires was aware that Ben knew the area around the camp, and once the guerrilla guides got them close to their destination, he would have Ben lead the way in territory he was familiar with.

In the dark of a moonless night, they returned to the *banca*s and sailed a short distance down the coast to the barrio of San Antonio, where they went ashore. Each team would take a separate route overland to avoid being detected by Japanese patrols. They would end at the internment camp as the sun was coming up so they could be in their assigned positions to attack at seven o'clock sharp.

As Squires went around checking everyone's gear, he saw that Ben had gotten his hands on a couple of fragmentation hand grenades, which now bulged in his pants pockets.

Ben Edwards was ready for his return to Los Baños.

A LONE, DRAB-GREEN C-47 SKYTRAIN MADE A ROUGH LANDING at Nichols Field, where combat engineers were still working feverishly to fill in craters and repair other damage to the runways.

The pilot was Major Don Anderson, of Davis, California, the youthful-looking commander of the 65th Trooper Carrier Squadron based in Leyte. His squadron flew the workhorse aircraft for carrying troops, cargo, and paratroopers in both theaters of war. They had arrived in the Southwest Pacific in summer 1943, flying their two-engine C-47s—the military version of the popular DC-3—from San Francisco to Australia, a trip that had taken them over water for a distance equal to about halfway around the world.

With the C-47's range of only a thousand miles at a cruising speed of 150 mph, that meant lots of island hopping. For most of the pilots, it also meant flying out of sight of land for the first time in their lives, not a comfortable feeling in bad weather or clear skies.

For months now, they had been based first out of New Guinea and then Leyte, flying troops and cargo wherever they were needed in the South Pacific.

Anderson was taken by jeep to division headquarters, where he met Henry Muller and Doug Quandt. Anderson confirmed that nine of his C-47s would arrive at Nichols Field on February 22 to drop a company of paratroopers at Los Baños at 7 A.M. the following morning.

Given the runway conditions, Anderson admitted his concern that the planes were now scheduled to take off in the dark. Fully loaded with paratroopers, they would be at their maximum take-off weight. If a pilot was unable to avoid a crater in the dark, one of his plane's front landing gears could snap off, and the aircraft could end up cartwheeling across the field. If its fuel tanks erupted, it could turn into a deadly inferno. The planes would have only their running lights to guide them around all the holes. Anderson asked Quandt to push back the time, even just fifteen minutes. Quandt thought it unlikely but agreed they could together ask the general.

After Swing heard Anderson out, he made one of his typical quick decisions. "Young man," he growled, nailing Anderson with his glare, "the jump time is seven o'clock sharp. You'd goddamn better be there."

Anderson spent a couple more hours being briefed by Quandt and Muller, who brought out maps, charts, and aerial photographs of the camp and the surrounding area. On a topographical map he noticed a low-slung hill just north of the drop zone. "We'll be coming in very low over that hill," he said. "We'd be sitting ducks for an enemy machine gunner there."

What he was thinking but didn't say was: *Hell, they could throw rocks and hit us.*

Muller told him recon scouts were just back from reconnoitering the area, and they had found no enemy positions on the hill. Also,

P-38 fighters would be providing cover in case of any enemy threats on the ground or in the air.

Anderson had never dropped paratroopers from such a low altitude. He would be leading the flight over Laguna de Bay, and when it was time they would slow down, descend, and move into three-plane V formations—known as "drop formations"—tucked tightly together. They would make only one pass. After the paratroopers left, the planes would climb to normal altitude and return to their Leyte base.

After the briefings, Anderson and his copilot, Captain Herbert Parker, of Jonesboro, Arkansas, were ready to return to Leyte to prepare the squadron for the upcoming mission. But before they left, Anderson wanted to take a peek at Los Baños Internment Camp.

He had a good idea what the planners at headquarters would have said about his flying over the camp. He would have been ordered not to do so because they wouldn't want to chance alerting the Japanese to the impending rescue mission. But he knew that planes flew back and forth over the area all the time on their way to and from Manila, so he didn't ask for permission.

Keeping the plane flying level and straight at five thousand feet so as not to attract attention below, Anderson gave Parker the controls so he could take a long, careful look out the cockpit window. He found the camp where he expected to see it south of Laguna de Bay, and easily located its long, distinctive barracks that looked just like the aerial photos. What shocked him though was the drop zone for the paratroopers.

From five thousand feet, it was about the size of a postage stamp.

SERGEANT CHARLES SASS, A TWENTY-FOUR-YEAR-OLD NATIVE of Kingston, New York, and the other men of B Company were not surprised when they were withdrawn from the fighting at Fort McKinley and sent to the rear. After all, they had been fighting for weeks and taking heavy casualties—one of them being Sass, when he was "knocked silly" a week earlier by a ricochet from a Japanese artillery shell that landed next to a ditch where he was taking cover. He bled from countless small punctures and metal splinters but nothing had been broken, and he was not out of action for any length of time.

What did surprise Sass and the others was that their assigned rest area turned out to be New Bilibid Prison in Muntinlupa. Everyone was relieved at least that the cell doors were left open.

Sergeant Charles Sass, spring 1944. *Courtesy Charles Sass.*

Sass joined the Army in December 1942, and the next spring was sent to Officer Candidate School, which he flunked out of before completing the six-week course—"they figured out I wasn't Eisenhower material." It was too late for him to rejoin his infantry outfit, which had left for Europe. After a few days hanging out in an empty barracks, he heard that the paratroopers were looking for volunteers and signed up. That took him to jump school at Fort Benning, where he discovered he was completely comfortable jumping out of an airplane. He was then shipped to New Guinea, where he had joined up with the 11th Airborne's 511th Parachute Infantry Regiment in time for Leyte.

The men of B Company were sequestered in the former penitentiary for a couple of days without their knowing what new mission they were waiting to be assigned. Rumors flew that something big was brewing. Everyone was guessing—correctly, as it turned out— that they had been spirited away to the prison to keep them separated and incommunicado in order to maintain mission security.

The secrecy ended on February 22 when John Ringler addressed his men. By then, they were used to Ringler's speeches of twenty-five words or less, and he didn't disappoint with extra verbiage now. He told them they were going to save the lives of more than two thousand civilian internees who had been prisoners of the Japanese for more than three years.

"We're going to do the most important thing we've ever done," he said, "and maybe we'll ever do."

Late that afternoon, the paratroopers boarded trucks and drove north for ten miles. When they arrived at Nichols Field, they found nine C-47s parked on the tarmac.

In the security of a guarded hangar, the paratroopers found their packed parachutes ready to go, along with extra weapons and ammunition. This is when they heard the details of the operation and were able to study maps and aerial photographs. It was explained how they would have to hit the ground running and get into the prison camp quickly to support recon before the guards had time to start killing the internees. They could expect the Japanese in the camp to fight back as ferociously as had the Japanese they had faced in the mountains of Leyte and, most recently, in the streets of Manila.

When Ringler said the altitude for the jump would be four hundred feet, the men stirred and mumbled to themselves.

"We'll be packing reserve chutes," he quickly added.

Most of the men in the hangar laughed; Ringler did not.

Everyone knew it would be impossible to deploy a reserve parachute manually in case the main chute malfunctioned because they wouldn't have the time or the altitude to do so. But paratroopers *always* wore reserve chutes. Ringler had decided days ago that telling his men "Don't worry about reserves because you're not going to have time to use them" would not be good for morale.

In truth, B Company's morale could not have been higher. Everyone was excited about the mission and ready to go. No outsider could have bought a seat in one of the C-47s from anyone in B Company. Sure, the mission sounded dangerous and they could take some casualties, but there was nothing new about that. After all the shooting and killing, the chance to "finally do something nice for people," as one young trooper said, was inspiring to everyone. Another paratrooper asked his buddy to write to his parents in case he didn't make it and let them know he was trying to save lives at the end.

That night, a team of Army cooks set up a kitchen and chow line out in the open, and the men of B Company were served their first hot meal in nearly a month: all-you-can-eat spaghetti and meatballs.

"Okay, guys," someone hollered. "The Last Supper!"

Everybody laughed, even Ringler.

Pup tents went up under the wings of the planes. This is where B Company would spend the night, though few troopers would get any sleep.

The regimental chaplain, Lee Edwin "Chappie" Walker, offered a nondenominational mass. A number of troopers, including Charlie Sass, accepted the last rites of their church. The chaplain looked out at the faces of the young men he had come to know so well in this war.

"Tomorrow, the world will be watching. May God be with you."

FOR HENRY MULLER, THE REPORT FROM A P-61 BLACK WIDOW, A twin-engine aircraft designed specifically for night operations, was nearly heart-stopping. Late on February 22, while on a night reconnaissance flight over the southern shore of Laguna de Bay, the three-man aircrew observed a long line of headlights entering the town of Los Baños.

Muller got on the phone and tried desperately to convince the Air Corps to send up another night mission to determine the latest whereabouts of the convoy since the report was a couple of hours old. But he was told that the P-61s and their pilots were done flying for the night.

It was midnight when he and Doug Quandt went to brief General Swing.

"All we know from this report," Muller began, "is that a long column of vehicles was observed entering Los Baños. As there are no U.S. units in that area, they must be Japanese. We don't know how many or from which direction they came or went. We don't know if it was reinforcements heading for the prison camp. We don't know if they were just passing through town."

If security had been breached—possibly leaked by a spy in one of the guerrilla groups—and the Japanese knew about the raid and had reinforced the camp, the U.S. units could be caught in a trap.

The question now was whether or not to call off the raid until further reconnaissance could determine if the situation had changed.

The amtracs, which would depart soon for their middle-of-the-night journey across Laguna de Bay, could be stopped. The paratroopers of B Company could be grounded. The diversionary column that was to head down Highway 1 could be held back. As for the Recon Platoon, they were already making their way through the jungle toward the camp, and there was no way to call them back or warn them. If they hit the guard posts at 7 A.M. as planned and tried to take the camp alone, they would be sacrificed.

Muller knew it was a close call for the general. "It's an unfounded report, sir," he added. "We're not sure what they are doing. We're not even sure how many trucks there were or where they went."

Swing nodded curtly. "Let's go ahead."

The only change Swing made to the plan was to put another battalion of paratroopers (2nd Battalion, 511th) on alert in the event they had to be sent down Highway 1 to fight off enemy reinforcements.

Muller spent the rest of the night worrying about all the things that could go wrong even if the Japanese had not reinforced the prison camp. The amtracs could get lost crossing the dark waters of the large lake. Hitting such a small drop zone with a company of paratroopers was not easy. Recon and the guerrillas might get lost or waylaid and not make it on time.

But something else was gnawing at Muller, too.

Given the recent surprise operations on Luzon that had freed prisoners at Santo Tomás, Old Bilibid Prison, and Cabanatuan, how many times in one month could Japanese prison-camp guards be surprised?

# FIFTEEN

# The Raid

*Raid: A military operation to temporarily seize an area in order to secure information, confuse an adversary, capture personnel or equipment, or to destroy a capability. It ends with a planned withdrawal upon completion of the assigned mission.*

U.S. DEPARTMENT OF DEFENSE

FIFTY-FOUR LOUDLY SCREECHING AMTRACS—RESEMBLING Sherman tanks missing their turrets—clanked along the ruined streets of Manila in the dead of the night. Although traveling in the dark so as not to alert the enemy to their movement, these war machines were not going to sneak up on anyone. The assignment given them in the raid on Los Baños was one for which they were neither designed nor their crews trained. It had been that kind of war for the 672nd Amphibian Tractor Battalion.

Corporal Dwight Clark, a twenty-one-year-old who was one of ten children born to a New Carlisle, Indiana, painting contractor and his wife, thought at one time that his motorized battalion would be facing German Tiger tanks in North Africa. That was what they had practiced for in the parched flatlands near Fort

Hood in Texas in 1943 as they learned how to drive, fight, and maintain their M-10 Tank Destroyers. These mammoth machines had been built to counter German blitzkrieg tactics by moving quickly to knock out enemy tanks. But just after the battalion finished its training, with an excellent score in its final tests, the war in North Africa ended.

A different armored vehicle was needed in the Pacific, and the battalion's tank destroyers were replaced with LVT (Landing Vehicle Tracked) Model 4As. Official designation: the Water Buffalo. Clark and the other men in the 672nd were turned into jack-of-all-trades for anything a three-man crew had to do to keep their amtrac operating.

The tractor battalion had arrived in the South Pacific in October 1944, and on January 9, 1945, carried troops ashore in the Lingayen Gulf assault landing. Powered by a nine-cylinder, 250-horsepower Continental aircraft engine, the sixteen-ton amtrac could go as fast as 15 mph on land and 5 mph in the water. Designed as ship-to-shore vehicles to carry in an open cargo compartment up to thirty infantrymen (or artillery pieces and small vehicles) to the beach, move inland for up to half a mile, and secure the beachhead with their .50-caliber (front) and .30-caliber (rear) machine guns until more troops arrived, the amtracs were then expected to return to the troopship and make another run until the landing was completed.

The amtracs were not built to be over-the-road vehicles; with sheet-metal tracks unsuited for paved or concrete roads, they could easily throw a track on a hard surface and be out of commission until replacement parts showed up. But given that the Japanese had blown so many bridges between Lingayen Gulf and Manila—leaving rivers to be forded by men, artillery, vehicles, and supplies—the amtracs were ordered to remain with the 37th Infantry Division and First Cavalry Division as they advanced toward the capital, and assist with river crossings.

The 672nd had been among the first U.S. units to cross the Pasig River that bisects Manila, connecting Laguna de Bay with Manila Bay. For a couple of weeks the men and amtracs had been bivouacked on the once-manicured fields of the Manila Polo Club, now chewed up by tank tracks. That's where, on February 20, the battalion was ordered to move out for an unspecified mission that would be launched three days later from the western shore of Laguna de Bay.

After taking aboard extra barrels of fuel, the crews fired up their smoking, backfiring engines, and the long, winding line of sawed-off tanks crawled forth on a zigzag route that found them moving by night and parked by day. The seemingly aimless drive ended on the third night when battalion commander Lieutenant Colonel Joseph Gibbs, a sturdy, thirty-six-year-old six-footer from Rosebud, Texas, ordered a hard turn to the east, which took them to Mamatid, the staging area for the raid on Los Baños Internment Camp.

Gibbs, a 1932 graduate of Texas A&M with a degree in civil engineering, had worked on soil conservation projects before the war while keeping his reserve commission, and went on active duty before Pearl Harbor. A polished, courtly officer older than most of his peers, he wrote home to his wife about his pride in "my boys and my battalion."

Major Henry Burgess, commander of the First Battalion of the 511th, was waiting for Gibbs and his amtracs at the staging area on the evening of February 22. After they came ashore the next morning near Los Baños, Burgess was to bring his battalion and the amtracs to the prison camp and start evacuating the prisoners. The plan, Burgess explained, was to have everyone out of the camp and on their way to safety across Laguna de Bay in no more than a few hours.

Burgess, a twenty-six-year-old from Sheridan, Wyoming, had been raised on a thirty-five-thousand-acre cattle ranch that sold horses to the cavalry. He learned to ride, shoot coyotes, and work on horseback from sunup to sunset, all of which qualified him to join the cavalry, which he did when he enrolled in the Wyoming National Guard the summer after his sophomore year at Harvard. Shortly after he graduated in 1940, his reserve unit was called to active duty. When the horse cavalry was disbanded, he joined the paratroopers.

Two days after being pulled out of action at Fort McKinley, Burgess's battalion—less B Company, which was already en route to Nichols Fields—was trucked southward, not on the main highway but, in order to preserve security, across bumpy dirt roads to Mamatid, twenty-five miles south of Manila and ten miles north of Los Baños.

This area was not yet in U.S. hands and was within range of enemy artillery located in hills to the west and south, so Burgess had his men set up a bivouac in a wooded area and keep out of sight during the day. This was where his troopers were first told about the raid, and everyone had the chance to look at maps and photos of the prison camp.

Late in the evening before the raid, Burgess and Gibbs strolled through the assembly area on the beach. Most of their men were sacked out on the sand or inside the amtracs. One of them was Pete Miles, who had been determined to join the raiding party even after Henry Muller advised him to stay at headquarters and get some rest. Pete knew he could help guide the amphibious force to the camp, and he felt he was owed the chance to go back and help free his friends.

Due to equipment breakdowns, the 672nd battalion had many more drivers and crewmen than amtracs these days, so Gibbs allowed men to volunteer for the mission to cross the large lake and "bring out some prisoners of war." Dwight Clark jumped at the opportunity to bring some people home. The 672nd soon had many more volunteers than amtracs.

Burgess explained to Gibbs that he and his men were to navigate in the dark across eight miles of open water, make three directional changes guided only by a compass, keep their fifty-four amtracs in a single-file column with no more than ten yards separation so they wouldn't lose sight of the one in front, and land on the designated beach near the town of Los Baños at exactly 7 A.M.

Gibbs knew that making all the course changes correctly was a tall order for his drivers and amtracs. They had never crossed an expanse of open, choppy waters like they would find in Laguna de Bay. Gibbs was not a trained navigator or even an amateur sailor. But he understood the value of precision. His training and work as a civil engineer had taught him that one small mistake could ruin a large project. With this mission, one navigational error along the way could cause the men to become lost or to arrive late. And without the amtracs, there would be no way to evacuate the internees.

Gibbs knew if he failed to bring his amtracs to the right place at the right time, the more than two thousand internees would have no way out.

JOE SWING WROTE TO HIS FATHER-IN-LAW, GENERAL PEYTON March, about the same worries that kept Joe Gibbs awake the night before the raid.

"All the bridges are out from Calamba on south," Swing explained, "so if I went after them by land, the devils would have plenty of time either to massacre the group or remove them further in the hills. Besides, half of the prisoners are so weak they couldn't walk the 10 miles to safety [to Mamatid], and with the bridges out and no way to transport them, the Japs could murder them with artillery fire."

The amtracs were so key to the evacuation that Swing decided he would ride in the lead vehicle. Burgess received orders from division headquarters to send an officer to pick up the general and bring him to the staging area where the amtracs would depart.

Lieutenant Robert Beightler Jr., a twenty-three-year-old Ohioan and 1943 West Point graduate, took a jeep and a driver to headquarters. After waiting around for Swing, they left with what Beightler thought was ample time. The young officer knew about handling generals; his father, Major General Robert Beightler, was commanding general of the 37th Infantry Division, known as the "Buckeye Division," which had fought in New Georgia and Bougainville and was now engaged in street-to-street fighting in Manila.

On the way back over unfamiliar roads with blackout lights on the jeep, they became lost. Burgess had promised that someone would be on the road with a flashlight to guide them down the dirt trail to the beach where the amtracs were assembled. But they found no roadside guide and bounced their way along bumpy roads in the dark until the driver slammed on the brakes, bringing the jeep to a stop with tires squealing. The front wheels stopped three feet from the edge of a hundred-foot gorge.

Beightler had never in all his life seen a man quite as angry as Swing at that moment; not because they had all nearly died by driving over a cliff, but because they were lost and screwing around so much that the general feared he would miss the departing amtracs. They groped around in the dark and finally found the path down to the beach.

They had been hearing the amtracs for several minutes, and stepped onto the beach in time to see the last one chugging away.

Swing unleashed more curses at Beightler, who had hoped to follow in his father's footsteps and make the Army a career. The general ordered the harried driver to take him back to headquarters, leaving a shocked Beightler, who was also supposed to have boarded one of the amtracs, on the beach contemplating his ruined military career.

The time was 5:15 A.M. The amtracs had left on schedule.

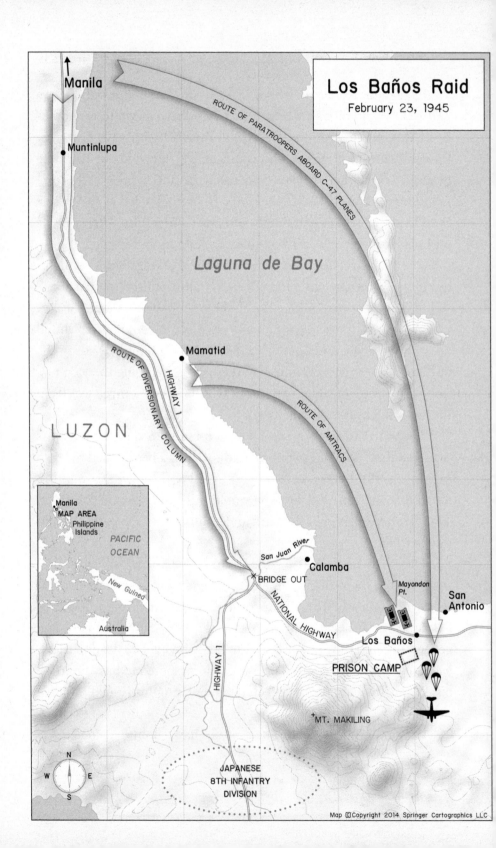

# Los Baños Raid
## February 23, 1945

Manila

Muntinlupa

ROUTE OF PARATROOPERS ABOARD C-47 PLANES

*Laguna de Bay*

Mamatid

ROUTE OF DIVERSIONARY COLUMN

HIGHWAY 1

ROUTE OF AMTRACS

L U Z O N

Manila
MAP AREA
Philippine
Islands

PACIFIC
OCEAN

New Guinea

Australia

San Juan River

Calamba

✕ BRIDGE OUT

NATIONAL HIGHWAY

Mayondon
Pt.

San
Antonio

Los Baños

PRISON CAMP

HIGHWAY 1

+MT. MAKILING

N
W  E
S

JAPANESE
8TH INFANTRY
DIVISION

Map ©Copyright 2014 Springer Cartographics LLC

LIKE THE PARATROOPERS HE WAS TO DELIVER TO LOS BAÑOS AT sunrise, pilot Alex Morley, a captain in the Army Air Corps with two thousand flight hours, spent the night on the tarmac at Nichols Field, sleeping on a canvas cot he kept in the plane for such times. Morley, a twenty-six-year-old from Cheyenne, Wyoming, had flown in with his copilot and crew chief the day before.

Alex Morley, C-47 pilot. *Courtesy Alex Morley.*

Morley's plane had been the first in the squadron to arrive over the field, and he circled a couple of times before landing because he hadn't liked what he saw below: wrecked planes strewn across the field and countless holes in the runway. After a cautious but safe landing, the other planes came in behind him, as if their pilots had been waiting to see if he crashed.

Now, at 5:55 A.M. on February 23, Morley was in the cockpit of his C-47, having completed the preflight checklist. He looked at his watch; five minutes to engine start-up and twenty minutes until takeoff.

With the squadron commander, Don Anderson, leading the way this morning, Morley and the other pilots would largely be following the leader. He knew from Anderson's briefing that the paratrooper commander wanted the nine C-47s to fly in a tight formation because of the narrowness of the drop zone and the need for his men to drop closely together on the small field. Anderson would bring them over the drop zone and radio the "go" signal when it was time for the jump. The other pilots would have to follow while avoiding a midair collision, given how close together the planes would be flying.

Morley had never before dropped paratroopers from four hundred feet—nor had any of the other pilots. Most jumps were from a thousand feet or higher. But Morley had faith they could do it and do it right—unlike another squadron of C-47s, whose pilots had dropped the same paratroopers at Tagaytay Ridge but scattered them over several miles because they didn't slow down their planes enough. Such a disorganized drop this morning would be a fiasco.

Twisting around to look out his side window, Morley could see the bulky shadows of the paratroopers silently climbing the ladder into his plane. Nobody was chatting or joking. Morley knew this was their quiet time, when each man was alone with his own thoughts. It was no time for frivolity, preening, or bravado.

Sergeant Charles Sass and the rest of B Company had started getting ready for the jump about 5 A.M. following a restless night under the stars after their spaghetti dinner. For these veteran paratroopers, the procedure was automatic. Sass first put on his chest harness over his olive-green fatigues. He slipped a web belt around his waist and hung from it two canteens filled with water, a bayonet, a first-aid kit, ammo pouches, and a trench knife. Across his chest he wore two bandoliers with more than a hundred rounds of M-1 ammunition. He also carried two thirty-round magazines for the BAR light machine gun someone else in his platoon carried.

He then buddied up with the guy next to him and each of them assisted the other in putting on their main T-5 parachute and harness. The main chute fit on the back and was secured by three snap hooks that fastened to the harness; two straps ran under the crotch, and a third went across the chest. The reserve chute was a large chest pack that fastened to the front of the harness with snap hooks. The metal handle that had to be pulled to deploy the chute was on the right side of the pack. The last item to go on was the bellyband, a wide strap that kept the reserve chute in place. Underneath this tight belt Sass stuck his M-1 Garand rifle, muzzle first, so he wouldn't lose it during the jump. Sass swore that an M-1 could topple a tree at a half mile, and he never went into combat with any other weapon— not even the M-1 carbine favored by other paratroopers because it weighed less and was easier to carry.

Groups of paratroopers—called a "stick"—were assigned to each plane by a sergeant who used a flashlight to read off the names. They lined up next to their assigned plane and did an equipment check for the man in front of them. They made sure the main parachute's static line was free and not looped under an arm or caught in a strap or webbing. One end of the fifteen-foot line was attached to the cover on the pack holding the main chute and the other would be snapped to a cable inside the plane.

When the trooper jumped, the line would go taut and rip off the pack cover, pulling out the contents. The prop blast would blow open the twenty-eight-foot canopy, and the static line would break free and remain with the plane. The opening time for the main canopy was approximately three seconds.

After they finished checking the man in front, everyone turned around and repeated the routine with the man behind. Only then was it time to board the planes, where they plopped down in metal seats set in facing rows along either side of the plane's cabin.

It was still dark out when the C-47s started up their noisy, sputtering engines, which soon settled down to a roaring drone.

The planes taxied down the tarmac in single file, with Anderson's in the lead. At exactly 6:20 A.M., he went to full power and released the brake. His plane started moving slowly down the dark runway, then began to build up speed, rattling and shaking like it would fall apart before lifting off. The runway was plenty long for C-47s, but Anderson wanted to bring his aircraft off the ground as quickly as possible to avoid as many of the potholes as he could. It was not the smoothest takeoff of his career, but they were off without a problem.

At 6:30 A.M., the last C-47 lumbered down the bumpy runway and went airborne, joining the rest of the squadron that had, one by one, gone up to a thousand feet and circled, waiting for all nine planes to form up.

"Got a problem, skipper," one of the pilots radioed Anderson. "My landing gear is not retracting. Can't keep up unless we red-line RPM."

It would be later learned that a ground mechanic at Nichols had neglected to pull the safety pins placed in the landing gear to avoid an accidental retraction of the wheels while a plane was on the ground.

A C-47 flying with its landing gear down would experience increased wind resistance and a significant loss of speed. If this had been a routine cargo run, Anderson would have sent the lagger back. But not this morning. He couldn't slow down the formation because it would make them late to the drop zone, and he couldn't let a plane of paratroopers fall behind.

"Goose RPM and go balls to the wall," said Anderson, even though he knew that holding full power for the entire flight could result in a blown engine. He just hoped that if this happened, it would be on the way back from the drop.

None of Anderson's pilots wore parachutes because there was no way for them to exit a C-47 during flight given how far the only door was in the back of the plane. They would not leave the controls. If a plane were hit by enemy fire or otherwise disabled, the pilots would stay with it all the way down.

Anderson led them all on a course out over Laguna de Bay.

The flight was a short twenty minutes.

He dipped his right wing to signal the squadron—which was flying in V formations of three planes each—that they should assume drop positions. In each of the Vs, the plane on the right, slightly above and behind the leader, retained its position, while the plane on the left crossed over and settled behind and slightly above the other two. All three planes were now stacked in a right-echelon formation that ensured none of them would overrun paratroopers jumping from a plane in front.

C-47s in right-echelon formation. *U.S. Army Signal Corps.*

Anderson also continued to bring them down lower. When he reached drop altitude, he leveled off, while continuing to slow down from 140 knots cruising speed. He wanted no more than 110 knots on his speed indicator when the paratroopers jumped so the shock of the chute opening would be less violent. It was quite a trick to slow down one of these lumbering transports without losing altitude or stalling the plane.

On Anderson's "Go!" signal, his copilot, Herbert Parker, flipped the switch that turned on a red light to the right of the jump door in the back.

Lieutenant John Ringler, who since takeoff had been standing at the opening created by the removal of the plane's set of double doors—large enough to drive a jeep through—had just watched the sun's fiery orange ball peek over the eastern horizon. He now yelled: "Stand up and hook up!"

The men sprang from their seats and formed a single line facing the back of the plane. They all snapped the ring on the end of their static line into the metal cable that ran overhead the length of the cabin.

"Equipment check!"

Everyone checked the static line of the man in front of him to make sure his ring was secured to the cable and the line was not caught anywhere.

As they approached the drop zone, Anderson saw two rising columns of white smoke; he had been told members of the division's Reconnaissance Platoon would mark the field with smoke grenades.

When the plane crossed the edge of the drop zone, Parker threw a switch that illuminated a green light next to the jump door.

"Close up!" Ringler ordered.

The paratroopers began pushing toward the door.

Realizing that the first man out would be a target for anyone on the ground with a mind to shoot at descending paratroopers, Ringler had at his feet an equipment bag, which he intended to kick out before he jumped and offer up as the first available target to any sharpshooters below.

A split second later, out went the bag, followed by Ringler.

A one-word chant now filled the cabin.

"Go! Go! Go! Go!"

Paratroopers are a thundering herd as they rush for the exit. Their job is to get out rapidly so they can land together and fight together. The cabin filled with the sound of heavy jump boots hitting the aluminum floor. As quickly as one man jumped and disappeared, the next man behind him followed, without hesitation or delay.

It was 7 A.M. exactly.

At ten o'clock the night before, shortly after Lieutenant George Skau's final briefing in the schoolhouse at Nanghaya, Terry Santos gathered his assault team and headed out on foot to the prison camp to be in position just outside it at sunrise. He had with him three recon members, all experienced scouts and veterans of Leyte: Vinson "Vince" Call, Lawrence "Larry" Botkin, and Barclay "Mick" McFadden. A dozen guerrillas joined this group, and Santos had one of the locals up front with him helping to guide the way.

They were being extra careful not to be spotted by enemy patrols or outposts, and several times during the night, they heard Japanese voices and quietly moved off in the opposite direction before circling back around. They wound their way through varied vegetation and terrain, the most difficult being flooded rice paddies. To cross them, they had to walk on narrow raised dikes, which made their silhouettes exposed on all sides. In places, they accidentally slid off the earthen banks and fell into muddy waters with a splash.

Santos had left behind his favorite weapon, which he had carried through most of the war: a .45-caliber submachine gun. In its place he had an M-1 Garand rifle. He had made the switch because of the gun towers at the prison camp. The long-barrel M-1 was more accurate for such kill shots. Not wanting to run low on ammunition, he wore two bandoliers with sixteen eight-round clips and another ten clips on his ammo belt. He also carried six hand grenades.

In a straight line, the distance they covered that night was about ten miles, but having to proceed cautiously and take a circuitous route added several miles and turned what should have been about a three-hour march into more than eight hours. When they were still half a mile from the camp, they came to a lone nipa hut.

Santos approached it alone and peered inside. A uniformed Japanese soldier was sitting up, cradling his rifle, sound asleep with a field phone next to him. It was obviously a listening post in the woods. Santos, his razor-sharp knife in hand, knew he could easily slit the sentry's throat and be on his way. He was tempted but held back. *What if they phoned and the guy didn't answer?* That could put the prison-camp garrison on alert. Santos sheathed his knife and silently backed away.

By the time Santos's team made it to their assigned sector at the southeast perimeter of the camp, they had only a couple of guerrillas still with them, including their loyal guide. The others had dropped off into the bush as they drew closer. He knew the Filipino fighters had developed their own ways, and even though they had been given plenty of rifle ammunition for this operation, they preferred using their machete-like bolos on their hated enemy. He suspected they would be waiting in the woods to ambush mano a mano any escaping Japanese.

Santos and his team dropped into a ravine that was marked "Boot Creek" on their map but was devoid of water. He checked his watch: 6:50 A.M. They still hadn't heard the approaching C-47s.

They moved closer to the guard posts they were assigned to attack, and the four scouts had just crested the opposite side of the ravine when a single shot rang out. It was too early—the paratroopers weren't yet overhead. Had someone beat the clock?

Santos and his team froze.

There were no more shots—only the predawn stillness.

The element of surprise had not been lost.


AFTER LEAVING NANGHAYA, MARTIN SQUIRES'S ASSAULT TEAM with recon members Gene Lynch and Wayne Milton, along with Ben Edwards and a dozen guerrillas, followed the same general route Ben had taken twice before.

When they were not far into their all-night trek, and just as they had started to cross a road outside the town of Los Baños, the guerrilla in front halted and passed word back that someone was on the road. Sure enough, Ben saw a flicker of a cigarette. Not knowing who it might be—and following Skau's strict orders to avoid any contact with Japanese—they retraced their steps and crossed the highway farther to the west.

Hours later, passing to the east of the prison camp, they rounded a small hill to the south before heading west toward the slopes of Mount Makiling, then turning northward. The sector they had been assigned, from which they would attack the camp, required the longest walk. Heading for the far northwest corner of the camp, they stayed in the dense woods about a thousand feet up the mountain slope so as not to be seen as they paralleled the camp's western boundary.

Squires had intermingled the Filipino guerrillas with his recon members. Suddenly, as it was beginning to grow light outside, he glanced back and realized that half of his column—including not only guerrillas but Lynch and Milton—was no longer following him.

Squires felt a cold chill that had nothing to do with the weather. With 7 A.M. rapidly approaching, his team was not in position, and he didn't even have all his recon guys. They had surely become separated in the dark woods; probably, he speculated, at the last Y in the trail. He decided to go back to gather his missing guys.

Looking at Ben, Squires knew it wasn't fair to send him back to face his former captors without a weapon. Squires had been carrying a .45 automatic in a leather shoulder holster since Leyte. A bit reluctantly, he now took off the holster and handed the powerful handgun to Ben, who checked to make sure the weapon was loaded, then slipped the holster over his head.

Squires told him to keep going with the guerrillas toward their assigned sector of the camp, and he would join them as quickly as he could. With that, Squires took off running in the opposite direction.

As Ben and the guerrillas got closer to the camp, they left the woods and took a shortcut through the yards of houses on Faculty

Hill. Without warning, someone's dog attacked one of the guerrillas. Reacting rather than thinking, the guerrilla shot the dog with a pistol.

The sound shattered the early-morning stillness and reverberated like a shot heard around the world. They froze to see what was going to happen next.

When nothing did, they moved swiftly into position, settling in some shrubbery outside the sawali-covered fence near the YMCA building. Ben could not see through or over the fence, but he knew a guard post was right on the other side, and it was manned by two guards round the clock. That was his team's target in the assault, and their entry point into camp.

All they could do now was wait for the planes and paratroopers. Those minutes seemed like hours to Ben.

At first, the drone of the C-47s was barely audible. But as it grew louder, the men's eyes turned to the sky. Then the planes were suddenly roaring overhead just east of the camp, coming in at an unbelievably low altitude—so low they looked like they might land nearby.

When the first parachute billowed open, Ben rushed the fence. Holding a grenade, he pulled the safety pin and tossed it over. After the explosion, he scaled to the top of the outer fence, jumped down, and crawled on his belly under the inner fence. As he got back on his feet, he saw two Japanese soldiers deserting a sentry post. He aimed his gun and fired. The bullet struck the guard in the middle of his back, and he fell to the ground dead. With no time to admire "the best shot of my life," Ben saw the other guard run to a nearby culvert and dive in.

Before Ben could react, one of the recon guys from another team showed up and flipped a grenade into the culvert as if he were throwing away an apple core. After the explosion, several guerrillas dragged the guard's broken body up to the road and delivered an unneeded coup de grâce with their bolos.

Bullets were now whizzing and whining past Ben from all directions. Tracer ammunition—one in every four or five rounds loaded with a pyrotechnic charge that lights up upon discharge and enables the shooter to follow the trajectory of his aim and make corrections—floated through the air around him like orange tennis balls.

When one bullet struck the ground in front of Ben, either metal fragments from the bullet or rock splinters hit his shins, causing small but painful wounds that began bleeding. Wearing the same khaki shorts he had worn during his escape, he chastised himself for not putting on long pants before he went to war.

Ben's assignment was to organize the evacuation of a nearby barracks that housed older men. Both frightened and elated, he now hurried for the barracks.

LIEUTENANT GEORGE SKAU AND HIS RECON TEAM WERE A QUARTER of a mile from the prison camp when he heard the drone of the planes. Inexplicably, their Filipino guide had become turned around in the dark as they crossed some interlocking rice paddies a while back, and they had lost valuable time.

At the sound of the approaching planes, Skau led his team on a flat-out sprint for the camp's main entrance near Baker Hall. With Skau was Tabo Ingles, the Hunters ROTC officer who had met with George Gray at the Espino home. Ingles had brought along several of his best fighters. Their target was key to the raid's success. They were to get to the stacked guns that the guards who were exercising had left in a building just inside the main gate. To do so, they had to be in position before the paratroopers jumped.

As they came to the front gate, they killed two sentries on duty and took out a stone pillbox with a grenade before anyone inside could get off a shot.

Now everything was happening lightning-quick.

The planes were overhead—billowing parachutes filled the sky and suddenly disappeared behind a tree line—gunfire and multiple explosions as other assault teams hit the camp simultaneously— the guttural sound of recon's BAR in the capable hands of big Robert Carroll as he fired the automatic submachine gun that could quickly gain fire superiority and overwhelm an enemy, first raking sentry posts and then dropping a half-dozen charging Japanese soldiers.

Skau and his team ran past the open field where the exercising Japanese soldiers had momentarily frozen in apparent shock before starting to run for the building fifty yards away that housed their weapons. Not taking the time to fire at them, Skau and his men sprinted past. When they reached the building that held the guards' stacked weapons, Skau tossed a white-phosphorus grenade inside. A loud explosion, and the building was soon engulfed in flames.

With no hope of arming themselves, the near-naked Japanese, now coming under fire in the field from several directions by recon scouts and guerrillas as they charged into the camp, desperately tried to flee. Those who weren't dropped on the exercise field by gunfire scattered into the woods like a herd of frightened deer.

Skau next bounded up the steps to the commandant's headquarters, a location he knew about from Ben and one he'd made a priority. As he kicked open the front door, the lone Japanese officer on duty inside bolted from behind a desk and dove for an open window.

Like a carnival trick shooter, Skau picked him off in midair. The young officer was dead before he hit the ground outside.

Terry Santos and his assault team attacked a machine-gun position at the southeast corner of the camp on cue. The woodpecker-like *rat-tat-tat* of a Japanese Nambu light machine gun, which Santos considered the most deadly infantry weapon in the Japanese arsenal, fired back at them but missed wildly.

Santos, Call, and Botkin poured a fusillade of rifle fire into the pillbox. Its earthen walls did not stop their bullets, and the enemy gunner was quickly silenced.

When a second Nambu opened up from another position, Call and Botkin were caught moving in the open. Call was wounded in the shoulder and unable to fire his weapon, but he managed to find cover. Botkin, bleeding profusely from a ricochet that hit him in the face, was pinned down by the enemy fire.

Staying low, Santos crawled through the tall grass to flank the gunner firing at them. He knew that the closer he came the safer he would be because the machine gun, fired atop a tripod, would be limited in its field of fire when aiming down and low.

When Santos was near enough, he rolled onto his back, took out a grenade, pulled the pin, and heaved it over his shoulder without looking.

The explosion silenced the second Japanese machine gun.

ON THE NIGHT BEFORE THE RAID, THE DIVERSIONARY FORCE made up of a battalion of glider infantry from the 11th Airborne's 188th regiment, along with a company of airborne engineers, the 472nd Field Artillery Battalion, and a company from the 637th Tank Destroyer Battalion, moved into place as planned to dissuade Japanese General Masatoshi Fujishige from sending elements of his Eighth Division to reinforce the prison-camp garrison.

The diversionary force was known as Soule's task force, for its commander, the forty-four-year-old Colonel Robert Soule, of Laramie, Wyoming. The stocky, sawed-off Soule, nicknamed "Shorty" for a reason, had already been awarded the Distinguished Service Cross—second only to the Medal of Honor—for commanding his regiment in action at Tagaytay Ridge. As senior officer on the Los Baños raid, Soule was named the assault commander of the operation, although he would be stymied all day with communication problems and unable to reach other units by radio.

Soule's nearly fifteen-hundred-man force had been trucked down Highway 1 until about 8 P.M., when the infantry disembarked and most of the empty trucks returned northward. The men rested among the headstones in a cemetery until 10 P.M. They then started out on their all-night, twenty-five-mile march through enemy-held territory, with their artillery and tank destroyers following so the ground troops didn't have to eat their dust. Arriving at their destination before sunrise, they set up positions on the north shore of the San Juan River, which was impassable to vehicles because of a blown bridge.

Shortly before 7 A.M., they heard the C-47s and looked up to see the nine-plane formation heading south. Right on time, their artillery opened fire on Japanese positions across the river and farther to the east, and the infantry waded across. Machine guns and mortars opened up from the opposite bank, where the Japanese were dug in.

One tank destroyer managed to cross the river at a shallow spot, but when it tried to climb up the thirty-foot bank on the other side, it kept sliding back. After several tries, it gave up and returned to the other side.

Watching this, one 188th trooper, Garnett Winfrey, reflected on how lucky it was that the internees were going to be evacuated by water because reaching them by trucks would not have been possible.

The first U.S. fatality of the day came when the tank-destroyer company commander, Captain Kenneth Dawson, of Louisville, Kentucky, was hit in the forehead by an enemy bullet while his unit was attacking a gun emplacement at a road junction.

As the troopers fought against the enemy combat outpost—placed at the river to delay any U.S. advance down Highway 1—Soule ordered one company to block the road that Japanese reinforcements would use to reach Los Baños. After breaking through at least one company of Japanese infantry, Soule's main force continued on, capturing an enemy position at Lecheria Hills next to National Highway, the road to Los Baños.

Shorty Soule's task force was putting up an aggressive fight and winning ground against entrenched defenders. How long they could hold the ground was another matter. Like everyone at 11th Airborne headquarters, Soule was thinking about the Japanese Eighth Infantry Division.

*When might they be coming up the road?*

THE HOURS LEADING UP TO THE RAID HAD BEEN NERVE-RACKING for Henry Muller at 11th Airborne headquarters, where he stayed close to the phone all night. When 7 A.M. came, he still knew little, other than the paratroopers had gotten off from Nichols Field that morning and the amtracs had left earlier that morning. As for recon, they had been out of touch for more than twenty-four hours, and he had no idea of their whereabouts.

The only unit they had contact with was Soule's diversionary task force, which had reported hitting the Japanese defenses at the San Juan River and Lecheria Hills

Muller was certain that General Fujishige had received word about the strong U.S. advance down Highway 1 toward his positions in the hills. It had been a loud advance, with not only the rumble of the tank destroyers, but also all the dust plumes sent up by decoy trucks that were dragging trees behind them to resemble the plumes of an advancing armored column. But would Fujishige believe that a large U.S. force with tanks was coming to fight him? Would it be enough to convince him to keep his forces in their defensive positions and not send reinforcements to Los Baños when he received news of the attack on the prison camp?

The surveillance flights Muller requested were now in the air over Highway 1 south of the San Juan River, watching for any signs of Japanese reinforcements on the move. Muller knew enemy units wouldn't be able to sneak through the densely forested hills and reach the camp in time to disrupt the raid. They would have to use roads. And if they did, they would be spotted by air surveillance and attacked first by P-38 fighters flying air cover. Then they would run head-on into Soule's task force, which would hold them as long as possible. At least, that was still the plan.

Muller picked up the phone and called the Air Corps duty officer.

"Any reports of enemy troop movements on Highway 1?" he asked.

"Nothing reported, sir."

Muller believed in the plan. Privately, he even thought it was perfect; they had thought of every possible contingency. However, the fact that *everything* would have to go right for the Los Baños raid to succeed was daunting. How could they expect that all the people and parts of such a complex operation would perform properly? Muller had learned these past months while the division had been in combat that in war things seldom worked out as planned.

Muller's thoughts kept returning to the prison camp and all the men, women, and children being held there. His biggest worry all along had been that they would be caught up in a violent gun battle.

Were bullets flying and explosions going off all around them right now?

## SIXTEEN

# Rescue

DOROTHY STILL HAD BEEN WORKING THE NIGHT DUTY SHIFT at the hospital for the past two weeks, and she was looking forward to returning to days because nights were so much about death and dying. Too often now, even a skilled nurse could do little for a patient other than say a prayer.

In the wee hours of February 23, another patient died. Dr. Nance had already made out the death certificate because he knew the sixty-six-year-old Briton would soon pass away. He listed malnutrition as the primary cause of death. He had written that diagnosis on many certificates in the last few months even though the Japanese had warned him not to use such terminology.

When the man's rattled breathing was finally silenced by death, Dorothy could only think, *Lucky you, may you rest in peace.* The only thing left for her to do was fill in the time and date.

The lack of food, severe weight loss, long hours, and heavy patient loads had worn Dorothy and the other nurses down beyond exhaustion. Even pushing gurneys and making up beds was difficult. It was not unusual for one of them to fall down simply because they lacked strength in their legs. Their hands shook when they gave an injection, handed out medicines, or assisted in the operating room. Dorothy had observed that Dr. Nance was similarly shaky during exams as well as surgeries.

They knew U.S. troops were fighting in Manila and were drawing ever closer to them, so it was no longer a question of *if* they would be rescued but how many of them would still be alive when the troops got to Los Baños.

One night recently, when Dorothy was almost asleep, she became aware that she wasn't breathing. *I must be dead,* she thought. It was not at all frightening but a pleasant feeling. *No more hunger, no more pain, no more war, just peace.* Then, to her surprise, she inhaled deeply. She woke up understanding that her time had not yet come. *God, if you have something else in mind for me, help me to be worthy.*

Her prayer was answered in part when she helped bring a new life into the world. But when twenty-seven-year-old schoolteacher Mildred McCoy, who was suffering from beriberi and malaria, went into labor, it turned into a long ordeal. In the middle of an overnight shift, Dorothy served as midwife and delivered a healthy baby girl named Lois at 2:20 A.M. on February 20, 1945. Lois's entry into the world was bested by six days with the birth of another girl, Elizabeth, born on Valentine's Day. It seemed the camp hospital had become a nursery as well as a death house.

Three days after Lois's birth, with her first-time mother still hospitalized, Dorothy looked after the camp's newest life amid all the misery and sickness. It was still predawn on February 23 when she heard little Lois's squeaky cries.

She took the baby into a linen closet so she could change her diaper in a warmer place. As she did, Dorothy realized how much the naked newborn resembled a plucked, underweight chicken. With large eyes set in an otherwise shrunken body, the baby had survived starvation in utero.

"You started off on the wrong foot, didn't you, little princess?"

Overly diluted powdered milk—the hospital's dwindling supply was reserved for newborns and the sickest infants—was a poor substitute for mother's milk, but whenever a malnourished mother was unable to breastfeed, there was no choice. Dorothy wrapped the baby securely in a small blanket and gave her a bottle with the watery formula.

Near the end of her shift, Dorothy sat at the hospital's nursing station in her regulation Navy sweater, with a tattered blanket over her legs to ward off the morning chill. On each patient's chart she wrote "2/23/45," and then jotted down any overnight progress notes for the day shift.

A few minutes before 7 A.M., the nurses coming on duty were preparing to take over. One of the orderlies peered out a window toward the field where the guards had gathered for their morning exercises and made a droll comment about their devotion to physical fitness.

"We could do calisthenics, too," Dorothy said without looking up, "if we were as well fed as they are."

A patient watching out a back window wondered out loud about the columns of white smoke rising nearby. No one had seen them before.

Suddenly Dorothy heard the *rat-tat-tat* of machine-gun fire, and her first thought was, *Oh, dear God! They're going to kill us!* Her second thought was about Lois. She rushed to the baby and took her into her arms. The gunfire was so deafening, she tried to cup her hands over Lois's ears to protect her hearing.

Another nurse, Margaret "Peggy" Nash, picked up baby Elizabeth, who was recovering from a burn on her back that had happened when a hot-water bottle put a blister on her tender skin. There was no way of knowing if the Japanese had decided to do away with them today or if U.S. troops were here, but either way, Nash thought, *Today we live or die—but at least this suffering is going to be over.*

Now the view out the window showed aircraft and descending parachute canopies.

The lead aircraft had the word RESCUE painted boldly on its side in tall black letters.

Margaret Sherk and Jerry Sams, whose "love baby," Gerry Ann, was thirteen months old today, were preparing to line up outside for morning roll call when the planes appeared overhead. When they saw the parachutes in the sky, Margaret instantly said they were the most beautiful sight she had ever seen. But at the sound of gunfire and explosions, they dropped into a drainage ditch with the baby and David.

"I'll bet we'll be out of here in two days," Margaret said joyously.

Jerry laughed. *"Two days?* Hell, if we aren't out of here in two hours, I'll be disappointed."

Ever adventurous in spite of being down to ninety pounds, Jerry climbed up to a barracks rooftop for a better look. He could see the field where the Japanese guards exercised; it now contained scores of half-naked dead bodies. Then a bullet whizzed through the barracks right below him, and he decided to rejoin his family in the ditch.

In the ditch, Margaret nursed Gerry Ann, who had no problem staying focused on breakfast in spite of all the explosions and gunfire. When things began to quiet down, they hurried back to the barracks, where they had their first face-to-face meeting with one of their liberators: a Filipino guerrilla. With a wide grin, he presented them with a lone chicken egg that had somehow come through unbroken. It was a lovely sight and quite a treasure, and it took Jerry less than ten minutes to hurriedly scramble it up and serve it to Margaret and David.

Next came the paratroopers—*big, beautiful American boys who looked like young gods from another planet,* Margaret decreed—striding through the barracks telling everyone: "Get ready to move. We're leaving here."

Charlie Sass of B Company was one of the paratroopers rushing into the barracks. In the first one he entered, he spotted a Japanese soldier at the back door firing his rifle from the hip. Sass felt the bullet whiz just inches above his head and raised his M-1. But as he did, the prisoners began pouring from their cubicles to greet their liberators.

The Japanese soldier ran out the door, slamming it shut behind him. As Sass ran past the internees, he was struck by how ragged looking and terribly thin they were, with bones and joints visible in their arms and legs. They reached out to touch him as if to prove that he was not an illusion.

When Sass reached the end of the barracks, he shoved open the door but couldn't see the guard. He took off in the direction he thought he might have gone. Sass rounded one corner and came upon a group of British internees calmly making tea. They insisted Sass join them, which, speechlessly, he did—for about two minutes, before finally having enough of this particular English custom.

"We're behind enemy lines!" Sass bellowed. "We're not staying!"

For B Company, the jump had gone exactly as planned, although it didn't start that way for Sass. No sooner had his parachute opened than he heard three distinct pops, followed by whistles. The pops were bullets fired at him and the whistles were bullet holes in his canopy, through which sunlight was shining. Sass considered trying to free his rifle so he could fire back, but then he landed hard. Two swings under the deployed chute was all the time he had, by far the shortest and quickest parachute descent of his life.

Only one trooper was injured in the jump when he landed atop the railroad tracks and twisted an ankle. Sass had landed close to Ringler, and the company commander hollered: "Sass, come with me!" In pre-raid briefings, Ringler had divided his company into three groups—one assigned to hit the camp from the north, another from the east, and a third from the south.

With Ringler, Sass and some other paratroopers hurried south. They came out through a ravine at the lower end of the camp near the chapel, then cut through the fencing with wire cutters to enter the camp.

It was then that Sass heard the unmistakable rumble of tank tracks.

"Jap tanks!" he hollered. "Bazookas forward!"

Ringler looked at him like he had lost his marbles.

"They don't have tanks, and we don't have bazookas."

About twenty minutes had passed since they stepped from the C-47s, and by the time they entered the camp, there was only sporadic small-arms fire, as most of the guards on sentry duty had either been killed by recon and the guerrillas in the first few minutes or taken flight.

The enemy tanks Sass thought he heard were the noisy amtracs lumbering ashore two and a half miles away. All the amtracs made it across in the pitch black even though at times a driver had to shut down his engine and listen for the growl of the amtrac ahead to make sure he hadn't lost contact and become separated. "Stay close, keep together!" were their standing orders.

They had been briefed about enemy patrol boats but didn't see any. They had also been told that a recon team would set up a smoke signal that would let them know they were in the right place at the right time. Sure enough, as they approached shore, just after seeing nine C-47s pass overhead, they saw two rising columns of green smoke marking each end of a sandy beach. The amtracs shifted into a three-abreast formation to speed the landing.

From his amtrac, Dwight Clark thought that whoever had planned all of this—the timing, the navigation, the beach, green smoke for "go"—had done a beautiful job. They received a few rounds of small-arms fire from Mayondon Point, but Clark and the other gunners didn't bother to return fire so that they could remain focused on getting ashore and reaching the prison camp.

Not everyone was as pleased. The paratroopers who had ridden across the lake in cargo holds of the amtracs were a miserable bunch. Amid a lot of hee-haws and gibes about the clanking and smoking machines that were as loud as city garbage trucks, they insisted to

Clark and the other amtrac crewmen that the only way to surprise the enemy was to drop in out of the sky like B Company was doing this morning.

Major Henry Burgess, who didn't like riding in these half tank/half boats any more than his men did, had crossed the lake in the lead amtrac with Joe Gibbs and navigated their route in the dark with only a handheld infantry compass. Once ashore, Burgess directed a company to secure the beachhead, handle the enemy position at Mayondon Point, and set up a roadblock on National Highway that went through the town of Los Baños.

He also ordered the two 75-mm howitzers off-loaded at the beach and made ready to fire. Then the amtracs, formed back into a single-file line with Burgess and Gibbs in the lead, took the road to the prison camp. Pete Miles, cradling an M-1 Garand, stood upright in the first amtrac, eagerly pointing the way.

About a mile inland, as they passed a nipa shack, a Japanese officer came outside, pulling up his pants and carrying a samurai saber. A machine-gun burst from the lead amtrac killed him instantly.

Back at the beach, when Clark had first heard loud rifle and automatic-weapons fire and explosions coming from the direction of the camp, he was certain the amtracs and the troopers with them would have to fight their way into the heavily defended camp. But by the time they approached the main gate—about 7:30 A.M.—things had quieted down noticeably.

The gate was open about two feet, and several guerrillas were pointing to a stone pillbox that guarded the entrance. The amtracs kept coming and someone looked inside the pillbox and found that its occupants were already dead, having been killed earlier by a hand grenade.

The lead amtrac drove through the wooden gate, splintering it. When they reached barbed-wire fencing, the amtracs mowed it down.

Burgess planned for the amtracs to drive right into the center of camp, making it easier to load up the internees. But it soon became clear that there wasn't enough room for all of the amtracs to park or maneuver inside the camp. With the exception of those needed to transport the nonambulatory internees, most parked in the open field outside the main gate near Baker Hall.

Burgess deployed his men in defensive positions. He had C Company move off down the road they had just taken so they were ready to engage any Japanese reinforcements that might show up. A Company was deployed outside the camp's perimeter to stop a Japanese counterattack through the woods.

Dorothy Still and the other nurses and orderlies had peered cautiously outside as the amtracs entered the camp. They watched as the first ones flattened the barbed-wire fences and turned into the circular drive in front of the hospital. An Army major and a colonel jumped out. The colonel went back to talk to the amtrac crews while the major strode toward the front of the hospital. Dorothy went outside to greet him.

"Good morning, I'm Major Burgess. Who's in charge here?"

"Dr. Nance is in charge," Dorothy said.

Just then Nance walked out of the hospital.

Burgess told Nance that everyone had to get out of the camp as quickly as possible. They discussed the best way to evacuate the sick and elderly from the hospital and various barracks.

Dorothy couldn't get over the sight of the U.S. soldiers, so much bigger and healthier than any men she had seen in years. They wore a new kind of helmet, not the "tin-pan things" of the First World War that were still being worn in 1941. And they all looked so lively and alert.

"Ma'am, what are you holding?" one of the soldiers asked.

Dorothy looked down at the bundle in her arms. She had forgotten she was holding baby Lois, who was now fast asleep. She showed the soldier the sleeping baby, then went back into the hospital and gave Lois to her mother. She told the worried woman about the American soldiers right out front.

"They've come to take us home," Dorothy said.

Outside, the amtracs dropped their tailgates, and the hospital patients and other nonambulatory internees were brought out. One of the first to be boarded was Margie Whitaker's father, Jock, who was now down to eighty-five pounds and "on his last legs."

During the gun battle earlier, Margie and her younger sister, Betty, had hidden in their barracks under the bed. When the first U.S. soldier came through telling everyone to be ready to leave, Margie asked if the Marines had landed. After all, she had been waiting so long for this day.

"Sorry, sister, Army paratroopers."

She and Betty rushed to the bathroom, where they brushed their teeth and washed their faces. The teenage girls—eighteen and four-teen years old—only then thought they were fit to be rescued.

As Ben Edwards walked through camp greeting old friends, he spotted two soldiers carrying Pete Miles on a stretcher, head-ing for an amtrac. Catching up with them, Ben asked Pete if he was wounded. Looking rather chagrined, Pete said no. He admit-ted he hadn't slept in three days and had simply collapsed from exhaustion.

They had not seen each other since separating at Nanghaya days earlier, when Pete headed off for 11th Airborne headquarters at Parañaque. Ben was shocked at how drawn and pale Pete now looked. His travels had taken their toll. Clutching the rifle he had been given for the raid, he asked Ben to keep it safe for him.

"I'd sure like to have it as a souvenir," said Pete, smiling.

Margaret and Jerry were delighted to see Dr. Nance standing up on the front amtrac with an Army major. The physician jumped down and hugged Margaret and shook Jerry's hand.

"You see," Nance said happily, "I *knew* you weren't supposed to go over the fence that night."

Margaret and Jerry walked with the children up to Baker Hall, where they climbed aboard a waiting amtrac. As soon as it filled up with about thirty internees, the driver started the engine and they rolled out of camp and up the road toward Laguna de Bay. When they approached the water, everyone was alarmed that there weren't any boats waiting to carry them across the lake. Had they come this far only to be stranded on the beach? Then it became clear that the vehicle wasn't stopping but had shifted into a lower gear and was heading directly for the water.

Margaret was horrified. *Surely this iron monster will sink with us inside!* The next thing she knew, they had entered the lake. When the water rose to about six feet, the tank started floating, and soon they were motoring across the choppy waters like a commuter ferry.

"It's amphibious," a grinning Jerry marveled.

The soldiers in the crew handed out C rations, chocolate bars, and real American cigarettes. If freedom hadn't felt entirely real for everyone yet, it started to become so with the ride across the lake in the floating tank with U.S. soldiers handing out goodies.

Margaret had already begun to look forward, not backward. At long last, she and Jerry could begin to straighten out the complications in their lives. War and imprisonment had brought them together, and she had found her true love. She intended to spend the rest of her life with Jerry and hoped he felt the same. But she was still married to Bob Sherk, a military POW, and she would now have to face all the pain and guilt that fact brought.

In another amtrac, Dwight Clark moved quickly from his assistant-driver position to the .50-caliber machine gun when they came under fire from Japanese snipers on the road leaving camp. Perched on the elevated gun platform outside the amtrac was a lady with a bundle in her arms. Twice, he asked her to move away, but she either didn't hear or was in a daze. Desperate to return fire, he jumped up, straddled her, and swung the gun toward the incoming fire.

He could see the muzzle flashes in the tops of coconut trees but not the snipers. Aimed for the treetops, Clark's machine gun unleashed showers of splinters, leaves, and shattered coconuts.

The whole incident was over in less than a minute, and only then did Clark hear a baby crying, and realized that the sound was coming from between his feet. The hot shell casings had bounced off the lady and rolled inside the bundle in her arms, which Clark was stunned to see held a newborn baby in a blanket. He saw that the hot ejects had burned the side of its little face. Clark felt terrible and apologized profusely to the woman, but the deed was done. He was sure he had scarred the baby for life.

By 11 A.M., flames were burning all around the prison camp. The fires had started earlier that morning when recon hit the garrison's guns and ammunition with white-phosphorus grenades, and quickly engulfed the Japanese barracks. But the paratroopers were having difficulty getting the internees to leave quickly—some were busy celebrating their liberation and others were laboriously packing up all their belongings even though they had been told one small bag only per person.

Ringler suggested to Burgess that they could get the camp emptied quicker by setting fire to the barracks, and the major agreed. Starting upwind in the camp's south, paratroopers began lighting fires in the tinder-dry structures. Some internees still couldn't just leave everything they owned. One man emerged from his barracks with a mattress on his back that a soldier promptly took away from him.

When the amtracs had loaded up, they departed for Laguna de Bay with approximately fifteen hundred men, women, and children. More than six hundred internees were left in the camp. Burgess addressed that assembled group.

"Your attention, please. It's going to be a long walk to the lake. We'll take it as easy as we can, but we can't loiter! You are to stay close together. We'll be around you on all sides. There may be snipers out there. If firing begins, lie facedown on the ground. Is that understood?"

Dorothy and two other nurses had stayed behind in case anyone in the last group needed medical attention. The rest of the hospital staff had gone out on amtracs with their patients. The trek to the lake began on the paved road leaving camp. Not far from the camp, they passed a dead Japanese soldier, whom all the internees looked at with interest. One of the internees spoke for them all when he said, "Too bad it's not Konishi."

Leaving the road, they followed a trail made by the amtracs through the woods as they headed for the shore. Paratroopers and guerrillas mingled with the internees providing assistance, and they formed a protective cordon along both sides of the column.

Though Dorothy and the other internees were still nearly giddy from the morning's events, she got the feeling that the Army guys weren't nearly as confident or relaxed as they looked. They remained alert, no noise escaped their notice, and they kept a close watch for any movement in the bushes or trees. Dorothy wondered if they knew something she didn't.

When they reached the narrow strip of beach, which was being protected by groups of paratroopers and guerrillas, Dorothy sat down on a log, kicked off her shoes, and rubbed her aching feet. It was the longest walk she had taken in years, and she was surprised she had made it.

The internees were told to wait on the beach for the return of the first amtracs that crossed the lake. It would be a couple of hours. Suddenly realizing how tired she was, Dorothy found the shade of a coconut tree to lie under and drifted off to sleep.

TERRY SANTOS, MARTIN SQUIRES, AND OTHER RECON MEMBERS joined the rear guard protecting the internees on their walk to the beach.

Earlier that morning, after destroying a pair of enemy pill-boxes, Santos found himself and his two wounded men pinned down by a third machine gun firing from a protected position on a knoll under a large tree. He kept shooting into the area until a platoon of paratroopers from B Company joined him. The new arrivals spread out and attacked the position, and the enemy gun was silenced.

Santos didn't realize that his faithful guerrilla guide had been shot until he was able to gather up his wounded comrades. He went over to check the man's vital signs, but he was already gone, having been struck in the chest.

Now, hours later, on the road to the beach, Santos talked to the men from other recon teams and learned that forty to fifty guards had been on duty at 7 A.M. Most of them were apparently killed outright in the attack, although counting dead bodies had not been anyone's priority that day. Santos reckoned that a lot of the camp's soldiers had made it into the woods. But he didn't think they had all lived to fight another day because he had heard enough shouts and screams coming from the woods to know that the guerrillas took care of many of them.

As for Squires, he told Santos about turning around just before 7 A.M. and going back to get the rest of his team. He found the two recon guys, Gene Lynch and Wayne Milton, waiting for him at a trail fork about half a mile away. They had reached the fork but didn't know which way to turn, and were waiting for him to come back. The three of them headed back as fast and as quietly as they could, but the battle started before they were in position. As they broke over the last hill and entered the camp, they passed the bodies of dead Japanese. Squires and his men had missed the fast-hitting attack and never fired their weapons.

Santos, who had expended more than a hundred rounds of M-1 ammo that morning and used all six grenades he brought, asked Squires why he had gone back instead of going ahead with the remaining men in his team. Martin said he was thinking about the firepower Lynch and Milton would add when they hit the camp.

Shortly after noontime, as everyone waited at the shore for the return of the amtracs, a lone single-engine plane circled several hundred feet overhead. It was a Stinson L-5, which was used as an artillery-spotter aircraft. But the passenger in the two-seater was not a forward observer trained in adjusting artillery fire from the air. It was General Swing. After missing the amtracs that morning, he had returned to headquarters and ordered up a plane and a pilot for later in the morning.

A young lieutenant assigned as the forward artillery observer for Burgess's battalion moved his shortwave radio into a clearing so he could better communicate with the plane. He was surprised when he heard Swing's voice come over the radio asking to speak to Burgess. The lieutenant hustled off and brought Burgess back to the radio. Swing asked for a report on the situation on the ground.

Burgess told the general that all the internees had been safely evacuated from the prison camp. He said the first load was en route to Mamatid in the amtracs, which would return in an hour or so to take the rest of the internees across. Burgess now knew there would be ample room in the amtracs for his men to ride back rather than having to march out and meet up with Shorty Soule's column to the west, as was originally planned. Burgess told Swing he would be able to bring out his battalion and recon in the amtracs. He added that he had suffered only four wounded.

"I'm very pleased," Swing said. Despite the brevity of the general's response, it was easy to hear the genuine relief in his voice. But Swing was not convinced that Burgess should leave just yet. He knew Burgess had to finish boarding the last of the internees in the amtracs when they returned, but he wanted to know if his battalion could then stay in the area, go through the town of Los Baños, and hook up with Soule, who was some eight to ten miles away, and was expecting Burgess to do just that. The general saw no reason to change the plan.

Dating back to Leyte, the 11th Airborne had a tradition of not giving up terrain or a tactical advantage once it had been achieved. But the reason that this tradition existed was that the 11th Airborne's first and only commanding general, Joe Swing, did not like giving up terrain or a tactical advantage to the enemy once it was achieved.

"Could you do this," Swing asked, "without heavy casualties?"

Rather than answer the question, Burgess turned off the radio.

Shortwave radio communications in that day were notoriously bad, and signals often went in and out due to weather or terrain. So the general would not have thought it strange that they were suddenly cut off.

What was surprising was that the young airborne major had pulled the plug on his commanding general. Burgess had decided he wanted to return with his men to Mamatid on the amtracs rather than march farther into enemy territory. His men were dog tired; they had been in combat for the past month and had gotten little sleep during the last forty-eight hours. They had only brought enough food and ammo for the raid, and they had given most of their rations to the hungry internees.

There was also the Japanese infantry division a few miles down the road. If the enemy division moved against Burgess, in strength, his battalion would be no match for them, and they might not be able to escape. He hadn't been able to make radio contact with Soule all day. Burgess had heard the ongoing battle and artillery fire for hours, and figured there had been a big fight at San Juan River or Lecheria Hills or both. A large enemy force could be coming between him and Soule. If that were true, and he couldn't reach Soule, they could be isolated with no support from the rest of the division and out of range of artillery other than their own two small 75-mm pieces.

The Harvard-educated, Wyoming cowboy told the lieutenant to

keep his artillery radio silent and to stow it because they wouldn't be using it again. Further communication might lead to a direct order that Burgess didn't want to carry out. He then watched the plane carrying Swing circle overhead a few more times before heading away.

An hour later, the amtracs returned, and Robert Beightler, the young West Point graduate who had endured Swing's wrath earlier that morning when they missed the amtracs, was on one of them. Beightler was Burgess's battalion intelligence officer, and each of them quickly caught up the other on what had taken place since they last saw each other.

When Burgess told Beightler about his radio communication with Swing, the young officer was surprised but not shocked. He knew that Burgess was as self-assured and strong-willed as General Swing. When Burgess admitted how relieved he was that Swing was not along on the battalion's mission—the general would surely have had his way about staying in the area and not giving up ground—Beightler realized that there might not have been a guide on the road that morning because Burgess wanted Swing to get lost and miss the departure of the amtracs.

By 3 P.M., as the last of the amtracs were loading and preparing to leave San Antonio beach, Japanese infantry were pushing closer and mortar shells began dropping nearby. The perimeter the paratroopers had formed around the landing beach shrank as they pulled back to board the amtracs, and this made the enemy that much bolder.

The last amtrac was a short distance away from water when Japanese troops swarmed onto the beach, firing rifles and machine guns. Tall geysers spouted in the water as mortar rounds chased the amtracs, whose drivers drove zigzag courses until they were out of range.

Dorothy was on that last amtrac. She stayed low but still peeked enough to see that no one had been hit or left behind on the beach. When it was safe, she sat up on top of the amtrac under the shade of her ragged old silk umbrella, the one valued possession she had brought with her. Slipping on an old pair of sunglasses that had made it through the war, she found the cool breeze off the water refreshing, even liberating.

"Nurse, one of the fellows down here passed out," said a soldier.

"Is there any way you can bring him up here?" she asked.

The unconscious internee was brought topside and placed between Dorothy and another nurse, Eldene Paige, with his head resting on Dorothy's arm. As a soldier held Dorothy's umbrella over them to protect the weakened man from the sun's glare, they monitored his pulse.

*Life* photographer Carl Mydans, who had been captured in Manila at the outbreak of the war and held at Santo Tomás until there was a limited prisoner exchange in 1943, had arrived in the second wave of amtracs from Mamatid. He now snapped an image that would immortalize a moment of human suffering and caring.

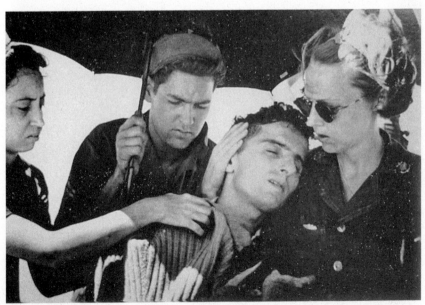

Nurse Dorothy Still, right, holding unidentified internee who fainted during evacuation on amtrac. Assisting is nurse Eldene Paige, left, as soldier shades patient. *Courtesy U.S. Navy Bureau of Medicine and Surgery.*

"Will he be all right?" asked the soldier with the umbrella.

"He'll be fine," Dorothy said. "He's been hospitalized many times. It was too hot for him down there, and he fainted."

The man soon regained consciousness, and when he did they placed him in a more comfortable upright position, where he remained safely in Dorothy's arms for the rest of the slow, noisy trip to freedom.

Dorothy Still had begun this war as a compassionate nurse, and on her last day of captivity, there was no reason for her to be anything else.

# SEVENTEEN

# "God Was with Us"

IT HAD BEEN A FRANTIC DAY AT 11TH AIRBORNE HEADQUARTERS. Henry Muller had not been able to communicate with any of the units in the raiding party. He had no idea how the rescue was proceeding until—more than five hours after it started—the first wave of amtracs carrying some fifteen hundred internees began arriving at Mamatid, where trucks and ambulances were waiting to take them to their temporary quarters at New Bilibid Prison. That meant more than six hundred internees were still in harm's way. So the tense waiting was not over.

Muller checked several times an hour with the Army Air Corps, and each time was told that air reconnaissance had not seen any enemy troop movements on Highway 1. This was confirmed by dispatches from Soule's task force, which said they were attacking Japanese defensive positions but were encountering no major enemy reinforcements. Whether the strong diversionary force had worked, or for some other reason, Fujishige had not sent troops toward Los Baños. Since this had concerned Muller most of all, he breathed easier once it was too late in the day for Fujishige to interfere with the operation.

Finally, at 5 P.M., Muller received the confirmation he had been awaiting. The second wave of amtracs with the last of the internees had safely crossed the lake to Mamatid. *They had done it.* The rescue mission he had envisioned when he first heard about the prison camp from the Filipino grower on Leyte three months ago had come to fruition. *More than two thousand men, women, and children held by the Japanese at Los Baños were now safe.*

Muller also soon learned that General Swing—circling over Soule's position in the L-5 aircraft—had radioed new orders now that the diversionary force had served its main purpose. They were to pull back from Lecheria Hills to the Highway 1 crossing at the San Juan River where the regiment had started at 7 A.M. and hold that position behind enemy lines until the battle in Manila was over and the rest of the 11th Airborne could turn south and attack Fujishige's division.

Soule would keep most of the ground and the tactical advantage his troops had won that day, which came at a cost of three KIAs—in addition to the tank commander, two 188th enlisted men, J. C. Doiron and Vernal R. McMurtrey, were killed by enemy fire at Lecheria Hills—and several wounded against well-dug-in defenders.

No other U.S. soldiers were killed in the raid on the prison camp. Two guerrillas from the Hunters ROTC, Atanacio Castillo and Anselmo Soler, were killed in the attack, and four guerrillas were wounded. The two wounded recon members, Vince Call and Larry Botkin, received first aid from the nurses at Los Baños before being evacuated in good condition. As for internee casualties, the most serious was a young woman internee, Margaret "Betty" Silen, who was shot in the hip. She had been among the first evacuated and would make a full recovery. Miraculously, she was the only internee reported hit by a stray bullet.

*No civilian fatalities.* Muller allowed that to sink in fully.

He hadn't slept for the better part of two days, but that night he fell exhausted into his cot. He did not go to sleep right away because his mind was still racing through everything that could have gone wrong. He fell into a fitful sleep, only to awaken in the dark soaked in sweat.

*For God's sake, stop it. It's all over. Everything that could have gone wrong didn't go wrong. Everything that had to go right did go right. Murphy's miserable law was suspended for twenty-four hours.*

With that, Muller closed his eyes and went to sleep.

WHEN MARGARET AND JERRY, EACH HOLDING A CHILD IN THEIR arms, stepped down from the amtrac at Mamatid beach, they were surprised to see that a number of Filipinos had come down to greet them, bringing coconuts, mangoes, and bananas. Speaking freely, the locals told them their own stories of recent atrocities committed by the Japanese against their people.

One Filipino grandmother, in the company of several younger women and a little girl, told Margaret that a few days earlier Japanese soldiers had raided a sugar plantation not far from there, and every male member of their family had been executed. The grandfather, the father, the young males, and all the boy children had been killed. This tragic story, and the sadness and quiet resignation on the faces of these grieving women, was something Margaret would never forget.

Amtracs arriving at Mamatid beach with internees after crossing Laguna de Bay.
*U.S. Army Signal Corps.*

Freed internees on Mamatid beach. *U.S. Army Signal Corps.*

Liberated internees boarded on a truck for New Bilibid Prison; food, freedom, and home. *U.S. Army Signal Corps.*

Army ambulances carrying liberated internees arriving at New Bilibid Prison. *U.S. Army Signal Corps.*

The freed internees climbed into open troop trucks and were driven fourteen miles north on paved and dirt roads to Muntinlupa, passing on the way crowds of Filipinos waving tiny U.S. flags and flashing the "V for Victory" sign.

As they approached a huge fortress with high walls and towers, everyone could see a large American flag flying atop one tall tower. They had arrived at New Bilibid Prison, recently liberated from the Japanese and selected by the military as the temporary refuge for the internees because it could accommodate thousands and could be defended against an attack.

The vehicles stopped inside a courtyard and the tailgates went down. As people climbed out of the trucks, Army MPs in the courtyard were announcing, "Milk and soup are being served," and pointing the way.

"Milk and soup . . ."

The food line was long but no one minded. Depending on which line one stood in, the hungry received a bowl of celery or bean soup served by Army cooks, and a cup of milk. Some went back for more three and four times, ignoring warnings that eating too much too quickly could make them ill. A full stomach was a new feeling everyone wanted to experience.

Bertha Palmer and her sons, John and Ronald, eat their first meal at New Bilibid after being liberated from Los Baños Internment Camp. *U.S. Army Signal Corps.*

There were other lines worth waiting in. The American Red Cross gave each internee a small tube of toothpaste and a toothbrush; the men were given shaving gear and the women powder and lipstick. Although Margaret found she couldn't care less about the makeup, she realized that they needed everything because the war and more than three years of captivity had taken everything from them except each other.

David got a pair of pajamas from the Mexican Red Cross and Gerry Ann her first frilly dress from the Philippine Red Cross. Every female internee received two cotton dresses, and the men got shirts and shorts. The new clothes hung on them all like scarecrows.

Margaret realized right away that they were once again inside a prison, but what a difference. That first night they slept on the floor in recently cleaned cells, but no one complained; after all, the unlocked cell doors were wide open, and their liberators were outside sleeping on the ground. Many people were too keyed up to go right to sleep. While Jerry, still weak from his recent hospitalization, slept after eating, Margaret took a stroll with the children, joining conversations and meeting the paratroopers who had risked their lives to rescue them.

After liberation: Jerry Sams holding Gerry Ann, who is keeping watch on a cup of milk her mother, Margaret Sherk, is holding, and David wearing a U.S. Army helmet. *Courtesy Gerry Ann (Sams) Schwede.*

The soldiers were eager to meet anyone from their hometown, as well as young, attractive American women. Some of the businessmen among the internees were so grateful to the soldiers they offered them postwar jobs. For a time, Charlie Sass had been one of the paratroopers visiting with the internees, but then he was overcome by a bone-weariness.

Surely they would be able to stay and rest for a day or two; Sass hoped there would be time to meet more internees and get phone numbers. He found a corner of the courtyard, laid out his gear on the ground, and was asleep within minutes.

At 5 A.M., the paratroopers were awakened in the dark.

"Get up. We're movin' out."

The fighting was still raging in the concrete fortifications of Fort McKinley as die-hard Japanese defenders were making their last stand.

The men of the 11th Airborne were going back on the line.

HENRY MULLER HAD HOPED FOR A CHANCE TO VISIT NEW BILIBID Prison and meet some of the folks the troops had rescued, but it never happened.

The next day was business as usual at 11th Airborne headquarters. It was almost as if the Los Baños raid hadn't taken place the previous day. Muller had expected to see jubilation on everyone's faces, but all he saw was a rush to get back to work. *I guess that's the way it is,* he thought. He recalled a line from an Army ballad: *There is no time for glory.*

Muller knew General Swing well enough not to expect him to come in and slap his officers on the back and say, "Good job, fellows." He was too much of a perfectionist; he expected a good job *always.* This day he stayed true to his character, and there were no backslaps or compliments handed out.

Swing did brag in a letter to his father-in-law, General March: "We pulled off a raid yesterday that would have made Knute Rockne envious in his heyday. As you know, it is seldom that everything clicks, but this time there wasn't a single miscue."

Swing mentioned in the letter that he had received congratulations from the man who had personally given him the mission to liberate the internees at Los Baños.

"Doug sent a wire saying it was 'magnificent.'"

The same day MacArthur's supreme headquarters issued a short press release quoting the general that read: "Nothing could be more satisfying to a soldier's heart than this rescue. I am deeply grateful. God was certainly with us today."

The rest of the world saw little in their hometown newspapers about the triumph in the Philippines that could count the number of innocents saved rather than the number of enemy soldiers killed or ground gained.

The lack of newspaper headlines about the prison camp raid was not a case of wartime censorship.

For on February 23, 1945, the same day as the raid, a combat photographer named Joe Rosenthal snapped an image of five soon-to-be-famous U.S. Marines raising the Stars and Stripes atop Mount Suribachi at a place called Iwo Jima.

# The Fate of Sadaaki Konishi

S ADAAKI KONISHI WAS CAPTURED BY U.S. FORCES IN LUZON ON
September 25, 1945, three weeks after the surrender of Japan. He
was processed on December 18, 1945, at Luzon POW Camp No. 1,
a secure detention facility established in Cabuyo, twenty-five miles
southeast of Manila.

Konishi was fingerprinted and measured at five-foot-four and
135 pounds, with brown eyes, black hair, and no distinguishing
marks. Born January
19, 1916, in Fukuoka
Prefecture on Kyushu
Island, he was married
(wife Tokiko) and had
one child. His POW
Basic Personnel Record
listed eleven years of education, his prewar oc-
cupation as farmer, and
his religion as Buddhist.

On November 23,
1946, a trial before a
military commission in
the case of *The United*

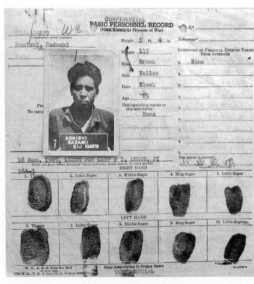

*National Archives, NARA.*

*States of America v. Sadaaki Konishi*, 51J-104279, began at the U.S. high commissioner's residence, a sprawling, Spanish-style building in downtown Manila.

Konishi was charged with violating the "laws and customs of war" in six specifications, including several having to do with the killing of civilian residents in and around the town of Los Baños. He was also charged with ordering or participating in the killing of American internee George Louis, and "devising and abetting a policy of gradual starvation" at the prison camp that caused widespread sickness, disease, and death.

The members of the military commission that would hear the case were all Army officers: commission president Colonel John L. Rice; Colonel William Hambry; Major Mamerto Montemayor of the Philippine Army; a veteran of Bataan, Major Raymond Ballweg; and Major Hugh Fkees.

Konishi's defense team had sought a delay due to their client's health. The prosecution called an expert witness, Captain Leon Karp of the Medical Corps, who testified that the defendant had "advanced pulmonary tuberculosis with cavitation," but his general condition was good. Dr. Karp recommended some safeguards to prevent the spread of TB, which is why Konishi wore a surgical mask during all court proceedings.

Chief Prosecutor Frank J. O'Neill, a civilian lawyer appointed by the judge advocate general, provided in his opening statement some background on Konishi after his arrival in the Philippines in January 1942 but prior to his arrival at Los Baños Internment Camp in July 1944.

"We choose to call his relations with the camp from then [July 1944] until February 23, 1945," explained O'Neill, "as phase one of his criminal career." Phase two, O'Neill went on, concerned Konishi's actions after the internees were liberated, when he was assigned to the Saito Battalion and carried out an order by General Masatoshi Fujishige to "ruthlessly wipe out hundreds of Filipino citizens . . . anybody who falls in their path, regardless of whether they are men, women, children or babies."

The prosecutor promised that the evidence would show Konishi to be a "contemptible soldier with a fierce hatred for everything American and a burning hatred for mankind in general. We will reveal what appears to be now a whimpering POW and show the swaggering brute he was during his tour in Los Baños, both at the camp and in the town."

The prosecutor then called his first witness, Fernando Bernardo, a resident of the town of Los Baños, who testified that Konishi had stopped him as he was walking along a road on February 28, 1945, and ordered him to join six other local men and "prepare tools for digging." Once they had assembled shovels and picks, Konishi took them to a wooded area where several dead bodies were covered by leafy branches from an acacia tree. He ordered them to dig a mass grave and bury all of the bodies. After they dug the hole and removed the foliage, they found four adult corpses, along with a boy of two or three years of age who was still alive.

"How did you find that out?" asked O'Neill.

"He was sitting up and one of his hands was tied to his mother's body. I heard him call, 'Mama,' and tell her he was hungry."

"Then what happened?"

Konishi told them to turn their backs, which they did. When they turned back around, they saw that the boy was dead.

"I noticed the wound of a bayonet," Bernardo said.

Ang Kim Ling, a Chinese boy who lived with his extended family in the small barrio of Anos three miles east of Los Baños, testified about visiting his grandfather's house on March 6, 1945. He said Konishi arrived that night with thirty or forty soldiers and told them they were bad people because they were pro-American and that he was in charge of killing them.

"And then what happened?"

"Then the Japanese started killing us."

"How were they killing you?"

"They bayoneted us. I was next to my grandmother, and the Japanese bayoneted my hands, and I fell down."

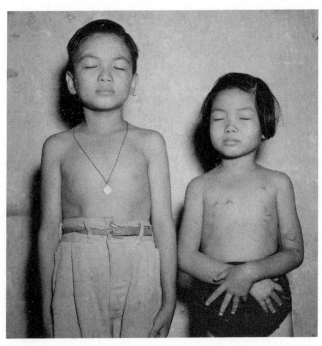

Ang Kim Ling, left, and his sister, wounded by Japanese troops who killed twenty-six civilians in the town of Los Baños on March 6, 1945. The boy testified against Konishi. *U.S. Army Signal Corps.*

"How many bayonet wounds did you receive that night?"

"Four."

"Was your sister with you that night?"

"Yes, she was with us."

"And how old was your sister at that time?"

"She was six years old."

"How many bayonet wounds did your sister receive that night?"

"Sixteen. They were all over her body. Arms, legs and breasts."

"Tell us how you happened to escape in the morning."

"I heard my sister whining, and I crawled out from under the dead bodies and dug her out."

"What bodies did you recognize?"

"My grandfather and grandmother. My father and mother. My uncles and aunts."

A total of twenty-six men, women, and children were killed that night.

Aurelio Almasan, a farmer, took the stand and explained how he came to be mayor of Los Baños on February 12, 1945.

"There was a rumor a few days earlier that Japanese were going to come to town and kill the Filipinos who lived there," he said. "Fearing that he would be killed, the mayor, the actual mayor, escaped. So they made me mayor."

In a deposition given to Army war crimes investigators a year earlier, Almasan indicated that the massacres in and around Los Baños started on February 21, 1945—two days before the raid on the prison camp—when three hundred Japanese soldiers came down from their bivouac on Mount Makiling and began an "extinction of all the civilians they could find." By the time the killings started, the mayor said, many townspeople had already fled for the woods or mountains, assisted by guerrillas. He estimated that six hundred to seven hundred residents were killed in and around Los Baños and the surrounding barrios between February 21 and March 6.

Former Imperial Japanese Army captain Chusiro Kudo was called to the stand to testify to the mass killings of civilians that took place in February and March 1945. Facing the specter of his own war crimes prosecution, Kudo was direct on some questions and evasive on others.

"When did you arrive in the town of Los Baños?"

"February 11, 1945."

"What was your job?"

"I was the commanding officer of the Kudo Unit of the Saito Battalion, 17th Infantry Regiment of the 8th Infantry Division."

It had been the Saito Battalion, other testimony would reveal, that engaged U.S. forces on February 23 and tried to prevent the evacuation of the Los Baños internees at San Antonio beach.

"During February 1945, did you receive orders to kill all guerrillas: men, women and children?"

"I got orders to kill all guerrillas."

"Did that order mean to you to kill all women and children?"

"If they lived in the same area as the guerrillas, they must then be killed the same as guerrillas. The order came from [General] Fujishige that all people who had connections with guerrillas must be killed."*

Kudo testified that he arrived on the grounds of the Los Baños College of Agriculture around 4 A.M. on February 27.

"Did you tell your men that everyone they found in the college grounds of Los Baños were to be killed?" the prosecutor asked.

"Yes, because we thought that area was a guerrilla area."

"Did you encounter any guerrillas?"

"We encountered shooting from the guerrillas."

"Were you present when the church was being burned?"

"Yes. There was shooting from behind the church. I took my platoon and attacked [the guerrillas]. When I left, there was not yet burning, but I saw it burning behind me later."

---

* The Fujishige Order, issued in January 1945 in a desperate attempt to defeat and punish guerrillas and their supporters and terrorize the populace in the towns and small barrios of Laguna province, stated: "The execution of the subjugation of the Fujishige Army Group security area will be done thoroughly. There's no question about the men and even to the women and children: kill them all." Fujishige was tried and convicted of ordering the deaths of more than 1,500 people. He was executed on July 17, 1946.

"While you were near the church, could you hear the cries of women and children in the church?"

"No. I never heard them. I saw some women appear in front of the church, and a hand grenade exploded."

*U.S. Army War Crimes Report No. 214:\* More than sixty residents, many of them entire families, took refuge in the Roman Catholic church on the college grounds. When the Japanese called for them to come out, some did, and were immediately killed. The remainder refused to leave the church and were immolated when the Japanese set fire to the church.*

"Do you know who hanged the priest in front of the church and bayoneted another one?"

"Headquarters men did it. When I attacked the church, we captured the two priests in the rectory and sent them to the battalion commander."

"Do you know what unit attacked the town of Maajas?"

*Report No. 214: On February 22, 1945, forty-five men, women and children from five families were forcibly taken from their homes in Maajas, a neighborhood (barrio) of Los Baños, by Japanese soldiers and killed.*

"I do not know."

"Do you know what unit attacked the town of Tadlak?"

*Report No. 214: On February 21, 1945, sixty-five men, women and children from ten families were taken from their homes in Tadlak, a neighborhood (barrio) of Los Baños, by Japanese soldiers and killed.*

"I sent one squad and attacked the west side of the town."

"Do you know what unit killed the civilians at Calamba?"

*Report No. 214: An estimated 1,500 citizens of Calamba, seven miles northwest of Los Baños, were massacred between February 12–15, 1945.*

"I do not know."

---

\* Investigation of "Case I-80 Los Baños, Laguna Province" was conducted from November 15, 1945, to December 15, 1945, by Captain Leslie J. Gobeyn and Lieutenant George C. Edwards, U.S. Army.

"Do you know the defendant, Warrant Officer Konishi?"

"I do not know."

A string of witnesses—practically the entire case against Koni-shi for his actions at Los Baños Internment Camp was proved by the testimony of former internees residing in Manila—were called to testify that the chief reason for the reduction of the food sup-plies in camp after July 1944 was the attitude and transgressions of Konishi.

Not only were there ample supplies in the locked warehouse, the witnesses testified, but local Filipinos were more than willing to pro-vide food to the internees. Konishi made a practice of turning away at the gate Filipinos who were bringing in carts of food. According to testimony, by September 1944, the internees were receiving about four hundred grams of food daily, and this steadily deceased to 150 grams or less by February 1945.

The commission heard that from Thanksgiving 1944 on, intern-ees lost on average a total of thirty to sixty pounds in three months, and were reduced to eating leaves, banana skins, slugs, dogs, and cats. The multitude of illnesses, diseases, and deaths that resulted were documented. Some former camp leaders, such as Dr. Dana Nance and committeeman George Gray, had managed to bring out of the camp many of their written reports and other documents, such as the minutes of committee meetings, autopsy reports, and complaints made to the commandant and Konishi about the food shortages and the rising illness and death rates among internees, much of which was submitted into evidence.

Former Los Baños internee Paul Hennesen, who was back work-ing for the U.S. State Department in Manila, described what he had seen on the morning that George Louis was killed. As he looked out the second-floor window of the camp church, he told of seeing Konishi and the commandant arrive at the scene where Louis lay wounded after being shot while trying to reenter the camp about

6:45 A.M. on January 28, 1945. Hennesen said he saw Konishi call for some soldiers, who arrived with a wood plank upon which Louis was placed and carried to the sentry box near the main gate. Hennesen saw Konishi take out the white-handled pistol from his holster and give it to one of the soldiers, who "went up to George and blew his brains out."

Konishi was defended by three American trial lawyers paid by the U.S. government—one of whom, Arthur Warner of New Jersey, would later be disbarred for a grand-theft felony conviction.

Konishi did not testify at trial.

On November 28, 1945—two months after his capture and while being detained at a POW camp in Rizal, near Manila—Konishi gave sworn testimony to Captain Leslie J. Gobeyn, acting investigating officer for the Army War Crimes Detachment. The prosecution submitted a transcript of that interview into evidence. The interview, during which U.S. Army sergeant Yoshiaki Ogita served as interpreter, was Konishi's only postwar statement. He gave it at a time when he might well have hoped that he would be able to avoid prosecution for war crimes.

**Q:** You were in charge of supplies including food for the internees at Los Baños Internment Camp. Is that correct?

**Konishi:** Yes.

**Q:** From October 1944 until February 23, 1945, would you say that the daily rations provided to the internees by the Japanese army was sufficient to keep the ordinary human being alive?

**Konishi:** In my opinion, that was not enough. If it had continued, they might starve. However, the allotment was the order from headquarters, and I just complied with that order.

**Q:** Where did you get the allotment of rations from?

**Konishi:** From the army supplies, from what was raised in the camp itself, and others were bought from Filipinos.

**Q:** Since you were in charges of supplies and food for the internees and since you considered the food and supplies inadequate to keep them alive, did you ever protest this matter or request additional supplies through the camp commandant or headquarters?

**Konishi:** I protested to headquarters. Whenever such complaints came from the internees, I always reported them to headquarters.

**Q:** If you considered the supplies inadequate to keep people alive, why didn't you undertake to get additional food from the neighboring area around the camp?

**Konishi:** The daily ration was determined by the army, and if I undertake such measures by myself, I would receive punishment.

**Q:** Do you know whether the internees requested permission to send out a detail under guard to supplement this starvation ration by gathering coconuts, bananas and other fruits growing in the area?

**Konishi:** Yes.

**Q:** Did you refuse that request?

**Konishi:** I had nothing to do with allowing prisoners out of camp.

**Q:** From October 1944 until February 23, 1945, did all of the prisoners begin to lose weight under the reduced ration?

**Konishi:** Yes, I believe so.

**Q:** During January and February 1945, do you know of a number of deaths in the camp resulting from malnutrition?

**Konishi:** I don't know exactly the number of persons who died, but I did hear of many persons dying of malnutrition.

**Q:** Do you know that the area in which the camp was located is one of the most productive in the world in coconuts, bananas and *camotes* [local sweet potatoes]?

**Konishi:** Yes.

**Q:** During January 7 to January 14, the entire Japanese garrison left the camp. Where did they go?

**Konishi:** To Manila, and some ran away to the hills.

**Q:** From January 14 to February 23, didn't the ration to the internees consist of approximately 500 grams of palay per person for three days?

**Konishi:** I don't know exactly the amount issued, but I know that it was decreased.

**Q:** Was there a policy of deliberate starvation of the internees?

**Konishi:** No, there was no such policy.

**Q:** Why then was no effort made to secure additional food for the internees?

**Konishi:** That was all determined by orders so I myself had nothing to do with it.

**Q:** The order which said that you couldn't go out and get additional food for the camp helped to cause starvation of the internees, didn't it?

**Konishi:** Yes, actually it caused deaths.

**Q:** On January 20, 1945, do you remember the killing of an American in camp?

**Konishi:** Yes.

**Q:** His name was Howard "Pat" Hell, wasn't it?

**Konishi:** I don't know anything about his name.

**Q:** Did you see the killing?

**Konishi:** No, I didn't, but I went out to look at the scene.

**Q:** How many times was Hell shot?

**Konishi:** He was shot twice.

**Q:** Where did you see the body?

**Konishi:** Outside the enclosure.

**Q:** Was he already dead when you saw him?

**Konishi:** He was pronounced dead when I saw him.

**Q:** Do you know who shot him?

**Konishi:** I think it was a guard.

**Q:** About a week later, another American was shot coming back to camp, wasn't he?

**Konishi:** Yes.

**Q:** Was that about January 28, 1945?

**Konishi:** I think so.

**Q:** Did you hear the first shot fired that wounded this man?

**Konishi:** Yes.

**Q:** Do you remember whether this man's name was George Louis?

**Konishi:** I don't know the name.

**Q:** A guard saw Louis coming in the camp that morning and fired a shot wounding him, is that correct?

**Konishi:** I am not sure of the facts.

**Q:** Did you see this man after he had been wounded?

**Konishi:** No.

**Q:** As a matter of fact, wasn't George Louis taken to a sentry box near the gate?

**Konishi:** I don't know.

**Q:** Didn't you go to that sentry box?

**Konishi:** No.

**Q:** Weren't you present when George Louis was executed?

**Konishi:** No.

**Q:** Didn't you as a matter of fact hand your pistol to a guard who executed George Louis while you were standing there?

**Konishi:** Positively no.

**Q:** If I tell you we have an American witness who saw you hand your pistol to a guard after which the guard placed your pistol against Louis' head and shot him, what would you say?

**Konishi:** I swear to God I wasn't there.

**Q:** Who ordered the execution of George Louis?

**Konishi:** I think it was the camp commandant, but I am not sure.

**Q:** Did you hear the second shot which killed Louis?

**Konishi:** I was not aware of it.

**Q:** How could you have been in camp and not hear it?

**Konishi:** I was not aware of it.

**Q:** You were in the camp that day, but you did not pay any attention to the second shot which killed him, is that so?

**Konishi:** This is the first time I heard he was executed in that sentry box. I heard the first shot because it was in the morning and it was quiet, but I did not pay any attention to the second shot so I was not aware of it.

**Q:** Do you remember what happened on February 23, 1945?

**Konishi:** Yes.

**Q:** Would you tell us what happened?

**Konishi:** In the morning American planes were circling overhead. I was still in bed at that time, and then I heard that paratroops had landed. I got out of bed, and then gunfire was from all directions. Then I heard orders for evacuation.

**Q:** Who gave those orders?

**Konishi:** I heard them from the camp commandant.

**Q:** Where did you go?

**Konishi:** We went out the front gate and went into the ravine. The paratroops were shooting at us. I went down the canyon and hid in the bushes. I stayed there until about 12 o'clock that night.

**Q:** Did other camp guards and staff go with you?

**Konishi:** Seven of us went to the ravine and hid in the bushes planning to escape to the hills, but the American tanks were seen on the road so we remained until 12 o'clock that night. Others who went out earlier escaped to the hills.

**Q:** Approximately how many camp guards and staff went away to the hills?

**Konishi:** About seven of us with our [camp] commandant Iwanaka.*

**Q:** When was the first day that you went to the town of Los Baños after the freeing of the internees at the camp?

**Konishi:** On the 27th of February.

**Q:** What were you doing there?

**Konishi:** I was ordered by the 17th Regiment of the 8th Division to investigate the routes taken by the American tanks and to make a report.

**Q:** Who gave you that order?

---

* After escaping the raid on the prison camp, Major Yasuaka Iwanaka, the camp commandant, took some of his staff to Alaminos, near Lipa, ten miles south of Los Baños. He was reported to have been killed the following month.

**Konishi:** My battalion commander, Saito, told commandant Iwanaka, and he gave me the order. Saito did not think that 2,000 people could be transported on these amphibian trucks, so they wanted to know the routes and the methods of transportation.

**Q:** How long did this work take you?

**Konishi:** Two days.

**Q:** On February 27, 1945, didn't you and your unit from the camp join with the Saito Battalion in an attack on the guerrillas occupying the college grounds?

**Konishi:** I remained in headquarters.

**Q:** Did you hear of an order being given to the Saito Battalion to kill all guerrillas, men, women and children before the college raid?

**Konishi:** I heard about an order from [Fujishige] to eliminate all guerrillas.

**Q:** On or about March 6, you were ordered to take charge of the detail that engaged in killing twenty-six Chinese civilians, weren't you?

**Konishi:** I didn't receive any such order.

**Q:** Why did you kill them?

**Konishi:** I didn't kill them.

**Q:** You were in charge of the detail on March 6, weren't you?

**Konishi:** My orders were just to receive food that was confiscated.

**Q:** Who ordered you to participate in the killing of the Chinese?

**Konishi:** I did not participate in that massacre. I was ordered by the battalion commander to confiscate the food.

**Q:** Were you just boasting when you told the Chinese family that you were in charge of killing them?

**Konishi:** I never said such a statement.

**Q:** Who killed George Louis?

**Konishi:** I think Lt. Kaseno, the captain of the guards.*

**Q:** What makes you think Lt. Kaseno shot George Louis?

**Konishi:** He was in charge of that.

**Q:** Did you carry a pistol?

**Konishi:** Yes, but I never used my pistol.

**Q:** Did anyone use your pistol for you?

**Konishi:** No.

**Q:** You were seen in the sentry box where George Louis was killed.

**Konishi:** It must be a mistake.

**Q:** Did you hear Fujishige make a speech saying that each man must kill seventy people?

**Konishi:** Yes, he gathered various battalion commanders, company commanders and other officers when he made that statement.

---

\* Lieutenant Kenkichi Kaseno accompanied Major Iwanaka to Alaminos, and was killed in March 1945.

**Q:** Were you present at the killing of Filipinos in the barrio of Tadlak in Los Baños?

**Konishi:** No.

**Q:** Were you present at the killing of Filipinos, men, women and children, at the church of the College of Agriculture?

**Konishi:** No.

**Q:** Were you present at the killing of 26 Chinese on March 6?

**Konishi:** No.

**Q:** Is there anything else you would like to add?

**Konishi:** To the best of my knowledge all what I have said is true.


The trial lasted through the holidays of 1946. Early in the new year, the case went to the five-member military commission for deliberations.

At 8:30 A.M. on January 15, 1947, the chief bailiff read a statement aloud to a courtroom gallery packed with former Los Baños internees: "In view of the intense interest which has been taken in the Konishi case, it is desired to guard against any demonstration whatever following the announcement of the verdict. It is desired that the verdict be received in complete silence by all spectators present."

The accused was escorted to his seat at the defense table, and commission members filed in wearing uniforms with campaign ribbons.

After dispensing with some formalities, the commission president, Colonel Rice, read a statement: "The Commission has heard and carefully analyzed and evaluated all the evidence in this case, and has based its findings solely upon the evidence. As a result, the

Commission arrived at a judgment and sentence in the case which will now be announced. The accused, Sadaaki Konishi, his defense counsel and the interpreter will take their positions in front of the Commission."

Konishi, his lawyers, and the interpreter arose and moved into position before the long table behind which sat the stony-faced commissioners.

"Sadaaki Konishi, the Commission, in closed session, and upon secret ballot, at least two-thirds of the members present at the time the vote was taken concurring in each finding of guilt, finds you:

*"Specification 1, guilty,"* of ordering a member of the Japanese Army under his control to kill James Gardner, a child who had been lying under the branches of an Acacia tree tied to the body of his dead mother, on February 28, 1945.

*"Specification 2, guilty,"* of permitting Japanese soldiers under his command to kill one named and sixty unnamed non-combatant Chinese and Filipino civilians on March 6, 1945.

*"Specification 3, guilty,"* of permitting Japanese soldiers under his control to attempt to kill two young Chinese, Ang Kim Ling and his sister, Ang Elisa, on March 6, 1945.

*"Specification 4, not guilty,"* of burning down homes in Los Baños.

*"Specification 5, guilty,"* of aiding and abetting a policy of general starvation at Los Baños Internment Camp between August 1, 1944, and February 23, 1945, thereby causing the death of four named Americans and numerous unnamed American and civilian internees.

*"Specification 6, guilty,"* of participating in the killing of George Louis at Los Baños Internment Camp on January 28, 1945.

The findings were then translated to Konishi by the interpreter, reading from a copy of the commission's statement. When he was finished, the interpreter nodded to the commission president.

Colonel Rice started again, reading now a much shorter statement.

"The Commission sentences you to death by hanging."

After the sentence was translated into Japanese, Colonel Rice ordered MPs to remove the convicted war criminal from the courtroom.

Konishi went quietly, his face still obscured by the mask.

This was the last the spectators would ever see of Sadaaki Konishi.


YEARS AND DECADES PASSED, BUT NO ONE WHO WAS INTERNED AT Los Baños could forget the name Konishi. Many found themselves wondering what had happened to their cruel camp villain.

In the late 1940s, there were news reports about Japanese war criminals being executed for their crimes, but Konishi's name never surfaced with the likes of Hideki Tojo and other notorious Japanese war criminals being hanged. Then, in the 1950s, after the United States and Japan signed a formal peace treaty that ended the occupation of Japan and restored that country's independence, reports surfaced that the convicted war criminals had been released by the new government. Is that what became of Konishi? Or, as some former internees speculated, had he cheated the hangman by dying of TB?

Maryknoll sister Louise Kroeger, of Maryknoll, New York,

Sadaaki Konishi, convicted war criminal. *National Archives, NARA.*

who had been held at Los Baños for seven months until the camp was liberated, wrote to an Army chaplain who she understood had come in contact with Konishi after his trial, in the hope of "settling once and for all the question I have always had about the last days of Konishi."

In a handwritten response dated May 21, 1983, Colonel John P. Wallace wrote to Sister Kroeger that he was the Catholic Army chaplain who supplied services to POW Camp No. 1, about ten miles from Los Baños, where war criminals were detained and executed.

"I have a record baptizing a Japanese war criminal by the name of Sadaski [*sic*] Konishi," Wallace wrote. "I baptized him on June 17, 1947, and he was executed on the same day. It was my custom to baptize shortly before execution to eliminate the need of confession as I couldn't understand Japanese. I visited this person repeatedly and instructed him in the Catholic faith through an interpreter. I do not remember whether or not he was [at] Los Baños Internment Camp as we never talked about their past as war criminals."

Sister Kroeger sent copies of the chaplain's letter to other former internees, and the information it contained became the gospel as to Konishi's fate. The story was reported in the 11th Airborne Division Association's newspaper, *Voice of the Angels,* and picked up by authors who wrote about Los Baños in the 1980s.

"There can be no question," wrote E. M. Flanagan, a retired U.S. Army brigadier general and unofficial historian of the 11th Airborne, "that Sadaaki Konishi went to his death by hanging on 17 June 1947."

One former internee, Carol Terry Talbot, before writing her Los Baños memoirs, *Escape at Dawn* (1988), telephoned the retired chaplain at his home in San Antonio, Texas. Wallace provided her with additional details. "Shortly after baptizing him," he said, "I walked with Konishi to the place of execution, witnessed it, and saw him buried."

A review of the chaplain's baptismal record for Konishi, a copy of which he sent to Sister Kroeger, shows two minor discrepancies: the spelling of his first name (Sadaaki not Sadaski) and his year of birth (1916 not 1914). Otherwise, the information matches with Konishi's POW personnel record, including the day, month, and place of his birth.

Konishi may indeed have been baptized at POW Camp No. 1 in the summer of 1947 by Chaplain Wallace and taken the Christian name "Peter," per the baptismal record. However, the Army chaplain could *not* have witnessed Konishi's execution and burial on June 17, 1947.

Sadaaki Konishi did not die that day.


ON JANUARY 15, 1947, THE DAY HE RECEIVED HIS DEATH SENtence, Konishi was transferred from the stockade at the U.S. high commissioner's residence in Manila to POW Camp No. 1 near Los Baños.

Konishi was still being held there on August 14, 1947, when his execution was "withheld until further notice" by written order of Douglas MacArthur. The reason: Konishi's appellate lawyer indicated he intended to file an appeal with the U.S. Supreme Court challenging the military commission's jurisdiction in the now-independent Philippine Republic.

By the autumn of 1948, with his execution still on hold, Konishi was flown to Japan. Upon his arrival at a military airfield, he was driven to Sugamo Prison, located six miles from the Imperial Palace in Tokyo. The prison, built in the 1920s, had been virtually untouched by the war, although almost everything around it had been leveled by U.S. bombs.

Sugamo was the most modern prison in the country. On the outside, only the high walls and tall gun towers betrayed the purpose of the otherwise nondescript group of buildings. The Japanese modeled its design and construction after the better European prisons, and used it primarily to hold political prisoners—anyone who the militarist leaders believed might interfere with their war plans. At war's end, the prison held some sixty political prisoners, all of whom the U.S. Army released.

Back view of Sugamo Prison, showing cellblocks and in foreground a gun tower. *Courtesy John L. Ginn.*

Konishi, a Class-C war criminal—Class-C criminals were those accused of "crimes against humanity," such as murder, extermination, and enslavement—entered Sugamo Prison on September 20,

1948. He was assigned to cellblock 5, which held only Class-C prisoners, all in solitary confinement. Like the others, his cell contained a table and chair, ceiling light, straw floor mat, and toilet. But Konishi stayed in the cell only one night.

Convicted Class-C Japanese war criminals outside their cells during daily inspection, Sugamo Prison. *Courtesy anonymous former Sugamo guard.*

Prisoners entering Sugamo were given a thorough medical examination. Konishi received his the next day. That exam, as well as the diagnosis contained in Konishi's medical file that came with him from the Philippines, revealed his advanced case of TB. To prevent him from infecting guards or other prisoners, Konishi was transported that same day to the U.S. Army's nearby 361st Station Hospital.

Five weeks later, on November 2, 1948, Lieutenant Colonel John Marren of the Medical Corps wrote the following to the commanding officer of Sugamo Prison about his patient: "Konishi's diagnosis is Pulmonary Tuberculosis, which has been proven to our satisfaction by repeated culture and microscopic examinations for Acid Fast Bacilli. Request that prisoner be transferred to a Japanese hospital . . . In an institution that deals exclusively with handling these cases, active treatment could more easily be pursued, thus making prognosis in this case more favorable."

Apparently unbeknownst to the Army physician, Sugamo Prison authorities did not transfer convicted war criminals under a death sentence to civilian hospitals, but only allowed their medical treatment at Sugamo's own dispensary or for more serious cases at a secure military facility. So Konishi remained at the 361st Station Hospital.

On March 30, 1949, Secretary of the Army Kenneth Royall wrote to the commander in chief, Far East, regarding the Konishi case. Given that Konishi's attorney had filed nothing with the Supreme Court in the past eighteen months, the solicitor general had informed the Army that there was "no longer any bar" to carrying out the sentence of death.

On April 12, 1949, MacArthur vacated his stay of Konishi's execution and ordered it to be carried out "at a time and place to be designated by the Commanding General, Eighth Army."

On April 27, 1949, Eighth Army headquarters directed the commanding officer of Sugamo Prison to "carry out the hanging of Sadaaki Konishi" on April 30, 1949.

The next day, First Lieutenant Ellis Coker, a combat veteran who had fought in Europe, arrived at the 361st Station Hospital with armed MPs to take Konishi back to Sugamo Prison. Coker was to be Konishi's hangman, although as a matter of prison policy this fact would not be revealed to the condemned man until he stood atop the gallows.

Coker was an accomplished executioner. He had hanged nearly all of the Class-C war criminals at Sugamo, which, to date, had numbered thirty-three. This included an especially busy night six weeks earlier, on February 12, 1949, when, using five side-by-side trapdoors on the gallows, he dropped eight war criminals to their deaths. That did not, however, break Coker's personal record of ten on August 18, 1948.

At Sugamo Prison, hanging had become a science. The weight and height of a prisoner was carefully measured, and the drop from the gallows adjusted so that a man's neck would snap instantly, and he wouldn't be left dangling and kicking, slowly strangling to death.

The lighter the condemned man, the longer the drop necessary for the rope to snap the neck. Although a broken neck ceased the flow of blood to the brain, death would be pronounced by a doctor with a stethoscope only after the heart stopped beating, which on average took ten minutes. Only rope made from manila hemp—a buff-colored fiber obtained from a species of plants native to the Philippines and named for the capital, one of the main providers of manila hemp—was used because of its strength.

A sergeant ordered the rope in big spools, cut pieces down to size, and straightened them by dropping them down an elevator shaft with a weight on the end. Then the same sergeant, who had learned his tradecraft at Nuremberg with the hanging of Nazi war criminals, tied the hangman's knots by winding the coils one atop the other until they totaled thirteen; always thirteen, never twelve or eleven. He then delivered the ropes to the gallows and secured them in place on an overhead beam above the trapdoors.

The Japanese had developed a technique in the 1930s for hangings at Sugamo Prison that appeared to be more humane than methods used elsewhere. A cone-shaped wooden block secured to the gallows by its own rope was released when the trapdoor was sprung, timed to strike the falling prisoner hard on the side of the head and render him unconscious a nanosecond before the noose broke his neck. A room filled with the blocks was found by U.S. Army personnel when they took over the prison. Once their purpose was determined, the blocks were used by the U.S. Army for executions at Sugamo.

The hangman's rope was used only once; afterward it was burned in a basement incinerator. The body of a war criminal hanged at Sugamo went directly into a simple wooden coffin and was driven under armed escort to a crematorium in Yokohama. The cremains of executed war criminals were not given to their families or anyone else, but disposed of so they wouldn't be made into martyrs with gravestones or shrines in their honor.

Coker and his guards delivered Konishi directly to Sugamo's Blue Prison, a small, separate building near the gallows that was used as a holding cell for the condemned. It was here that Tojo spent his last hours. That evening, an official group crowded into Konishi's small cell. In addition to Coker, there was an interpreter and five witnesses, all Army officers who certified they observed the time and date of his execution being read in his own language, and Konishi acknowledged that he understood the contents of the execution order.

Army policy required that notification of the exact time of his execution be announced to a prisoner at least twenty-four hours beforehand. Thereafter, they could receive a visit from clergy and request a last meal, which at Sugamo typically consisted of rice, miso soup, raw or broiled fish, bread, jam, and coffee or tea.

Two nights later, near midnight, guards entered Konishi's cell. They placed a heavy restraint belt around his waist, with chains that went to manacled ankles and wrists. An extra chain went between his legs from front to back, which rendered him unable to raise his hands above his waist. So constrained, he could only take short, choppy steps.

He was escorted into a courtyard lit by a few tall lights.

The building with the gallows was a hundred yards away.

The slow walk of the prisoner sheathed in chains that rattled and jangled with each step lasted three or four minutes.

As they entered the brightly lit death house, Konishi was taken before the seated witnesses. He was identified by name and serial number as he passed by them. Execution of a Class-C prisoner required two official witnesses to certify that they had seen the hanging, but tonight there were five witnesses—four U.S. Army officers and a sergeant.

They climbed the thirteen steps to the top of the gallows.

Coker was waiting there. He made sure Konishi was positioned over the first trapdoor. Then Coker placed a black hood over Koni-shi's head, followed by the hangman's noose. He adjusted the rope so that the coiled knot was up behind the left ear. Once that was secured, Coker stepped back a few feet to a wooden-handled me-chanical lever.

There was nothing left for anyone to do or say, so Coker pulled the lever, and the trapdoor sprang open with the sound of a rifle shot.

The trap was sprung at thirty-three minutes after midnight, April 30, 1949.

Sadaaki Konishi was pronounced dead fourteen minutes later.

SOME 5,700 JAPANESE WERE INDICTED FOR WAR CRIMES AFTER World War II. Of these, 4,500 were convicted in trials held in Japan and elsewhere in the Pacific region; 525 received life sentences, 2,944 were sentenced to lesser prison terms, and 920 were executed.

Sugamo Prison, where Sadaaki Konishi and other Japanese paid the ultimate price for their crimes against humanity, no longer exits. It was demolished in 1971. In its place is a sprawling amusement and shopping complex named Sunshine City, with a sixty-story high-rise that was Japan's tallest building at the time of its completion in 1978. In one corner of the complex is a small, well-manicured park where a flat stone marks the location of the prison's gallows. A message in Japanese reads: "Pray for Eternal Peace."

# Dramatis Personae

**Edwards, Ben.** *Los Baños internee.* Ben's return to the United States was short-lived; within a year he was back in the Philippines with his wife, Ruth (née DeLany), whom he met before the war and with whom he had a whirlwind courtship upon his return to Chicago. He went back to work for Pan American Airways in Manila, then in 1948 accepted a job with Caltex Petroleum Corporation.

He bought land to farm not far from Los Baños, raising chickens and growing crops such as corn, okra, sunflowers, and tomatoes. Ben enjoyed bird and duck hunting with Filipino friends, former guerrillas he had met during the war. He also saw a lot of his old friend Pete Miles, who lived and worked in Manila, and

Ben Edwards (seated, far right) after the war (1946) with some of his Filipino friends, former guerrillas who took part in the Los Baños prison-camp raid. *Courtesy Ann (Edwards) MacDonnell.*

who died of a sudden heart attack in 1962. (The other internee with whom Ben and Pete escaped, Freddy Zervoulakos, moved to America, served ten years in the U.S. Navy, and died in 1998 at the age of seventy-four.)

In 1965, Ben transferred to Saigon for a year, then to Hong Kong for another year, and finally to Seoul, South Korea, for ten years. He retired in 1977 to a home on eight acres of forested land on Bainbridge Island, Washington. Ben died in 2010 at age ninety-one.

Postwar celebration at the Manila Hotel. Left to right: Ben Edwards; Arsenio Lacson, a former guerrilla who became a journalist and was elected mayor of Manila (1952–1962); his wife, Luchi; Ben's wife, Ruth; and Pete Miles. *Courtesy Ann (Edwards) MacDonnell.*

**11th Airborne Division.** The division's Reconnaissance Platoon and Company B of the 511th Parachute Infantry Regiment were awarded the Presidential Unit Citation for their roles in the Los Baños rescue. There were five airborne operations in the Pacific Theater against the Japanese, three of which—including Los Baños—were made by 11th Airborne paratroopers. Division paratroopers served as General Douglas MacArthur's honor guard during the Japanese surrender ceremonies aboard the USS *Missouri* in Tokyo Bay on September 2, 1945. MacArthur selected the 11th Airborne to be the first U.S. Army division to occupy the Japanese homeland. During

World War II, no 11th Airborne trooper deserted or was captured. The division was permanently deactivated in 1965.

**Muller, Henry, Jr.** *Lieutenant Colonel, G-2 Intelligence, 11th Airborne Division.* Muller stayed in his position with the airborne division for the rest of the war. During the occupation of Japan, he became assistant G-2 of the Eighth Army prior to returning to the United States to be the aide-de-camp to General Courtney Hodges, commander of the First Army. He served in the same position to General Walter Bedell Smith. When Smith was appointed director of the Central Intelligence Agency, Muller was selected to be an assistant to the director for two years. Following a tour with the Army's deputy chief of staff for operations, he was selected as the deputy commanding general of the 101st Airborne Division in Vietnam. Two years later he was named commanding general of the Infantry Training Center at Fort Polk, Louisiana. He retired as a brigadier general in 1971 after thirty-two years of service.

Over the years, he has taken pride in knowing that the Los Baños rescue mission became a legendary benchmark for military intelligence, planning, and execution of a raid behind enemy lines, and has been studied at military staff and command schools in the United States and elsewhere. "I've been told that General Swing often commented when addressing 11th Airborne reunions that the Los Baños raid would not have been possible 'without perfect intelligence,'" Muller says. "I only wish the general had said that to me back in 1945."

Muller is ninety-seven, and lives with his wife, Cathryn, in Santa Barbara, California.

**Nance, Dana.** *Los Baños internee and camp physician.* In April 1945, Dana rejoined his wife, Anna, and three children in New Orleans, where they had spent the war years. In 1946, Dana was awarded the Presidential Medal of Freedom, the nation's highest civilian honor, for meritorious and lifesaving services rendered to his fellow internees from 1942 to 1945.

The Nance family settled in Oak Ridge, Tennessee, where Dana opened a private surgical practice. Dana and Anna both immersed themselves in civic affairs. About Dana, a local newspaper editor later wrote: "On first glance [he] could appear gruff and, because of his size and the verve with which he moved, maybe even a little menacing. But the warmth of his approach was then almost immediately obvious. A total can-do person, Dana refused to be put off by naysayers."

After Anna died in 1981, he remarried in 1986, and died the following year in Bryn Mawr, Pennsylvania. He was eighty-two years old.

**Sams, Jerry and Margaret (Sherk).** *Los Baños internees.* A week after the liberation of Los Baños, Margaret learned that her husband, Bob Sherk, had been killed in November 1944 when a Japanese transport ship carrying 1,600 U.S. military POWs being taken to Japan to work in the mines was mistakenly bombed by U.S. planes. She had trouble reconciling the unfairness of him enduring the hardships of a POW camp for three years only to be killed by American bombs just months before he would have been liberated. Her having delivered such a hard blow to him a year earlier was a cross she would bear for the rest of her life.

Nevertheless, she was devoted to Jerry Sams, and they married in January 1946, although they always celebrated the day they met at Santo Tomás in September 1942 as their true anniversary. Margaret and Jerry had two more children. Jerry became a specialist in the nation's missile program, and worked as assistant technical director at Cape Canaveral. They bought a home in Atherton, California, near the campus of Stanford University, and in 1969 Jerry founded Data Optics, a small, innovative high-technology firm.

They always kept at least a month's worth of food supplies at home because they never wanted to go hungry again. "The only good things about the war and our captivity," Jerry often said, "was that we met each other and had our daughter Gerry Ann." They retired to a 153-acre ranch near Chicago Park, California. In 1987, they went on a tour of the Philippines, returning to Los Baños for the first time. Margaret thought she was over those painful years, but when she walked in the front gate and read the plaque about the internment camp, she burst into tears.

Writing about the experience in her memoir, *Forbidden Family*, helped. "If I am ever unfortunate enough to be interned again," she wrote, "I pray that Jerry will be with me. He has more imagination in a minute than most people have in a lifetime." Jerry died in 2007 at age ninety-six. Margaret died in 2011 at age ninety-four.

**Santos, Terry.** *Lead scout, Reconnaissance Platoon, 11th Airborne Division.* After the Philippines campaign ended, he and Martin Squires were aboard an Army plane that would take them to Okinawa. Before the plane took off, Lieutenant George Skau and another officer came aboard, looking for seats. There were none available, so Skau ordered Santos and Squires off. The two enlisted men deplaned, although Squires did so begrudgingly. He did not care for Skau, and cared even less after the recon lieutenant threatened to court-martial him for turning back on the trail the morning of the raid and not being in position with his team at 7 A.M. Santos talked Skau out of such punitive action, pointing out that with the mission's great success, there was no reason to do anything that would reflect badly on recon.

As the aircraft carrying Skau approached Okinawa, which was obscured by a smoke screen put up by U.S. ships to hide from kamikaze attacks, it crashed into a mountainside, killing all aboard. "See, Martin?" Santos remarked to his friend. "Lieutenant Skau saved our lives by kicking us off that plane."

Santos and Squires, along with the other members of recon,

were awarded the Silver Star Medal, the nation's third highest military decoration, for their role in the Los Baños raid. When Santos returned home, he attended San Francisco State University on the GI Bill and became a hydraulic engineer. He retired in 1986.

In 2006, Santos, then eighty-five years old, was leaving a restaurant in broad daylight when he was jumped by a mugger. As he had learned to do more than sixty years earlier, Santos reacted swiftly to neutralize the threat, bringing up his wooden cane hard between the legs of the mugger, who yelped in pain and went down. Santos then "went to work on him" with the curved end of the cane to make sure he wouldn't get back up. A lady walking her dog across the street called the police.

When paramedics arrived, the only person who required a ride to the hospital was the much younger mugger, who had multiple broken ribs and cracked kneecaps. A police officer looked at the elderly man wearing the "World War II Veteran: I Served with Pride" baseball cap.

"You did that?" she asked.

"No," Santos said, "my cane did."

Asked if he wanted to file a complaint against the man being taken away by ambulance, Santos declined. "He's suffered enough."

Santos is the last surviving member of the Recon Platoon. At age ninety-three, he lives in San Francisco.

**Squires, Martin and Margie (Whitaker).** *Reconnaissance Platoon (Martin) and Los Baños internee (Margie).* After the war, Martin returned to his parents' home in Bellingham, Washington, where Margie was living with her family while attending college. Margie's mother gave a talk at the Rotary Club about the family's wartime experience and rescue at Los Baños, about which the local newspaper published an article that Martin's mother read. She encouraged her son to call the young woman in town he had helped rescue. He was tired and not ready to be social, and he had already been jilted by a woman he thought was waiting for him, so he said no. After several more days of her nagging, Martin said in frustration to his mother, "Mom, why don't *you* call her?"

She did, and when Margie came on the line she handed him the phone. That led to a first date, and a year and a half later, Martin and Margie were married. Martin returned to college on the GI Bill and graduated from the University of Washington with a degree in fisheries. After working as a warden for the state department of game, he went to work for Boeing, where he was a quality assurance engineer for thirty-two years before retiring in 1984.

Margie Whitaker and Martin Squires shortly before their wedding, 1947. *Courtesy Margaret (Whitaker) Squires.*

When Margie finished college, she taught elementary school. They had three children, all of whom Martin taught to fish and enjoy the great outdoors. In retirement, he and Margie toured the United States in their RV. Margie had "fifty-two wonderful years with my hero husband" before he died in 2000 at age seventy-nine. Margie, age eighty-eight, lives in Des Moines, Washington.

***Still, Dorothy.*** *Los Baños internee and U.S. Navy nurse.* Ten days after the liberation of Los Baños, an admiral's plane arrived in Manila to take the eleven Navy nurses to Leyte, where soon after landing Dorothy fainted from exhaustion before a group picture could be taken in front of the admiral's tent. After she recovered, a chair was brought out for her and the picture was snapped with everyone on their feet but her.

Liberated Navy nurses with Vice Admiral Thomas Kincaid, commander of the U.S. Seventh Fleet, who welcomes them in Leyte. In their honor, his mess served a steak dinner with all the trimmings, which Dorothy Still, seated at left after fainting, was too weak to eat. *Courtesy U.S. Navy Bureau of Medicine and Surgery.*

Dorothy Still during a publicity tour speaking at Long Beach, California, shipyard, 1945. *Courtesy Dan Danner.*

The nurses all received the Bronze Star and the Prisoner of War Medal. Dorothy went on a ninety-day recuperation leave to regain her health, and was then assigned to Bethesda Naval Hospital, Maryland. Being one of the country's newest heroes, she was sent around the country on a saving-bond drive, giving talks to enthusiastic crowds. While she was proud to represent the Navy Nursing Corps, Dorothy felt unworthy of the public acclaim.

"I had simply sat the war out in a prison camp," she wrote in her 1995 memoir, *What a Way to Spend a War,* "being neither particularly brave nor courageous." She believed she had "just done my job as a nurse."

She left the Navy in 1947 and married a sound technician. She was pregnant with their third child in 1956 when her husband, Golburn Danner, died while covering a political convention. She returned to work as a nurse. In the mid-1970s, Dorothy reconnected with Tom Terrill, an internee she had met at Los Baños; they soon married and had some good years together. Dorothy died in 2001 at age eighty-six.

**Vanderpool, Jay.** *Major, guerrilla coordinator, 11th Airborne Division.* One of the "unsung heroes" of the Los Baños raid, according to Henry Muller, Vanderpool did not take part in the actual raid but was away on another mission on February 23, 1945, helping to feed Filipinos evacuating from war-torn Manila. However, he had crossed Laguna de Bay more than once coordinating with various guerrilla units about their participation in the operation.

"The Los Baños raid was a great U.S. Army accomplishment and major Allied accomplishment," Vanderpool said in his 1984 oral history. "The guerrillas did an excellent job; everyone did. There was enough glory for everyone involved that day."

A veteran of the wars in Korea and Vietnam, Vanderpool is honored in the Army Aviation Hall of Fame for his early experimentation in the mid-1950s in ordnance and airmobile tactics for helicopters, many of which are still used today. He retired a full colonel, and died in 1993 at age seventy-six.

**Los Baños newborns.** The two newborns the nurses at Los Baños protected during the raid and took to the amtracs for the ride to freedom grew up to work in the medical field. Elizabeth John (Thomas), born on Valentine's Day 1945, graduated from the University of California, San Francisco, School of Medicine in 1979, and had a long career specializing in internal medicine. She retired in 2009 and lives in Oakland, California. Lois McCoy (Bourinskie), born three days before the camp was liberated, graduated from Providence College of Nursing in Oakland, California. She sent a graduation announcement to the Navy nurse who delivered her at Los Baños: Dorothy Still.

Lois worked as a registered nurse in Vancouver, Washington, for thirty years until her retirement in 2010. Lois was the baby burned by hot ejects from amtrac gunner Dwight Clark's machine gun. In 1998, Lois's phone rang and a man asked if she was "baby Lois from Los Baños?" Lois said yes. "I heard you cry. Do you have a scar on your face?" She assured him that she did not.

Dwight had spent half a century certain he had scarred her for life. Lois and Dwight met the next year when she accepted his invitation to speak at a reunion of the 672nd Amphibian Tractor Battalion (belatedly awarded, in 2011, a Presidential Unit Citation for its role in the Los Baños rescue operation). They stayed in touch by phone, letters, and e-mail, and—according to Dwight's two daughters—he treated Lois like a third daughter. Dwight became a minister and teacher. He died in 2012 at age eighty-eight.

Baby Lois, born at Los Baños Internment Camp three days before liberation, with her mother, Mildred McCoy, late 1945. Upon their return home, Lois was hospitalized for many weeks suffering from malnutrition. *Courtesy Lois (McCoy) Bourinskie.*

# Sources

Complete book publication details are supplied in the bibliography. U.S. military records such as unit histories, action reports, and war diaries, as well as records pertaining to war-crime trials and sentences, are available at the National Archives II, College Park, Maryland. U.S. Army command histories, communications, and personal papers are collected at the U.S. Army Military History Institute, Carlisle, Pennsylvania. Oral histories and other information pertaining to the U.S. Navy Nursing Corps are available from the Bureau of Medicine and Surgery, Washington, D.C. Military personnel records are accessed at the National Personnel Records Centers, St. Louis, Missouri. Oral histories of former wartime prisoners are available at the Andersonville National History Museum, Andersonville, Georgia. Documents and histories pertaining to the internment of Catholic nuns are at the Maryknoll Mission Archives, Ossining, New York. Historical records about World War II in the Southwest Pacific are available at the MacArthur Memorial, Norfolk, Virginia. Interviews and archival research were conducted in Los Baños and Manila by the author's research assistant, Jose Custodio, based in the Philippines.

## Chapter One: The Fall of Manila

Ben Edwards oral history (1988); Ben Edwards letter to Mr. and Mrs. Thomas D. Costello (October 1941); author's interviews with Buck Edwards (2013), Portland, OR, and Ann MacDonnell (2013), Vancouver, BC; William Rivers, "Los Baños Recollections"; James McCall, *Santo Tomás Internment Camp: STIC in Verse and Reverse;* Lewis Watty, "A Prisoner of the Japanese"; Headquarters XIV Corps, Office of the Inspector General, "Report of Investigation of Atrocities by Members of the Japanese Imperial Forces in Manila and Other Parts of Luzon, Philippine Islands"; Dorothy Still Danner oral history (1991); Dorothy Still Danner, *What a Way to Spend a War;* oral histories of Navy nurses Bertha Evans (1992), Mary Rose Harrington (1994), Margaret Nash (1992); *Navy Medicine,* Jan./Feb. 2003; Diane Burke Fessler, *No Time for Fear;* Evelyn Monahan and Rosemary Neidel-Greenlee, *All This Hell;* Russell Brines, *Until They Eat Stones;* G. R. Sams, Andersonville NHS oral history (1995); U.S. Marine Corps and U.S. Coast Guard service records; author's interview with Gerry Ann Schwede (2013); U.S. government statistics regarding American civilians held in prison camps by the Japanese: http://www.bacepow.net; author's interview with Schwede; Margaret Sams "Dear Friend" letter (April 28, 2004); Elizabeth Norman, *We Band of Angels;* Margaret Sams, *Forbidden Family.*

## Chapter Two: Prisoners of the Japanese

Sams NHS oral history (1995); Sams, *Forbidden Family;* Margaret Sams letter to Paul Shea (Sept. 12, 2004); Margaret Sams, "Always Remember"; Sams, "Dear Friend"; Celia Lucas, *Prisoners of Santo Tomás;* Sams, *Forbidden Family;* Danner oral history (1991); Nash oral history (1992); Harrington oral history (1994); oral history of Ann Bernatitus (1994); Judith Johnson, "Laura Cobb: A Kansas Nurse in a Japanese Prisoner of War Camp"; Norman, *We Band of Angels;* Still, *What a Way to Spend a War;* author's interview with John Montesa (2014); John Montesa, "Boxcars on a Narrow Gauge Railway"; John Montesa, MacArthur Memorial oral history (2010).

## Chapter Three: Los Baños Internment Camp

Rivers, "Los Baños Recollections"; Montesa oral history; Marcelino Macapinlac, "The Historical Geography of Los Baños During the Japanese Occupation"; Fernando Bernardo, "UPLB: A Century of Challenges and Achievements"; Alex Calhoun, "Remarks Made to the Committee by Colonel Utunomiya"; Margo Tonkin Shiels, *Bends in the Road;* Donna Marchetti, *Saving Grace;* Lewis Watty, "A Prisoner of the Japanese"; Herman Beaber, *Deliverance! It Has Come!;* Anthony Arthur, *Deliverance at Los Baños;* Henry Yarborough, Andersonville NHS oral history (1999); Sams NHS oral history; Sams, *Forbidden Family;* Dorothy John Horn, *The Cage: A Memoir and Diary of a Young Girl's Internment in World War II;* Norman, *We Band of Angels;* Danner, *What a Way to Spend a War.*

## Chapter Four: Sky Soldiers

Author's interviews with Henry Muller (2012–2014); Henry Muller, "You're a Young Paratrooper" and "Listen As You Have Never Listened Before"; 11th Airborne Division: "History and Tribute"; Dwight D. Eisenhower Library; Henry Burgess, *Looking Back;* E. M.

Flanagan Jr., *The Angels: A History of the 11th Airborne Division;* author's interviews with Terry R. Santos (2012–2014); Larry Alexander, *Shadows in the Jungle;* Colonel John Crump, "Sgt. Terry Santos, U.S. Army (Ret)"; www.AlamoScouts.org.

## Chapter Five: "You'll Be Eating Dirt"

Penny Lernoux, *Hearts on Fire;* Danner oral history (1991); Nash oral history (1992); Harrington oral history (1994); Danner, *What a Way to Spend a War;* Norman, *We Band of Angels;* Johnson, "Laura Cobb: A Kansas Nurse in a Japanese Prisoner of War Camp"; Edwards, oral history (1988); Rivers, "Los Baños Recollections"; Robert Allen, *Philippine War Diary;* Arthur, *Deliverance at Los Baños;* Dana Nance deposition, Army Intelligence dossier; Report No. 155, Army War Crimes Branch; Frances Cogan, *Captured;* Sadaaki Konishi, POW Basic Personnel Record (Dec. 18, 1945); Testimony of Sadaaki Konishi, public trial exhibit (Nov. 28, 1946); Marchetti, *Saving Grace;* David Robbins, *Broken Jewel;* Grace Chapman Nash, "The Gallant Buccaneer of Los Baños"; George Mora, "My Los Baños Diary"; Doris Rubens, *Bread and Rice; United States v. Sadaaki Konishi,* Opinion of the Board of Review (1947); Report to the Commandant, "Hygiene and Sanitation" (Oct. 1944); committee letter to commandant (November 16, 1944).

## Chapter Six: Return to the Philippines

Douglas MacArthur, *Reminiscences;* Gordon Sullivan, "Leyte," U.S. Army Center of Military History; Flanagan, *The Angels; Time* magazine, Nov. 20, 1944; "Down but Not Out," *Time,* Dec. 2, 1991; Santos interviews (2012–2014); Martin Squires, "A Good Lesson" and "Reminiscing"; Martin Squires letter to E. M. Flanagan Jr. (Dec. 20, 1984); author's interviews with Margaret Whitaker Squires (2012–2014); Samuel Eliot Morrison, *History of the United States Naval Operations in World War II, Vols. 12, 13;* Richard Keith, "The Fog of War," *Voice of the Angels* (March 2014); Muller, "Listen as You Have Never Listened Before"; Gerald Walker, *My Most Memorable Christmas;* James Clayton, *The Years of MacArthur, Vol. 2, 1941–45;* Walter Krueger, *From Down Under to Nippon;* Joseph Swing letter to Peyton March (Dec. 1944); Arthur, *Deliverance at Los Baños;* Muller interviews (2012–2014).

## Chapter Seven: Freedom Week

Danner, *What a Way to Spend a War;* Robbins, *Broken Jewel;* Katherine Ellis Brown, "Diary of Katherine Ellis Brown"; James McCall, "List of Deceased," *Santo Tomás Internment Camp;* Grace Chapman Nash, "The Gallant Buccaneer of Los Baños"; Dana Nance, "Hygiene and Sanitation" report, Feb. 2, 1945; Shiels, *Bends in the Road;* Cogan, *Captured;* Danner oral history (1991); Montesa interview (2014); Sams, *Forbidden Family;* Margaret Sams, "Memories of Living in Internment Camps"; Margaret Sams letter to Paul Shea (July 30, 2001); Margaret Whitaker Squires, *Land of the Morning;* Sr. Louise Kroeger, "Report on Los Baños" (1945); Margaret and Martin Squires, Andersonville NHS oral history (1995); author's interview with Whitaker Squires (2012); Horn, *The Cage;* Beaber, *Deliverance! It Has Come;* Rivers, "Los Baños Recollections"; Donald Roberts, "Angels to the Rescue," Military Heritage (2001); Frederic Stevens, *Santo Tomás Internment Camp;* Mora, "My Los Baños Diary"; Marchetti, *Saving Grace.*

## Chapter Eight: Under the Cover of Darkness

Jay Vanderpool oral history (1983); Edward Dissette, *Guerrilla Submarines;* Clay Blair, *Silent Victory;* Muller interviews (2012–2014); MacArthur, *Reminiscences;* Proculo Mojica, *Terry's Hunters: The True Story of the Hunters ROTC Guerrillas;* David Rutter, *Olga's War;* Jay Vanderpool letters to E. M. Flanagan Jr. (1984); Flanagan, *The Angels.*

## Chapter Nine: The Killings

Interview with Daikichi Okamoto, *Escape at Dawn;* Sister M. Colman, "Internment in Manila, Los Baños, P.I."; John Halsema, "The Liberation of the Los Baños Internment Camp"; R. A. Arthur, "The Fate of Lt. Konishi"; Rubens, *Bread and Rice;* Cogan, *Captured;* Marchetti, *Saving Grace;* Horn, *The Cage;* Arthur, *Deliverance at Los Baños*; Mora, "My Los Baños Diary"; Nance, Army Intelligence dossier; Monahan and Neidel-Greenlee, *All This Hell;* Danner, *What a Way to Spend a War;* Danner oral history (1991); *United States v. Sadaaki Konishi,* Opinion of the Board of Review (1947); Report No. 155, Army War Crimes Branch; Minutes of the Los Baños Executive Committee (1945); Robbins, *Broken Jewel;* Joseph Vernick, "Stranded"; Montesa interview (2014); Santos interviews (2012–2014).

## Chapter Ten: "Do It Right, Joe"

Santos interviews (2012–2014); E. M. Flanagan Jr., *The Los Baños Raid;* Arthur, *Deliverance at Los Baños;* Squires letter to Flanagan (Dec. 20, 1984); Henry Muller letters to author (June 1 and June 12, 2014); Robert Eichelberger, *Dear Miss Em;* Swing letter to March (January 1945); Vanderpool letters to Flanagan (1984); Vanderpool oral history (1983); Robert Ross Smith, *Triumph in the Pacific;* Flanagan, *The Angels;* Angela Perez Miller, Oral History Project, the University of Texas at Austin; "American POWs of Japan," Asia Policy Point (Dec. 14, 2011); Linda Goetz Holmes, *Unjust Enrichment;* MacArthur, *Reminiscences;* author's interviews with Muller (2012–2014).

## Chapter Eleven: The Escapes

Edwards, oral history (1988); Pan American World Airways, "Return from Hell: Pan Americans Liberated from Jap Internment Camps"; Rivers, "Los Baños Recollections"; Administration Committee's "Summary of Events Leading to the Rescue of Los Baños Internment Camp"; Arthur, *Deliverance at Los Baños;* Brown, "Diary of Katherine Ellis Brown"; B. F. Edwards, "Los Baños Internment Camp: Escape and Liberation," *Bulletin of American Historical Collection* (April/June, 1985); Ben Edwards letter to Sister Louise Kroeger (Nov. 14, 1983); Ben Edwards letter to Mr. and Mrs. Thomas D. Costello (March 4, 1945); interviews with Edwards (2013) and MacDonnell (2013); Rutter, *Olga's War;* Leonardo Nuval, *Remember Them Kindly;* Gustavo Ingles, "The Inside Story: The Liberation of Internees in Los Baños"; Mojica, *Terry's Hunters;* Flanagan, *The Los Baños Raid.*

## Chapter Twelve: The Los Baños Force

U.S. Department of Defense, Joint Publication 1-02: Dictionary of Military and Associated Terms; XIV Corps Extract, "Operations on Luzon: Chapter VIII, Los Baños";

Muller interviews (2012–2014); Henry Muller address, San Diego, CA (Feb. 5, 1999); Henry Muller address, Los Baños, CA (Feb. 25, 1995); Henry Muller, "Setting the Record Straight," *Voice of the Angels* (June 2002); Donna Marchetti's interviews with Henry Muller (April 13–14, 2000); Henry Muller letter to Donna Marchetti (Feb. 7, 2001); Henry Muller letters to George Doherty (1994–1995); Flanagan, *The Los Baños Raid;* Vanderpool oral history (1983); Jay Vanderpool letter to David Blackledge (March 17, 1982); Vanderpool letters to Flanagan (1984); 11th Airborne Division Headquarters, "Report on the Los Baños Operation" (March 17, 1945); Arthur J. Coleman letters to E. M. Flanagan (August 1984); Santos interviews (2012–2014); Crump, "Sgt. Terry Santos, U.S. Army (Ret)"; Alexander, *Shadows in the Jungle;* B. F. Edwards, "Los Baños Internment Camp: Escape and Liberation," *Bulletin of American Historical Collection* (April/June, 1985); Edwards letter to Mr. and Mrs. Costello (March 4, 1945); Donald J. Roberts II, "Angels to the Rescue," Military Heritage (Aug. 2001); Horn, *The Cage.*

## Chapter Thirteen: "Rescue Must Come Soon!"
Whitaker Squires interviews (2012–2014); Squires NHS oral history (1995); Whitaker Squires, *Land of the Morning;* Administration Committee's "Summary of Events Leading to the Rescue of Los Baños Internment Camp"; Monahan and Neidel-Greenlee, *All This Hell;* Brown, "Diary of Katherine Ellis Brown"; Mora, "My Los Baños Diary"; C. Edwina Todd, "Nursing Under Fire"; Horn, *The Cage;* Jerry Sams, "War in the Pacific" (2006); Sams, NHS oral history (1995); Schwede interviews (2013); Sams, *Forbidden Family.*

## Chapter Fourteen: "The World Will Be Watching"
John Ringler, "The Los Baños Raid," *Winds Aloft* (Fall 1999); Paul Aswell, "The Airborne Mission and Lt. John Ringler," *Airborne Quarterly* (Spring 1995); Donna Marchetti's interview with John Ringler (2000); Flanagan, *The Angels;* "Daring Rescue Overshadowed," *Omaha World-Herald* (Sept. 6, 1997); author's interviews with Charles Sass (2013–2014); Edward Lahti, *Memoirs of an Angel;* Edwards, "Los Baños Internment Camp: Escape and Liberation," *Bulletin of American Historical Collection;* John Fulton, "Los Baños," *11th Airborne Division;* Muller interviews (2012–2014); Herbert J. Walker, "Trooper Carrier Mission," *Airborne Quarterly* (Spring 1995); Charles Sass, "The Story of Me and My Times"; author's interviews with Jack McGrath (2013); John Ringler video interview, "War in the Pacific" (2006); "Rescue at Dawn," History Channel (2004); Arthur, *Deliverance at Los Baños.*

## Chapter Fifteen: The Raid
Arthur Coleman, "Life and Times of the 672d Amtrac," *Voice of the Angels* (Dec. 1998); Coleman letters to Flanagan (1984); Dwight Clark, "History of the 672nd Amtracs at Los Baños," *Voice of the Angels* (March 2007); "Rosebud, Texas Man Directs Sensational Raid to Free 2,146 Prisoners"; Bob Dill, "The 672 Amphibian Tractor Battalion: Unsung Heroes of the Los Baños Prison Raid," *Voice of the Angels* (Dec. 2001); Bronze Star Medal Citation, Headquarters 37th Infantry Division (Nov. 1945); Burgess, *Looking Back;* Headquarters 11th Airborne Division, "Report on the Los Baños Operation"; Muller interviews (2012–2014); Joseph Swing letter to Peyton March (Feb. 24, 1945); Robert

Beightler, "Los Baños," *Voice of the Angels* (Vol. 125); Robert Beightler, "A Swing and a Miss," *Winds Aloft* (July/Oct. 1989); Dwight Clark, "The Los Baños Prison Raid"; Flanagan, *The Los Baños Raid;* author's interviews with Alex Morley (2013–2014); H. J. Parker, "Trooper Carrier Mission," *Airborne Quarterly,* Spring 1995; Fulton, "Los Baños," *11th Airborne Division;* Crump, "Sgt. Terry Santos, U.S. Army (Ret)"; Santos interviews (2012–2014); Terry R. Santos, "The Recon Platoon at Los Baños," *Winds Aloft* (circa 1987); Edwards, "Los Baños Internment Camp: Escape and Liberation"; Arthur, *Deliverance at Los Baños;* Edwards letter to Mr. and Mrs. Costello (March 4, 1945); Flanagan, *The Angels;* Dominick Suppa, "What I Remember About Los Baños"; author's interview with Martin Moen (2013); Paul Shea's interview with Martin Moen (2006).

## Chapter Sixteen: Rescue

Danner oral history (1991); Danner, *What a Way to Spend a War;* oral histories of Navy nurses Harrington (1994) and Nash (1992); Edwina Todd, "Nursing Under Fire"; Nora Kinzer, "Armed Forces Nurse Day," Arlington Cemetery (May 4, 1984); Lois McCoy Bourinskie interviews (2014); Lois McCoy Bourinskie, "Rescue and Reunion"; Sams, "War in the Pacific" (2006); Sams, NHS oral history (1995); author's interview with Schwede (2013); Sams, *Forbidden Family;* Donna Marchetti notes of 511th PIR reunion (July 2000); Charles Sass, "I Jumped at Los Baños"; Dwight Clark, "The 672nd Amphibian Tractor Battalion: Los Baños and World War II"; Dill, "The 672 Amphibian Tractor Battalion: Unsung Heroes of the Los Baños Prison Raid"; author's interview with Paul Junkroski (2014); Burgess, *Looking Back;* Flanagan, *The Los Baños Raid;* Arthur, *Deliverance at Los Baños;* Whitaker Squires interviews (2012–2014); Edwards, "Los Baños Internment Camp: Escape and Liberation," *Bulletin of American Historical Collection* (April/June, 1985); Henry Burgess's speech at thirty-fifth Los Baños anniversary reunion (1980); Santos interviews (2012–2014); Martin Squires letter to E. M. Flanagan Jr. (Jan. 1, 1984); Beightler, "Los Baños," *Voice of the Angels* (Vol. 125); Robert Beightler's letter to Paul Shea (June 2001).

## Chapter Seventeen: "God Was with Us"

Muller interviews (2012–2014); Frank Quesada, "Freedom at Dawn"; Sams, *Forbidden Family;* Carol Terry Talbot and Virginia Muir, *Escape at Dawn;* Charles Sass interviews (2013–2014); Swing letter to March (Feb. 24, 1945); MacArthur telegram to XIV Corps (Feb. 24, 1945); MacArthur press release (Feb. 24, 1945); Chairman of the Joint Chiefs of Staff, Washington, D.C. (Feb. 25, 1993).

## Epilogue: The Fate of Sadaaki Konishi

Sadaaki Konishi, POW Basic Personnel Record; *United States v. Sadaaki Konishi,* Public Trial Record; Aurelio Almazan deposition (Nov. 26, 1945); Report No. 214, "Los Baños Massacres," U.S. Army War Crimes Branch (Dec. 1945); Rino Francisco, "The Agony of Laguna"; Jose Custodio, "The Destruction of Batangas"; Talbot and Muir, *Escape at Dawn;* Flanagan, *The Los Baños Raid;* John Ginn, *Sugamo Prison, Tokyo;* Delivery Receipt,

Sugamo Prison (Sept. 20, 1948); Discharge or Permanent Transfer, Sugamo Prison (Sept. 21, 1948); John Marren letter to commanding officer, Sugamo Prison (Nov. 2, 1948); Kenneth Royall letter to Commander in Chief, Far East (March 30, 1949); Douglas MacArthur letter to Commanding General, Eighth Army (April 12, 1949); W. H. Edwards, headquarters, Eighth Army, letter to commanding officer, Sugamo Prison (April 27, 1949); Release of Prisoner from 361st Station Hospital (April 28, 1949); author's interviews with former Sugamo prison guard (2014); witness certificate, Sugamo Prison (April 30, 1949); death certificate, Sugamo Prison (April 30, 1949).

# Appendix

# The Camp Roster

THE LAST ROSTER OF LOS BAÑOS INTERNMENT CAMP WAS typed by internee Carol Terry in February 1945 on a 1920s manual typewriter. Retrieved by George Gray as the camp was being evacuated, this list has been recognized by the U.S. government as the official camp census. A total of 2,147 American and Allied prisoners of the Japanese were rescued at Los Baños on February 23, 1945; some individuals named herein did not live to see liberation but died due to beriberi caused by starvation or other diseases or were executed by the Japanese after the list was compiled.

*American*
Adams, Elbridge M.
Adams, Gustav Adolph
Adams, Owen
Adams, Welba S.
Adrian, Kathleen Halloran
Adrian, Michael Joseph
Agnes, Sister Inelda
Agnes, Sister Regina
Ahern, Hilary
Aimee, Sister Marie
Aiton, Felicimo L.

Aiton, Joe E.
Aiton, Josepha D.
Albert, Daniel Louis
Ale, Francis Harvey
Allen, Robert Coleman
Alness, Mark Gerhard
Alphonsa, Sister Mary
Alsobrook, Anthony Leonidas
Amstutz, Elda
Ancilla, Sister Marie
Anderson, Charles Richard
Anderson, Charles Stewart

Anderson, Oscar William
Anderson, Theodore Maxwell
Andrew, Sister Mary
Ankney, William Edgar
Antoinette, Sister M.
Apelseth, Clement Anders
Appleby, Blanche
Aquinata, Sister M.
Arana, Bernardina
Arana, Cesar
Arana, Esther
Arick, Melvin Ray
Arida, Jodat Kamel
Armstrong, Robert Worthington
Ashton, Sidney
Assumpta, Sister M.
Augustus, Sister Mary
Avery, Charles William
Avery, Henry
Axtman, Boniface
Ayres, Glen Edwin
Babbitt, Winfred Howard
Backman, Herbert
Bagby, Calvin T.
Baker, Rowland John
Balano, Felix
Baldwin, Rena
Barnaby, Catherine
Barnes, Charles Irwin
Barnes, Evelyn Crew
Barnes, Richard Porter
Barter, Fred
Bartgis, Fred
Barth, Phyllis Ludwig
Bartlett, Mildred Glaze
Bartlett, Sydney Stockholm
Barton, Roy Franklin
Bateman, Jack
Bateman, John James
Bateman, Sallie
Bauman, William McComb
Baxter, Cecil Marie
Baxter, Sidney

Bayley, Harold Raymond
Bayouth, Khallel Assad
Beaber, H.
Beata, Sister M.
Beaty, Truman Carlson
Bebell, Clifford Felix Swift
Beck, Emsley William
Beck, Francis Harold
Becker, Frank Emil
Bee, Edwin Joseph
Beeman, Frank Robert
Beeman, Maude Rona
Beeman, Narvel Chester
Beeman, Raymond Richard
Beeman, Wallace Earl
Begley, Charlie
Beigbeder, Frank Michael
Bennett, Frank Cantillo
Benninghoven, Edward Robert
Berger, William Harris
Bergman, Gerda Ottelia
Besser, Leo
Bezotte, Fred
Billings, Bliss W.
Binsted, Norman S.
Binsted, Willie M. G.
Birsh, Charles
Bissinger, George Henry
Bissinger, Winifred Allen
Bittner, Joseph
Blackledge, David
Blackledge, Helen
Blackledge, Robert
Blair, Herbert E.
Blair, Susan
Blake, Lila
Blake, Mary
Blake, Owen A.
Blakeley, Mildred M.
Blalock, John
Blanchard, Harold Mason
Blanton, Charles Maxwell
Blanton, Dale Lincoln

Blechynden, Claire Louise
Blue, Harry Coleman
Bogacz, Francis
Bogle, Edwin Carmel
Bolderston, Constance
Bollman, Benjamin B.
Bollman, Elsie K.
Bollman, J. W.
Bollman, Lynn B.
Bond, Leo
Bonham, Rex
Boomer, Louise Charmian
Boomer, Joseph
Boston, William
Boswell, Eleanor Madaline
Bousman, H.
Bousman, James
Bousman, Martha
Bousman, Nona
Bousman, Tom
Bowker, Bayard Jordan
Bowie, Harold Dewell
Bowie, Leah Lourdes
Bowie, Paquita Rodriguez
Boyce, Leila Susan
Boyce, Viola Ceres
Boyd, Joseph
Boyens, Ernest
Boyers, James Simon
Boyle, Philip
Bradfield, Elizabeth Shortridge
Bradely, Brant
Bradney, Reuel
Bradanauer, Frederick W.
Bradanauer, Grace A.
Bratton, Charles Henley
Brazee, Albert John, Jr.
Brazee, Nancy Agnes Erwin
Brendel, Oswood Roland
Brigitine, Sister
Brink, John William
Brink, Maude E.
Brink, Myron

Brink, Pamela
Brink, Robert Arlington
Broad, Wilfred
Brock, Joe O.
Brockway, Alex Grove
Brockway, Merna Morris
Brook, Walter Leroy
Brooks, Horace
Brown, George
Brown, Harry John
Brown, Helen Margaret
Brown, Katherine Ellis
Brown, Mary Martha
Brown, Nell McAfee
Brown, Ray
Brown, Richard Sefton
Brown, Roy H.
Browne, Leslie
Browne, Pilar
Browne, Robert
Brush, John Burk
Brush, Lois Bogue
Brushfield, Elizabeth
Bryan, Arthur
Bryan, Edgar Robeson
Bryan, Winifred
Bucher, Anna L.
Bucher, George Scott
Bucher, Henry H.
Bucher, Henry H., Jr.
Bucher, Louise S.
Bucher, Priscilla J.
Buckalew, Donald Howland
Buckles, Frank Woodruff
Budlong, Vinton Alva
Burke, Harry Taylor
Burkman, Charles Harris
Burlingame, Walter Michael
Brunham, Edward Frank
Burns, Francis
Burns, James
Burns, James (2)
Burrell, Louie Grant

Burton, Edith Ganz
Burton, Harry Royal
Burton, James Edward
Butler, John Nicholsen
Bulter, Linnie Marie
Cadwallader, Helen
Caecilius, Sister M.
Cain, Claude Oliver
Cain, Thomas
Caldwell, William A.
Calhoun, Alexander Dewey
Calvert, John Ellis
Calve, Elisa Warbaugh
Cammack, Larue
Campbell, Guilford E.
Campbell, Leo Lee
Campp, Anthony L.
Canson, John
Capen, Morris Noel
Caritas, Sister M.
Carlisle, Mabel Burris
Carlson, Alvin
Carlson, Imogene Ina
Carlson, Lawrence
Carlson, Mark
Carlucci, John (Boniface)
Carpenter, Henry
Carson, Hilton
Carter, Roland van
Carty, George B.
Carty, Eleanor May
Carty, Jean Pearl
Casanave, Andres
Casanave, Emilio
Casanave, Grete
Casanave, Pedro, Jr.
Casanave, Pedro Andres
Casanave, Peter A.
Casanave, Rachel Olive
Casanave, Teresa E.
Casanave, Theodore
Casey, Edward
Cashman, Michael

Cassel, Henry D.
Cassell, Marie
Cassell, Marion Reedy
Cassell, Maurice Arnold
Cassidy, John Patrick
Catherine, Sister M.
Cease, Forrest Lee
Cecil, Robert E.
Celeste, Sister M.
Chambers, Bunnie, Sr.
Chambers, Bunnie, Jr.
Chambers, Isidra
Chambers, Katherine
Chambers, Maria
Chantal, Sister M. de
Chapman, Corwin Clyde
Chapman, Mary Frances
Chapman, Virginia Dewey
Chase, Leland Preston
Chatman, Littleton
Cheek, Jesse Willard
Chester, Harold Dean
Chester, Pearl Eileen
Chestnut, James Edward
Chew, John Hamilton
Chichester, Robert Oxley
Chickese, Ernest
Childers, Ralph Leroy
Christensen, Edward
Christensen, Joseph
Christie, A.
Chisholm, Robert
Cillo, Thomas
Clare, Joseph-Mother M.
Clark, Andrew
Clark, Rush Spencer
Claude, Henry Louie
Clayton, Noel
Clifford, Carl Gaines
Clifford, William Dennis
Clingen, Herbert Signer
Clingen, Ida Ruth
Clingen, Robert Fraser

Cobb, Laura May
Coffey, Henry A.
Cochran, Donald Lewellyn
Cofer, Newton
Coggeshall, Roland Roberts
Cogswell, Gladys Jessie
Cole, Birnie
Cole, George Edward
Cole, Minnie
Coleman, Barbara M.
Coleman, Marjorie K.
Coleman, Marshall L.
Coleman, Patricia C.
Colin, Paul J.
Collier, Leonard Hooper
Collins, Joseph Davis
Collins, Thomas James
Colman, Sister
Conant, Ellsworth Thomas
Conant, Juanda June
Conant, Myra Belle
Cone, Hector Anthony
Congleton, Lucy E.
Conner, Herman Burt
Connors, John
Conway, Joseph Michael
Constance, Sister M.
Cook, Alfred D.
Cook, James William
Cook, Maude Rose
Cook, William Sherman
Cook, W. Thomas
Cooper, Hugh Price
Copello, Thomas George
Copper, Robert Gamble
Corbett, Daniel
Cornelison, Bernice
Cort, Marcus Robert
Corwin, Alvah Oatis
Crabb, Josephine Rosalie
Craven, Louise Broad
Craven, Osgood Coit
Crawford, Joseph Claypole

Crawford, Robert Allan
Crawford, Virginia Hale
Crist, Ann Bennett
Crist, Lynn Levi
Croft, Patty Gene
Croft, Selma Marion
Croft, William Frederick
Croisant, Everett Albert
Cromwell, Robert Horace
Croney, Dorothy Fain
Crooks, William
Crosby, George Howard
Crothers, Ellen N.
Crothers, John Young
Cullens, James Wimberly
Cullum, Leo
Cumming, Clarence Warder
Cumming, Ernest
Cumming, Milton Weston
Cumming, Patrick
Cunningham, Frederick Noel
Curavo, Leonard Alexander
Curran, Elmer Hege
Curran, Howard H.
Curran, Hugh McCollum, Sr.
Curran, Hugh McCollum, Jr.
Custer, Theodore Hart
Dahlke, Gustav A.
Dahlke, Inga Hedwig
Dakin, Bess May
Dakin, Charles Austin
Dale, Billie Ann
Dale, Donna Lee
Dale, Edna Lee
Dale, Frank Emmit
Dale, Melvin Eugene
Dale, Roberta M.
Damrosch, Elizabeth H.
Damrosch, Leopold
Damrosch, Leopold, Jr.
Danie, Amelia Louise
Danie, Antony Joseph
Davey, Laura Emily

David, Sister M.
Davidson, Abraham
Davidson, Arthur Dewain
Davis, Marian Electra
Davis, Maureen Neal
Davis, Roger William
Davis, Rosella A.
Davis, Sun Ye
Dayton, Earl Tresiliam
Deam, Mary L.
Dean, Harry Wilson
Decker, Louis
De Coito, Ann I.
De Coito, Louis
Decoteau, Joseph
Dedegas, Basil
Deihl, Edith Jolles
Deihl, Renzie Watson
De La Costa, Frank A.
De La Costa, Jan
De La Fuente, Pelegrin
Delaney, Frank Lorraine
De Loffe, John
De Martini, Louise V.
Deppermann, Charles
Depue, Rodney Albert
Detrick, Herbert J.
Detrick, Lulu H.
Detzer, Linus William
DeVries, David Andrew
DeVries, Gene
DeVries, Gladys L.
DeVries, Henry William, Sr.
DeVries, Henry William, Jr.
Dewhirst, Harry Daniel
DeWitt, Clyde Alton
Dick, Thomas William
Dincher, Frederick
Dingle, Leila
Dingman, Arthur
Divine Child, Sister Mary
Doig, Leroy Dorry, Jr.
Doino, Francis

Dominica, Sister M.
Dorothy, Sister
Dow, William
Dowd, Austin
Dowling, Richard
Downing, Donald Clark
Doyle, Emily Norma
Doyle, Joseph Desmond
Downs, Darley
Dragset, Ingie
Dreyer, Karl Olaf
Drost, Leonard
Dudley, Earl C., Sr.
Dudley, Earl C., Jr
Dudley, Susie Hall
Dugas, Alfred Frederick
Dustin, Herbert Warren
Dwyre, Allen Louis
Dyer, Althea C.
Dyer, Harlan L.
Dyer, June L.
Dyer, Mary
Eanswida, Mother M.
Earl, George Richard
Eaton, Gertrude Mary
Eaton, Leon Schultz
Ebbesen, Frank E.
Eddy, Arthur Louis
Edwards, Benjamin Franklin
Edwards, Herbert Kenneth
Edwards, John
Edwards, Mary Constance
Eison, George Simon
Ekstrand, Martin Eugene
Eldridge, Lawrence
Eldridge, Norma
Eldridge, Paul H.
Eldridge, Retha
Eleanor, Sister Frances
Elizabeth, Sister M.
Elliott, Francis Roy
Ellis, Adele Marie
Elstner, Josephine Elmer

Elwood, Joseph Donald
Emerson, Ause
Epes, Branch Jones, Sr.
Epes, Branch Jones, Jr.
Epes, William Fitzgerald
Erdman, Joseph James
Erickson, Eric Oscar
Erickson, Harry Eric
Evans, Bertha Rae
Evory, Harold William
Ewing, Margaret Greenfield
Ewing, Roy Emerson
Fairweather, Barbara Hayne
Fasy, Carroll
Fawcett, Alfred Edward, Sr.
Fawcett, Alfred, Jr.
Feely, Gertrude
Felicidade, M. Mary
Felix, Harold (Raphael)
Fernandez, Carmen Mary
Fernandez, Gregoria
Fernandez, Joaquin Jose
Fernandez, Juanina Mary
Fernandez, Mary Louise
Ferrier, John William
Ferrier, Theresa Diana
Fidelis, Sister M.
Fielding, Ralph
Fisher, Arthur George
Fisher, Frederick Russell
Fisher, Ruth Lincoln
Fishman, Alvin William
Fittinghoff, Nicholas Alexander
Fleisher, Henry
Fleming, Joseph Lamar
Fletcher, Charles Falkner
Flint, Alvin Lovett
Flint, Sarah Viola
Florence, Paul Billington
Flores, Joe Tatani
Florez, Juanita R.
Florez, Julietta Lee
Florez, Ramona Samilpa

Fluemer, Arnold William
Fonger, Burton
Fonger, Leith Cox
Fonger, William Henry
Ford, Charles Emery
Ford, Henry Tagros
Ford, William Munroe
Forney, William Thomas
Fowler, Ernest A.
Fox, Frank Christopher
Fox, Henry
Fox, James Joseph
Fox, James Roy
Fox, Mattea
Fox, Vincent Altizo
Francisco, Louis Joseph
Frantz, Daniel David
Fraser, Elvie
Frederica, Sister M.
Fredenert, M. M.
Freeman, Edward Francis
Freeman, Frances Mary
Freeman, Jo Fisher
Fricke, Herman Henry
Fricke, Dorothy
Friedl, Joseph
Fuller, Sumner Bacon
Gabrielson, Carl William
Gaffke, Albert A.
Gaillard, John Gourdin
Galassi, Dominico
Gallaher, Robert Franklin
Gallagher, Harry Joseph
Gallapaue, William Earl
Gallit, Henry Emil
Galway, Howard
Gardiner, Clifford A.
Gardiner, Elizabeth A.
Gardiner, William A.
Gardner, Claude Dennis
Garmezy, Samuel
Garrett, Elwood Llewellin
Garrigues, Dwight N.

Gavigan, Tripp G.

Genevieve, Sister Rose

Georgia, Sister M.

Gesemyer, Arthur K.

Gesemyer, Georgie C., Sr.

Gesemyer, Georgie C., Jr.

Gewald, Myrtle F.

Gibson, Alvin Harvey

Giles, Vinton Sela

Gilfoil, Katherine

Gilfoil, Katherine N.

Gilfoil, Lydia Alice

Gilfoil, Mary Louise

Gilfoil, Patricia Ann

Gilfoil, William Scott

Girard, Edward

Giucondiana, M. M.

Gisel, Eugene

Gladys, Sister M.

Glunz, Charles

Glunz, Henrietta H.

Godfrey, M. M.

Goebel, Otto John

Goldman, Edmund

Golucke, Louis Harold

Goodwin, Martin Luther

Gordenker, Alexander

Gordon, John J.

Gorzelanski, Helen Clara

Gotthold, Diana

Grady, Virginia H.

Gray, Bernice Louise

Gray, Edward James

Gray, George

Grau, Albert

Graves, Arthur

Greer, Henry

Griffin, Elizabeth G.

Griffin, Frank

Grishkevich, Vitaly Ippolit

Grode, Leo

Gross, Morton Robert

Guicheteau, Arnold J.

Gunder, Jack H.

Gunnels, Robert Lee

Guthrie, Mary J.

Guthrie, Richard S.

Guthrie, Romelda A.

Guthrie, William E.

Haberer, Emanuel Julius

Hacker, Leonard

Hackett, Alice

Hackett, John Alexander

Hageman, Marshall N.

Hale, J. Willis

Hale, Velma M.

Haley, Arthur Edward

Haley, James

Hall, Norman Shannon

Hallett, John Bartlett

Ham, Hugh Mack

Hammill, Dena M.

Hammill, Richard L.

Hammill, Rogers N.

Hammond, L. D. Lloyd

Hamra, Adeeb Joseph

Hancock, Lawrence Kelly

Hancock, Mary Edna

Hannings, Richard Edward

Hanson, Donie Taylor

Hanson, Rolf Hinnen

Hard, Herbert William

Hard, Marie Lucille

Hardy, Beverly Earl

Harms, Lloyd Frederick

Harper, Anita Mae

Harper, Arthur Edward

Harper, Betty Jane

Harper, James Albert

Harper, Steven Phillip

Harrah, Orville

Harrah, Rose Marie

Harrell, Richard Maxted

Harrington, Mary Rose

Harris, William S.

Harrison, Phillip Francis

Harshman, Albert N.
Harshman, Anita Wichman
Hart, Herbert Henry
Hart, Joseph Chittendon
Hartnett, Ernest
Hatcher, Benjamin Carlile
Hause, Charles David
Hausman, Louis Michael
Haven, Lewis Quincy, Jr.
Hayme, Carl
Haynes, Albert
Headley, Donald Grant
Healy, Gerald
Healy, John
Heath, George Eddy
Hebard, William Lawrence
Heery, Joseph Marion
Heesch, Henry John
Heichert, Murray Baker
Hell, Jan Howard
Hellis, Herbert Dean
Henderson, Barclay C.
Henderson, Dorothy Gardiner
Henderson, George William
Hendrix, Daisy
Hennel, Charles
Hennesen, Maria Alexandrina
Hennesen, Paul
Herndon, Alice Patterson
Herndon, Rees Frazer
Hertz, Harold Emerson
Hess, Arlene F.
Hess, Hudson S.
Hess, Lois Ellen
Hess, R. Bruce
Hess, Robert R.
Hess, Victor Glen
Hess, Viola Ruth
Hibbard, James F.
Hicks, John Thomas
Highsmith, Jerome
Hight, Allen H.
Hiland, George S.

Hildabrand, Carl
Hileman, Arthur Daniel
Hill, Alva J.
Hill, Jay Ward
Hill, John
Hill, Martha M.
Hill, Samuel W.
Hinck, Dorothy A.
Hinck, Edward M.
Hinck, John A., Jr.
Hinck, Mary L.
Hinck, Robert
Hindberg, Walter
Hinkley, Jay Augustus
Hinsche, Otto
Hobson, Henry
Hochreiter, Charles J.
Hodge, Julia M.
Hodges, Catherine Taylor
Hodges, Harry Mead
Hoffmann, Winifred
Hogenboom, David Lee
Hogenboom, Leonard Samuel
Hogenboom, Ruth Groters
Hogenboom, Stephen
Hokanson, Marie Corp
Hokanson, Mons
Holt, Jack Berger
Holt, Truman Slayton
Holy Name, Sister M.
Honor, Dorothy Y.
Honor, Herbert C.
Honor, Herbert, Jr.
Honor, Vera O.
Hood, Thomas Dewitt
Hook, Emil V.
Horgan, Gregory
Hornbostel, Johanna Mario
Horton, Frank
Hoskins, Colin Macrae
Hoyt, Jackson Leach
Hubbard, Charles R.
Hubbard, Christine

Hubbard, William Augustus
Hudson, Clay Menafee
Hudson, Lewis Clifton
Hudson, Primitiva Bertumen
Hughes, Harry Bloomfield
Hughes, Hugh John
Hughes, Russell
Hughes, Samuel Alexander
Hull, Edwin Miles
Hunt, Darcy Swain
Hunt, Phray O.
Hunter, John Jacobs
Hyland, Walter
Harpst, Earl Michael
Iddings, Paul Loren
Immaculate Concepcion, S. R. M.
Innis, Charles
Innis, David
Innis, David James
Innis, Donald
Innis, Frances
Innis, Joseph
Irvin, Tom B.
Irvine, Bessie
Irwin, Henry
Isabel, Sister M.
Jackson, Myrtle
Jacobs, Louis Welch
Jacobson, David
James, Elizabeth
Jamieson, William
Janda, Marie Wagner
Janda, Robert Lee
Jarlath, M. M. of S. T.
John, Rees Hopkin
Johnson, Cherokee Chickasaw
Johnson, Frederick Arnold
Johnson, Henry S.
Johnson, Ralph Murdoch
Johnson, Seneca O.
Johnson, Thomas W.
Johnson, Walter
Johnston, Doris

Johnston, William W.
Jones, Andy
Jones, Bernard Edwin
Jones, Charles Ernest
Jones, Elvis Everett
Jones, Ethel L.
Jones, Frank Dehaven
Jones, Muriel Gertrude
Jones, Robert Berian
Jones, William Henry
Jordan, Thomas Mark
Julian, Frederick
Juravel, Carl
Jurgenssen, August John
Jurgenssen, Jennie Grace
Justin, Sister M.
Kahler, Stannie Daniel
Kalkowsky, Adam Edward
Kapes, David
Katz, Anne
Katz, Frances Valerie
Katz, Isabella
Katz, William Allen
Kahn, Maurice
Kaminski, Nicodemus
Kavanagh, Joseph
Kay, Joseph Kerop
Kailen, Ernest
Keiley, Daniel James
Kelly, Harold Maxwell
Kemery, Mona Mae
Kemp, Oley C.
Kern, Helen
Kerr, Joseph
Ketchum, Gladys Esperanza
Keys, Harold Harte
Keys, John Dewitt
Kidder, Lucia Booth
Kidder, Stanley Rast
Kiene, Clarence Kirk
Kiene, Mildred Evelyn
Kienle, Alfred
Kilkenny, Edward Michael

King, Carl Philip
King, Josephine Cook
King, Mary Barbara
Kingsbury, Stanley Carlos
Kinn, Leo
Kinney, John Thomas
Kinsella, John Sylvester
Kitzmiller, Blaine John
Kitzmiller, Owen
Kleinpell, Robert Mensson
Klippert, Edward
Knaesche, Herman
Knowles, Sambuel Etnyre
Koestner, Alfred U. S.
Kolodziej, Antonio
Kramer, Amelia
Kramer, Donald
Kramer, Effie
Kramer, Georgette
Kramer, Harry
Knutson, Gilman Darrell
Koons, Harry Montford
Koons, Thelma Donnelly
Krause, William Owen
Kringle, Harry
Kuhlman, William Henry
Kundert, Paul Denton
Lacey, Betty
Lacey, Kristin
Lacey, Sharon
Lacey, William Edward
Lacy, Merrill Ghent
LaFouge, Edward Rudolph
Lam, Bo Ming
Lamb, William Lee
Lambert, Frederick Dankilla
Landis, Audrey Blanche
Landis, Frederic
Landis, Patricia A.
Landis, Richard
Landis, Roderic
LaPointe, William F.
LaPorte, Margaret

LaPorte, Otto
Lappin, Leslie Everett
Lauriat, Frederick
Lautzenheiser, Ora Ezra
LaVigne, Ernest Henri
Lawry, Gordon Langford
Lawton, Betty Estelle
Lawyer, Jerome
Leary, John (Jack) Thomas
Leary, Paul
Lederman, Daniel Bishop
Lee, Charlotte Kingsbury
Lee, C. W.
Lee, David
Lee, Elfred M.
Lee, Fred M.
Lee, James Milton
Lee, Margurite
LeForge, Roxy
Leighton, Ethel Packard
Leisring, Lawrence
Leitch, James Elmer
Leland, James Arthur
Leland, Rosamond Cooper
Leland, Shirley Mae
Leonarda, Sister M.
Lesage, Alphons Gerard
Lessner, Eva
Lessner, Hilda
Levy, Ruben
Lew, Wah Sun
Liggett, James Paul
Liles, Lawrence Poland
Limpert, John William
Lind, Niles John
Linn, Harold Adolphus
Lochboehler, Bernard
Logan, George Lafayette
Lombard, Harold Webster
Lombard, James Dino
Lord, Montague
Louis, George James
Lovell, Glenn Howard

Lovell, Ruth Patterson
Lowry, William Arthur
Lubarsky, Saul
Lucy, Sister Mary
Lundquist, Carl Axel
Luckman, Elsie Marion
Lyon, Herbert
McAfee, Clauda
McAfee, Leo Gay
McAfee, Robert
McAllister, Margaret
McAnlis, David
McAnlis, Jean
McAnlis, Josephine
McAnlis, Ruth
McAnlis, William
McBride, John Henry
McCaffray, Arthur
McCalister, Jacob
McCandlish, William Foster
McCann, James
McCarter, Edward Lee
McCarthy, Floyd Arthur
McCarthy, Marian Florence
McCarthy, William Ransom
McCarty, Leroy
McCarty, Edward Charles
McCloskey, Robert E.
McClure, Carl Hamlin
McClure, Ryanna
McCoy, Lois Kathleen
McCoy, May
McCoy, Oscar Gervius
McCune, Joseph Gerhardt
McDonough, Charles A.
McEntee, Samuel Sanders
McGaretty, Howard Carson
McGovern, Lee
McGrath, Peter William
McGrew, Kinsie
McGuiness, Joseph
McGuire, Grace Ann
McHugh, Patricia Willis

McIntosh, Melville Ethelbert
Mckay, Jean
McKee, Robert
McKeown, Hugh Michael
McLey, Harold J. G.
McMann, Frank Patrick
McMann, James
McMann, John
McManus, Ambrose
McMullen, Joseph
McNamara, Francis Robert
McNicholas, John
McSorley, Richard
McStay, John
McStay, John Curry
McVey, Bunnie Cecilia
McVey, Charles David
McVey, Grace Alice Mary
McVey, Mary Cecilia
Mabry, Frank M.
Mabry, Opal Marie
MacDonald, Alyse Louise
MacDonald, Bob
MacDonald, George
MacDonald, Helen
MacDonald, John
MacDonald, Kenneth
MacDonald, Margaret
MacIntosh, James
MacKinnon, James Bowie
MacLaren, Donald Ross
Madigan, Francis
Madsen, Elmer
MaGee, George Lyman
MaGee, Mary Elizabeth, Sr.
MaGee, Mary Elizabeth, Jr.
MaGee, Philip Donald
Magill, Charles Newton
Mahoney, John Joseph
Makepeace, Lloyd Brenecke
Malmstrom, Charles Clarence
Mangels, Franz
Mangels, Henry Ahrends

Mangels, John F.
Mangels, Margaretta Hermine
Mangels, Nieves
Mangels, Nieves Chofra
Mankin, James Percy
Manser, Daniel Leonard
Marcella, Sister M.
Margerita, Sister M.
Margulies, Ruben
Marion, Sister Cecilia
Marsden, Ralph Walter
Martin, Clarence
Martin, D. P.
Martin, Edgar
Massey, Charlotte
Masson, Philip
Matthew, Sister Rose
Matthews, William Jerome
Maura, Sister Bernadette
Maurashon, Sister
Maxcy, Joseph
Maxey, Wilburn
Maxwell, William Allen
Mayer, Harry O'Brien
Meagher, Bernard Joseph
Meagher, Zora Simmons
Mee, Louis
Meinhardt, Ruth
Melton, Jesse Edgar
Merrill, Robert Heath
Merritt, Isaac Erwin
Messinger, George Marion
Metz, Carmen Adoracion
Meukow, Coleman Arian
Meukow, George Osakina
Meukow, Nina Ruth
Meukow, Walter Trendal
Meyer, Gus Henry
Miles, Daniel Walter
Miles, Prentice Melvin
Miller, Charles Henry
Miller, Dorothy Veronica
Miller, Gilbert Charles

Miller, Helen
Miller, John Joseph
Miller, Maxine Margaret
Mills, John Andrew
Millward, Samuel James, Jr.
Miravalle, Andrew Nino
Miriam, Sister Agnes
Miriam, Sister Louise
Miriam, Sister Thomas
Missmer, George Washington
Missler, Carl Edward
Mitchell, John
Mitchell, Thomas
Mitchell, William Thomas
Moak, Conway Columbus
Mock, Charles Gordon
Mollart, Stanley Vincent
Monaghan, Forbes
Montesa, Anthony Joseph
Montesa, Edward William
Montesa, Henrietta F.
Montesa, John Phillip
Montgomery, Antonia Cantilo
Montgomery, Ethel Denise
Montgomery, Everett Verden
Montgomery, Fern Asunsano
Moore, Charles F.
Moore, Emma G.
Moore, George
Moore, Joseph Oliver
Moore, Joseph W.
Moore, Leonard C.
Moore, Mae Dancy
Moore, Patricia E.
Mora, Ernest Joseph
Mora, George Castro
Mora, Iberia Ortuno
Moran, Lawrence Richard
Morehouse, Francis B.
Morehouse, Phyllis Brenda
Morehouse, Winifred Louis
Morison, Walter Durrell
Morning, John

Morris, Leroy
Morrision, Carson C.
Morrision, Helena V.
Mortlock, Frank Oliver
Moss, George Herbert
Mudd, Maurice
Mueller, William Fred
Muldoon, Anthony Gregory
Mulry, Joseph
Mulryan, Alma Steiger
Mulryan, James Raymond
Munger, Henry Weston
Munger, Louralee Patrick
Murphin, William
Murphy, John Joseph
Murray, William Elmer
Myers, Kenneth Robert
Myers, William Tyner
Naftaly, Lillian Saidee
Naftaly, Nancy Nataly
Naido, Joseph
Naido, Ruth Louise
Nance Dana Wilson
Nash, Gail Blackmarr
Nash, Grace Chapman
Nash, Margaret Alice
Nash, Ralph
Nash, Ralph Stanley
Nash, Roy Leslie
Nathanson, Nathaniel Arthur
Nau, Catherine Ludwina
Neal, James
Neal, Pauline
Neibert, Alice Julia
Neibert, Henry Edward
Neikam, William L.
Nelson, Thomas Page
Nelson, Valley
Newcomb, Water Cattell
Newgord, Julius Gerard
Nicholas, John Middleton
Nichols, John Randolph
Nichols, Leonard David

Nicholson, James Francis
Nicholson, John
Nicholson, William
Nicol, Celeste Claire
Nicol, Charles Bertram
Nicol, Fedora Mary
Nicol, Jacqueline Winifred
Nicol, Normal Arthur
Nicoll, David
Nokes, Wilbur Charles
Norton, Alfred
Nuger, Isaac
Nuttall, Edmond
O'Boirne, Vincent
O'Brien, John Robert
O'Brien, Michael Wilbur
Obst, Thomas James
O'Conner, Clarence
Ode, Carsten Linnevold
O'Hara, Kathleen F.
O'Hara, Lorraine Betty
O'Hara, Michael Joseph
O'Hara, Michael Joseph, Jr.
O'Haver, Goldie Aimee
Ogan, William Clarence
Olivette, Sister M.
Olsen, Lillian Agnes
O'Malloy, John Bryan
O'Neill, James
Oppenheimer, John
Osbon, Bert Paul
O'Shaughnessy, Martin
Oss, Norman Alfred, Jr.
O'Toole, John Patrick
Overton, Elbert Monroe
Owens, Hoyle Williams
Pacheco, Michael Angelo
Paget, Cyrus
Paige, Eldene Elinor
Palmatier, Ellery Leroy
Palmer, Clarence Hugh
Palmer, Mildred Ailene
Pangborn, Wallace

Parham, Archer Brandon
Parker, Bertha F.
Parker, Bertha Helena
Parker, Helen Dorothy
Parker, Roy Lester
Parker, Wilbur Clarke
Parquette, William Stewart
Parish, Edward John, Jr.
Passmore, Fred J.
Patricia, Sister M.
Patricia, Sister Marie
Patterson, Myron
Pauli, Ralph
Pawley, Charles-Thomas
Pearlman, Max O.
Pearson, Cecil Leroy
Peck, Lawrence Leroy
Peek, Elvin Roland
Penny, Harold Ray
Pepper, Charles John
Perfecta, Sister
Perkins, Willie Ray
Perry, Walter Lee Gihon
Pflug, Emma
Philip, Dorothy Suzanne
Phillips, Eleanor Marie
Phillips, Howard Lester, Sr.
Phillips, Howard Lester, Jr.
Pickell, William H.
Pickens, Henri B.
Pickering, Camille Elaine
Pickering, John Kuykendall
Pierce, Margaret Helen
Pirassoli, Charles William
Pitcher, Susie Josephine
Plowman, Claire Elizabeth
Plowman, Elizabeth Oxford
Plowman, George Harden
Pohl, Gordon Robert
Pollard, Harriet Emma
Pond, Helen
Porter, Lloyd Thomas
Posner, Irving

Precino, Thomas
Preiser, Rosa Christian
Preston, Rose Marie
Price, Walter Scott
Priestner, Joseph
Purnell, John Ferguson
Purnell, Lillian Cottrell
Putney, Harry Bryan
Quillinan, Frank William
Quinn, Grant
Raleigh, Daniel Mead
Rand, Grace
Rast, Beni
Ratcliffe, Jesse Walker
Raymond, Mona
Reardon, Francis
Redard, Alexander James
Redempta, Sister M.
Reich, Bertha Harris
Reid, William Robert
Reilly, Matthew
Reinhart, James H.
Reith, Joseph
Repetti, William
Repikoff, John
Reuter, James
Rey, Sister Maria del
Reynolds, Ralph Leonard
Rhudie, Ada Woodsworth
Rhuide, Oscar Peter
Rice, Williard Lamont
Richards, Edwin Franklin
Richards, Mary Fielding
Riddle, Henry Hampton
Rider, Frank Jackson
Riffel, Dorothy Ann
Riffel, Esther N.
Riffel, Gordon William
Riffel, Retta Leona
Riffel, William E.
Riley, Charles
Rively, William
Rivers, William Richard

Rizzuti, Oarm
Robert Marie, Sister
Roberts, Elizabeth
Roberts, Galien Sofia
Roberts, Odin Gregory
Robertson, Joseph H.
Robie, Merle Steel
Robinson, Charles A.
Robinson, Graham Post
Robinson, Leslie D.
Robinson, Roberta May
Rodgers, Frances
Roebuck, Brooks Waldo
Roebuck, May Ephrom
Roehr, Oscar Carl
Roehr, Pauline Marie
Roeper, Ludwig Earl
Rohrbaugh, Olive
Rohrer, Helen Brian
Rohrer, Samuel Lewis
Rosabella, Sister
Roscom, Jerry Nicholas
Rose, Sister Catherine
Rose Jude, Sister
Rose Marie, Sister
Rosella, Sister
Rosenthal, Leon
Rosier, Warren
Ross, Ervin Clinton
Ross, George
Ross, Gladys Mary
Ross, Lillian
Routhier, George Silvio
Rowland, M. Elston
Ruane, John
Runyon, Richard Earl
Rurka, Steve
Russell, Aida B.
Russell, Diana Marie
Russell, Earl Edwin
Russell, Theresa White
Ryall, Theodore Lee, Jr.
Rydberg, Carl Gunnar

Safino, Esther A.
Sager, Frederick James
Salamy, Abraham George
Salet, Elizabeth Ann
Salter, Russell
Samara, Edward Thomas
Samara, Saleem George
Sams, Gerald R.
Sampson, James Stewart
Sanborn, Donald George
Sanders, Albert J.
Sanders, David J.
Sanders, Edna F.
Sanders, Florence Smith
Sanders, Phillip Herman
Sands, Martin Paul
Sands, Mildred Marie
Satterfield, Frederick Malone
Saunders, Emma
Saunders, Frank, Sr.
Saunders, Frank, Jr.
Saunders, Norma Louise
Sayre, Bruce
Scaff, Alvin Hewitt
Scaff, Lawrence A.
Scaff, Mary Lee
Scarlett, Jane Agnes
Scarlett, William John
Schechter, Seymour
Scheidl, Rudolph John
Scherer, Doris
Scherer, Morris C.
Scherer, Richard
Schermerhorn, William H.
Scheuermann, Dennis Friday
Scheuermann, Gustav John
Scheuermann, Gwendolyn Marta
Scheuermann, Helen Friday
Schier, Kathleen Grant
Schier, Samuel Saunders
Schmidt, Richard Joseph
Scholastica, Sister M.
Schoppe, Leonard Albert

Schoppe, Lillian A.

Schroeder, Louis

Schorth, Max Brune

Schubert, Edward C.

Schuster, Helene Jeanete

Schuster, Helene Rothmeister

Schuster, John Howard

Schworer, Donald Valentine

Scofield, Donald Eugene

Scott, Elizabeth Steele

Scott, Joe Edwin

Scott, Lyle Cecil

Seals, Margaret Mildred

Sechrist, David P.

Sechrist, Harold

Sechrist, John W.

Sechrist, Marguerite

Shaffer, William Robert

Shapiro, Herman

Shaw, Herbert Wesley

Shaw, Kate Sibley

Shaw, Walter Ray

Sherk, David Robert

Sherk, Gerry Ann

Sherk, Margaret Coulson

Shimmel, Edith

Shoemaker, Abbott Paul

Shropshire, Harry Wesley

Shurdut, Joseph Moses

Siena, Sister M.

Silen, Elizabeth Jean

Silen, Joan Bradford

Silen, Margaret Elizabeth

Silen, Shirley Ann

Silloway, Merle

Simatovich, Nicholas Joseph

Simmons, Ernest Edgeworth

Sklenar, Anthony Joseph

Small, Elizabeth Studavant

Small, Frank Sylvester

Small, Helen Elizabeth

Smallwood, Robert

Smith, Alfred Whitacre

Smith, B. Ward

Smith, Dewey Woods

Smith, Harry Josselyn

Smith, Harry Thurston

Smith, Joseph John

Smith, Paul L.

Smith, Stephen L.

Smith, Viola R.

Smith, Willard Horace

Smoyer, Egbert M.

Snead, Elizabeth B.

Snead, Mary Carol

Snead, Paul Kindig

Snead, Paul Laurence

Sniffen, Genevieve Marie

Sniffen, John Mark

Snyder, Gaines

Snyder, Mary Lucille

Snyder, William Raymond

Soares, John Stanislas

Sottile, Frank Joseph

Spatz, Oswald

Spear, Earl Franklin

Spencer, William Meek

Spencer, William Robert

Sperry, Henry M.

Stacy, Gertrude Rosie

Stahl, Alfred Joaquin

Stancliff, Leo

Stark, Clarence Theo

Starr, John Bernal

Stearns, Mary Jean Stephens

Steffens, Raymond Harold

Steven, Oswald Barnard

Stevens, Leslie Eugene

Steward, Basilia Torres

Stewart, John Norman

Stiver, Edna Theresa

Stiver, Joseph Alfred

Stocking, Charles Samuel

Stokes, Henry Milton

Stoll, Eugene Leo

Stoneburner, Edna

Strong, James Walter
St. Thomas, Federico, Jr.
Stuart, David Lennox
Stubo, Knutty Christian
Stumbo, John David
Stump, Irene J.
Stump, Lawrence
Stumpf, William Jerome, Jr.
Sturm, Stanley Marcellus
Sudhoff, Raymond George
Sullivan, Edward
Sullivan, Russell
Suro, Reuben
Swanson, Ruth Pauline
Sykora, Frank
Tabor, John
Tapia, Edwin Joseph Jones
Taylor, William Leonard
Taylor, Willis L.
Tekippe, Owen
Terrill, Thomas Star
Terry, Albert Henry
Terry, Carol Louise (Talbot)
Terry, Joseph Edward
Teurnee, Maurice Conrad
Theophila, Sister M.
Theudere, M. Mary of S. P.
Thomas, Antonita B.
Thomas, Dollie Mae
Thomas, Florence A.
Thomas, Howard Wilton
Thomas, Robert Lee
Thompson, David Bill
Thompson, Floyd Addison
Thompson, Leslie Daniel
Tinling, Don
Titlow, Marian Phillips
Todd, Carrie Edwina
Todd, George, Jr.
Todd, Noel
Todebush, Ralph Bernard
Tootle, Mildred Caroline
Torkeson, Edward

Treubig, John F.
Tribble, Jesse Lee
Trogstad, Martha Bowler
Tuck, Ernest E.
Tuck, Helen G.
Tuite, Thomas
Tulloch, James Garfield, Jr.
Tulloch, William James
Tutten, Daniel Eugene
Ullman, Frank
Ullman, Tamara Alexis
Urquhardt, Edward J.
Urquhardt, Maud J.
Urquhardt, Stanley P.
Vandenburg, Charles Osborn
Vandenplas, Pierre Gaston
Vernick, Joseph Barry
Vicroy, Sigle Allen
Villar, Charles Herman
Vincent, Louis Lester
Vinson, Olivert Castille
Vinson, Thomas Chalmers
Vitalis, Sister Mary
Vogelgesang, John
Von Hess, Jack C.
Voss, William Frederick
Wagelie, Cunval Andreas
Wagner, John Robert
Wagner, Rudolph
Wahlgreen, Beulah King
Walker, Alfred Francis
Walker, Harold
Walker, Orian Love
Wallace, Frank Byron
Waples, James Francis
Ward, William Vines
Wareham, Johnson Matthew
Warner, Carl
Warner, Mary Delilah
Warren, Fred Prince
Warren, Harry Pre
Waterstradt, Albert Edward
Wathen, John David

Webster, Walter, Jr.
Weems, Alexander Murray
Weibel, Mary Eileen
Weil, Charles William
Welborn, George
Welch, Leo
Wells, James
Wells, Jessie
Wenetzki, Charles Eduard
West, Glenn Key
West, Hester D.
Wester, Arthur W.
Westmoreland, Graham Bradley
Westmoreland, Victoria Maria
Wheeler, Hiram Albert L.
Wheeler, Ida Ellen
Wheeler, Robert Antony
Wheeler, Robert J. M.
Whitaker, Evelyn Eddy
Whitaker, Helen Elizabeth
Whitaker, Jocelyn Alfred
Whitaker, Margaret Evelyn
Whitaker, Septimus Tom B.
White, George Henry, Jr.
White, Nathaniel Walker
Whitesides, John Garrett
Whitmoyer, George Irwin
Wichman, Daniel Lee
Wichman, Douglas
Wichman, Ernest Hermsen
Wichman, Gladys Caroline
Widdoes, Alice S.
Widdoes, H.W.
Wienke, Carl Ludwig
Wienke, Carmen Aurora
Wienke, Edward Peter
Wienke, Elizabeth Carmen
Wienke, Frederick Johan
Wienke, Mercie Christina
Wienke, Theresa Victoria
Wienke, Violet Alma
Wilcox, Lyle
Wilcox, Wendel

Wilder, Charlie
Wiley, Samuel
Williams, Clyde Scott
Williams, Gordon L.
Williams, Greta R.
Williams, Jack
Williams, Leona H.
Williams, Roy Harold
Willmann, George J.
Wills, Hugh Clarence
Wills, Ida Gertrude
Wills, Jane S.
Wilson, Anita Marie
Wilson, Edward John
Wilson, Harold Norman
Wilson, James Reese
Wilson, Jesse Smith
Wilson, John
Wilson, John Brownlee
Wilson, Wilbur Scott
Winn, Charles Robert
Winn, Ethel May
Winship, S. Davis
Winsor, Christine
Wislizenus, Claire Alberton
Wittman, Arthur Carl
Wolff, Charles
Wolfe, Carrie A.
Wolfe, Leslie
Wolfgram, Ida Mae
Wolfgram, Leroy Herbert
Wood, Joseph Palmer
Woodin, Charles Wesley
Woodrooff, William Dickey
Woods, Robert Gordon
Woodworth, Ruth A.
Workman, Doris Therese
Workman, George Welman
Workman, Helen Marie
Workman, Katherine Marie
Workman, Lillian Ann
Workman, Mildred Josephine
Worthen, Helen Margaret

Worthen, Thomas Roy
Wright, Lourdes Dizon
Wright, Randall William
Wright, Tobias Henry
Yankey, Mary Louise Curran
Yankey, William Ross
Yarborough, Alta Lenna
Yarborough, Henry Edward, Jr.
Yard, Lester Hollaster
Yartz, John
Yearsley, Helen Ellison
Young, Robert Alexander
Young, Roman
Young, William H.
Zervoulakos, Alfred Gregory
Zigler, William McKinley
Zillig, Martin

### British

Aaron, Jean Margaret
Aaron, John David
Aaron, John Maurice
Airiess, Eric Mather
Aitkens, John Reginald
Albine, Sister
Aldred, Herbert
Allen, Constance
Allen, Elizabeth
Allen, Margaret
Allen, Phillip
Anderson, David
Andrews, Nadia
Andrews, Ronald V.
Arnovick, Charles
Arnovick, George M.
Arnovick, Mary M.
Azevedo, Beatrice
Azevedo, Olga
Bairgrie, Alexander
Baigrie, Bertha
Baildon, Aimee
Balfour, William
Balis, David

Balis, Jenny
Barnes, Katherine
Barnes, Kenneth
Barnes, Robert
Barnes, William Frank
Barr, Fiona
Barr, Margaret
Barr, Ronald
Barrett, Cecil
Beck, Arthur Charlesworth
Beebee, Walter Willis
Beeman, Sarah
Behenna, Dorothy
Bennett, Lillian
Bentley, Edward
Birchall, James Richardson
Black, James
Blair, Leslie
Blechynden, Lindsey DeClarke
Boddington, Dorothy
Boddington, Richard John
Bonner, Norman Ellis
Bosch, Edward Henry Brett
Boswell, George James
Bradshaw, John William
Brambles, Elizabeth
Brambles, Grace
Brambles, James Christopher
Brambles, Margaret Lillian
Brambles, Patricia
Brambles, Ralph
Brambles, Ralph Douglas
Bramwell, Edward Kennedy
Bramwell, Helen L.
Breson, Lillian
Brewster, Charles
Brooks, Anna
Brooks, Cyril H.
Brooks, Kenneth S.
Brooks, Leonard C.
Brooks, Rose E.
Buckberrough, Rosa
Buhler, Charles

Burn, Robert
Burn, William Angus
Bush, Edward Stanley
Cameron, John Fraser
Celestine, Sister M.
Chapman, Maurice Bonham
Chong, Charles
Christian, Frederick
Clark, Wallace Robert
Clarke, Esther Millicent
Clarke, Evelyn Victoria
Cohen, Florence Frances
Corfield, Isla
Corfield, Gillian I.
Corley, Thomas Ekstrom
Coxon, Jane Margaret
Crabbe, Kenneth Murray
Creech, Henry
Crewe, James
Curtis, John Shearme
Dalgleish, Mabel Emily
Dalgleish, Mabel Margaret
Da Silva, Augustus
D'Authreau, John Harold
Dickson, Elsa Fanny
Dodd, Gloria Lydia
Dodd, Reginald Morris
Dodd, Zina Andreevna
Dolores, Sister Maria
Donald, William
Dos Remedios, Henry Joseph
Douglas, William
Doull, Agnes
Doull, William
Dow, James Frederick
Drysdale, Thomas Douglas
Duncan, Ian Murray
Dwyer, Thomas
Ethelburga, Sister M.
Fairweather, James Edwin
Falkner, Angeles Martin
Falkner, James Albert
Falkner, Ronald D.

Fitzgerald, Desmond S.
Fox, Catherine Mary
Fox, Charles James
Fox, Christopher Charles
Fox, Lawrence
Fox, Patrick James
Fox, Stephen George
Frampton, Amy Beatrice
Frampton, Muriel
Freckleton, Thomas
Geddes, Eric
Geddes, Jean Frances
Gertrude, Sister Lane Fox
Gillett, Bertram John
Gordon, Mary
Gordon, Matthew Dobie
Grant, Helen Gordon
Gray, Irene Betty
Green, Louisa
Green, Michael John
Greenland, Lucy Violet
Griffith, Owen Ambrose
Grimmant, David Henry
Haigh, Annie
Haigh, Jesse
Haigh, Renee Mary
Haigh, Victor Alfred
Hails, Henry Forster
Hallowes, Elsie Mary
Hamblett, James
Hanson, Frank Raymond
Hardcastle, Charles Otterson
Harris, William Francis Geo.
Hayes, Jean
Hayes, Kathleen Elizabeth
Hayes, Michael Aloysius
Haymes, Maxwell Freeland L.
Hearn, Martin Everard
Hill, Rowland George
Hodges, Arthur J.
Hodges, Eleanora
Hoey, Richard C.
Hoey, Ruth C.

Hollyer, William George
Horridge, George Redvers
Hughes, Donald Francis
Humphries, John Hugh
Hurley, Patrick
Hutchison, David Dick
Irvine, Jean
Ismail, Sheil Salim
Jackson, James Gregory
Jamieson, Stewart
Jaques, Stanley Heath
Jay, John Leslie
John, Dorothy A.
John, Helen M.
John, Kathleen Elizabeth
John, May
Jones, Henry Victor
Jordan, Kathleen Agnes
Kane, John William James
Kay, Aubony Taylor
Kennedy, Eileen
Kennedy, Erna V.
Kennedy, Kathleen M.
Kennedy, Robert C.
Kennedy, Robert C., Jr.
Kew, Cecil
King, Agnes Isabel
King, Charles Forrester
Kotliar, Betty
Lee, Anise
Legg, John Alexander
Leith, Henry Earl
Leith, Mair
Leith, Rosemary
Leyshon, Frank Howard
Ligertwood, Charles Liddell
Lloyds, Edwin William
McClure, Lawrence Maxton
McGinness, Thomas John
McGregor, Robin
McKerchar, Ian
McLeod, Hugh
McMaster, John Wilson

McMaster, Norah Helen
McWhirter, Hugh Fergus
MacIntyre, Norah Peal
MacIntyre, Ronald
MacKay, Kathleen Mary M.
MacLaren, William Hart
MacLean, Hector James Hilder
MacLean, Margaret
MacWilliam, Jean Cowan Shanks
MacWilliam, Richard Niven
MacWilliam, Scott
Malcolm, Harry Redd
Malpas, William Richard J.
Mann, William Ronald
Mather, William Gladston
Maxima, Sister M.
Meadows, Gordon
Medina, Elfrida Elizabeth
Miller, Charles Walter
Miller, David Carlton
Miller, Patricia Ann
Miller, Robert Walker
Miller, Vera Alexandra
Moore, Calvert Hildabrand
Morley, Howard
Morris, Robert Owen
Morrison, Geoffrey Lionel
Morrison, Robert Alexander
Naismith, William Cunningham
Nathanson, Jean L.
Nathanson, Marie Emsley
Nelson, Archibald Graham
Newgord, Esther
Newsome, Peter Noel Vesey
Nicolson, John
Norton-Smith, Kenneth James
Oliver, Violet Lillian
Palmer, Bertha Lucy
Palmer, John Blything
Palmer, Ronald Singleton
Parker, Herman Vercomb
Parquette, Rosemarie Dorothy
Paterson, James

Paterson, Mary D.
Patey, Walter Bruce
Particia, M. M.
Pedder, Gerald Herbert
Pedersen, Gwendolyn Florence
Perry, David Henry
Philomena, Sister Marie
Piatnitsky, Olga Pavlovna
Piercy, Arthur
Pollard, Arnold
Pollock, Yvonne Celia
Pope, Harvey Collie
Porter, Robert John
Price, Arthur
Price, Elizabeth Sible
Price, William Samuel
Prismail, Allen
Proudfoot, Alexander
Prout, James Ormand
Quinn, Bernard Alphonsus
Redfern, Foster
Reich, Joseph
Reid, George William
Richardson, William Bryan
Robertson, Howard Laird
Roche, Barbara Pavlovna
Roche, Mary Roberta
Rodda, Hababah
Rodgers, Albert G.
Rodgers, Marcus G.
Rodgers, Rosa N.
Royston, John
Rushton, George
Rushton, Violet Edith
Ryde, Sonia
Sawyer, Paula Adelatie
Schelkunoff, Vladimir Peter
Scott, David Alexander
Serephins, Sister Mary of the
Sinclair, Jeffrey Whitfeld
Small, William Valentine
Smith, Arthur Linton
Smith, George Albert

Smith, Joan Marie
Smith, John Alwynne George L.
Smith, Louis
Smith, William A.
Spackman, Harold C.
Spackman, Winifred D.
Steel, James Laurie
Stephens, Sydney
Stratton, Joseph Grant L.
Strong, Martin
Symonds, John
Templer, Angela Mary
Templer, Ann Hazel
Templer, James Robert
Templer, Jennifer S.
Thomson, Elizabeth Marie
Thomson, Robert Allison
Tomkin, Anna Georgvina
Tonkin, Marguerite Janet A.
Tonkin, Matthew McNair
Tonkin, William Charles Geo.
Turner, William
Tyre, Alexander James
Watson, William
Watt, Effie Margaret
Watt, Olive Charlotte
Watty, Lewis Thomas
Webb, Frank Hardy
Whittal, Henry Cecil
Wightman, Arthur John
Wightman, Eglington John
Wightman, Ethelgiva Frances
Wightman, Irene Nellie
Wightman, William Dana
Willder, Katie Agnes
Williams, Hugh Hosking
Williams, John Joseph
Williamson, Margaret
Wilson, Ian Thurburn
Wilson, Walter James
Windle, Wilfred Edwin
Wood, Charles John
Wooding, Wilfred

Wright, Arthur
Wulfildan, M. M.
Yewen, Nina Efgenievna
Zacharias, Hans

## Australian
Bargallo, Amelia
Bargallo, Salvadora
Best, Francis
Blanchard, Mary
Byrne, Joseph
Cruice, William
Deane, Patrick
Dougherty, John Hercules
English, Leo
Gygar, Andrew
Holt, Bridget Trist
Holt, Edna May
Hughes, Allen John
Jackson, Gordon
Kemp, Joy Elizabeth
Laycock, Kathleen
Laycock, William Murray B.
McCarthy, Charles
McGuire, Mary Kathleen
MacMaster, John Dunlop
Nield, Frederick Bodin
O'Donnell, Gerard
Pinkerton, Stanley Corey
Pinkerton, Velma
Richards, Thomas Robert
Ridley, John Edwin
Sagor, Amy Lida
Sexton, Francis
Smith, Flora Beryl
Taylor, Betsy Doris
Taylor, Charles
Thomas, George Frederick
Walsh, Francis

## Canadian
Abarista, Sister Mary
Alphonse, de Ligori

Angeline, Sister Mary
Ann Celine, Sister Saint
Ann Marie, Sister
Arcand, Ulric
Begin, Joseph
Benoit, Mother Mary of Saint
Bernard, Sister M.
Bleau, Albert
Brouillard, Rodrigue
Charter, Catherine
Charter, Luckey Kathleen
Charter, Thomas Henry
Christophe, Soeur Saint
Clotilde, Sister M.
Dalmis, Michael
Desmarais, Camille
Everista, Mother
Frician, Sister M.
Gabriel, Sister De-Anuncion
Gabriel, Sister S.
Geofferey, Joseph
Gustav, Sister Saint
Harper, Ella Mae
Hodgson, Francis Xavier
Holloway, Glen Irwin
Humphries, Robert Maxwell
Jarry, Andre
Jepson, Leon Baynes
Joseph de Bethlehem, Sister
Lawton, Herbert
Loptson, Adulsufinn Magnus
Loptson, Faith C.
McCullough, Henry
McKenney, Warren Evans
McKenzie, Catherine
Madeline Marie Barrat, Sister
Marie de Preciux Sang, Sister
Mathiew, Soeur Saint
Maurice, Sister Mary
Mooney, Luke Henry
Murphy, William J.
Nicol, Arthur Louis
Paget, Kathleen M.

Paget, Margaret E. J.
Paget, William H. W.
Palmer, Blanche Evelyn
Philp, George Ansel
Pierre Claver, Sr. S.
Rene, M. M.
Rosemonde, M. M.
Shaw, Alice Florence (Beyes)
Victorice, M. M. of Saint
Williams, William C.
Ymer, M. M. de Saint

### Netherlands
Aalten, Hans van
Alarda, Sister M.
Albana, Sister N.
Aldenhuysen, Godfred
Alice, Sister M.
Alphonsa, Sister M.
Anastasia, Sister M.
Bathildis, Sister M.
Bieschop, Roosegaade J. Philip
Blans, Thomas
Blewanus, Gerard
Boggiam, Max
Borght, Francisco van der
Bos, Maria Theresa
Burer, John
Cajetani, Sister M.
Canisia, Sister M.
Coenders, John
Corsten, Andrew
Croonen, Joseph
Decorata, Sister
DeHaan, Isaac
Dekker, John
DeWit, E.
Donata, M.
Dyk, Francisco van
Egonia, Sister M.
Engelen, Felite van
Es, Roelof van
Evangelista, Sister M.

Fransen, Martinus
Gentila, Sister M.
Glansbeek, Reinier van
Groonen, Josef
Groot, Petrus
Hagen, Jan van
Hartog, William
Hendricks, Nicholas Wilhelmus
Houben, Arnold
Intven, Joseph
Janssens, Alberta
Janssens, Marius Cornelus
Jonkerguuw, Hubertus Josephus
Joseph, M.
Jurgens, Constans (Bishop)
Keet, Teodoro
Kemperman, Richard
Kilb, Antony
Loo, Cornelio van der
Lutgardis, M.
Magdala, Sister M.
Margretta, Sister M.
Mees, Gregory
Mees, William
Michels, Derk Aw.
Modesta, Sister M.
Notenboom, Jacobus Cornlis
Odyk, Anton van
Oomen, Antonius Paulus
Opstal, Van William
Polycarpa, Sister M.
Raben, Karel Hendrik
Reimers, Christian Hendrik
Reoinjen, Henricus van
Ruyter, Jan
Schaeffer, Johannes Henricus
Slangen, Peter
Sleegers, Henry
Smits, Andrianus
Steyger, Adrianus
Tangelder, Gerardo
Timp, Pedro John
Tonus, Cornelio

Trienekens, Gerardus F.
Van der List, Petrus J.
Van Overveld, Antonio
Van Vlierden, Constant Matthys
Verhoven, Joseph
Vincent, Jacobus
Vlasvelo, Pedro
Vrakking, Johan
Werff, Alice Catherine
Werff, Milagros Herrera
Werff, Pieter Hildebrand
Werff, Wanda Oliva
Werkhoven, Jacobux
Willemina, M.
Willemsen, Bernardus J.
Zegwaard, Francis Henry

### Norwegian

Aanonsen, Nels Marion
Abrahamsen, Blarne William
Christensen, Yugvar Kjell
Eilertsen, Thomas
Einarsen, Ruben Helmer
Monsen, Olaf
Oyen, Nils
Pedersen, Erling Bjoern
Petersen, Knut Selmer
Petersen, Trygve

### Polish

Adelski, Borys
Bieniarz, Edward
Gang, Samuel Sam
Hirschorn, Marcus
Keller, Harry
Krzewinski, Ludwig
Lerner, Helen
Lounsbury, Irene Olshenke
Mingelgruen, Wilhelm
Neuman, Rudolph Ham
Propper, Norbert
Rabinowicz, Icko
Rabinowicz, Mordchal

Sackiewicz, Alexander
Sackiewicz, Wladyslaw
Sielski, Wladyslaw
Sielski-Jones, Yadwiga Teresa
Soroka, Samuel Chaim
Strzalkowski, Henry
Szpigielman, Marek
Wahraaftig, Oswald
Werbner, Izydor

### Italian

Bulli, Angelo
Coll-Mellini, Helen
Ghigliotti, Giuseppe
Ghigliotti, Lourdes
Gircognini Lorenzo
Gircognini, Manuela
Gircognini, Maria Lisa
Gislon, Antonio
Givseppefranco, Altomonte
Mellini, Rudolph
Vigano, Angelo
Vigano, Augusto
Vigano, Camilla
Vigano, Frederico
Vigano, Maria
Vigano, Tuillo

### Nicaraguan

Carcamo, Carmelo Noguera

### French

Dreyfus, Jules

# Bibliography

Adevoso, Eleuterio "Terry" L. Recollections of Thirty Years Ago: Second World War. Years in Southern Luzon. Unpublished.

Adevoso, Eleuterio Lavengco. *A Personal Story: 50 Years*. Manila, PI: Guaranty Press Inc., 1989.

After Action Report. "The Los Baños Operations." General Headquarters, U.S. Philippine Island Forces, Hunters–ROTC Guerrillas, March 18, 1945.

Agoncillo, Teodoro A. *The Fateful Years: Japan's Adventure in the Philippines, 1941–45*. Manila, PI: R. P. Garcia Publishing Company, 1963.

Alexander, Larry. *Shadows in the Jungle: The Alamo Scouts Behind Japanese Lines in World War II*. New York: NAL Caliber, 2009.

Allen, Robert Coleman. Philippine War Diary: A Prison Camp Saga. Unpublished manuscript, 1991.

Armamento, V. Brigoli. *The Indomitable*. Pasay City, PI: The Viking, 1972.

Arthur, Anthony. *Deliverance at Los Banos*. New York: St. Martin's Press, 1985.

Baclagon, Uldarico S. *Filipino Heroes of World War II*. Manila, PI: Argo Printing & Publishing House, 1980.

———. *Military History of the Philippines*. Manila, PI: St. Mary's Publishing, 1975.

Beaber, Herman, and John S. Beaber. *Deliverance! It Has Come!* Global Publishing Bureau, 2001.

Bernardo, Fernando A. "UPLB: A Century of Challenges and Achievements." Manila, PI: University of the Philippines Los Baños Alumni Association, Inc.

Blackledge, David W. The Liberation of Los Baños. Unpublished manuscript, 1969.

Blair, Clay, Jr. *Silent Victory: The U.S. Submarine War Against Japan*. Annapolis, MD: Naval Institute Press, 1981.

Brackman, Arnold C. *The Other Nuremberg: The Untold Story of the Toyko War Crimes Trial*. New York: Morrow, 1987.

Breuer, William B. *Retaking the Philippines*. New York: St. Martin's Press, 1986.

———. *Geronimo! American Paratroopers in World War II*. New York: St. Martin's Press, 1991.

Brines, Russell. *Until They Eat Stones*. New York: J. B. Lippincott Co., 1944.

Brown, Katherine Ellis. Diary of Katherine Ellis Brown (Vittaly). Unpublished.

Bruce, Colin John. *Invaders: British and American Experience of Seaborne Landings 1939–1945*. Annapolis, MD: Naval Institute Press, 1999.

Burgess, Henry A. *Looking Back: A Wyoming Rancher Remembers the 11th Airborne and the Raid on Los Baños*. Missoula, MT: Pictorial Histories Publishing Company, 1993.

———. Reminiscences of the 11th Airborne Division Raid on Los Baños. Unpublished manuscript, 1981.

Burgess, Mary. *Both Sides of the Canvas*. Bloomington, IN: AuthorHouse, 2004.

Calhoun, Alex. Remarks Made to the Committee by Colonel Utunomiya. Unpublished memorandum, May 31, 1943.

Cates, Tressa, R.N. *Infamous Santo Tomás*. San Marcos, CA: Pacific Press, 1981.

Clayton, James D. *The Years of MacArthur, Volume 2, 1941–45*. Boston: Houghton Mifflin, 1975.

Cogan, Frances B. *Captured: The Japanese Internment of American Civilians in the Philippines*. Athens, GA: University of Georgia Press, 2000.

Colman, Sister M. Internment in Manila, Los Baños, PI. Unpublished.

Crouter, Natalie. *Forbidden Diary*. New York: Burt Franklin & Co., 1980.

Custodio, Jose Antonio. "The Destruction of Batangas." *History from the People, Vol. 4*. Manila, PI: National Historical Institute, 1999.

Danner, Dorothy Still. *What a Way to Spend a War: Navy Nurse POWs in the Philippines*. Annapolis, MD: Naval Institute Press, 1995.

Devlin, Gerard M. *Paratrooper!* New York: St. Martin's Press, 1979.

Doherty, George. The Souls of the Valiant. Unpublished.

Dilley, Michael F. *Behind the Lines: A Critical Survey of Special Operations in World War II*. Havertown, PA: Casemate Publishers, 2013.

Dissette, Edward, and Hans Christian Adamson. *Guerrilla Submarines*. New York: Bantam Books, 1980.

Edwards, Buck. *P.O.W.—A Philippine Odyssey*. Portland, OR: Benjamin F. Edwards III, 2013.

Eichelberger, Robert L. *Dear Miss Em: General Eichelberger's War in the Pacific, 1942–1945*. Westport, CT: Greenwood Press, 1972.

———. *Our Jungle Road to Tokyo*. Nashville, TN: Battery Press, 1989.

Elleman, Bruce. *Japanese-American Civilian Prisoner Exchanges and Detention Camps, 1941–45*. New York: Routledge, 2006.

Ewing, Alice Damberg. *Courage and Deliverance: Our Mother's Story*. Coralville, IA: F. E. P. International, 2006.

Fessler, Diane Burke. *No Time for Fear: Voices of American Military Nurses in World War II*. East Lansing, MI: Michigan State University Press, 1996.

Flanagan, E. M., Jr. *Airborne: A Combat History of American Airborne Forces*. Novato, CA: Presidio Press, 2003.

———. *The Angels: A History of the 11th Airborne Division.* Novato, CA: Presidio Press, 1989.

———. *The Los Baños Raid.* Novato, CA: Presidio Press, 1986.

Francisco, Rino A. "The Agony of Laguna: Japanese Reprisals Against Civilians During the Occupation." *History from the People, Vol. 4.* Manila: National Historical Institute, 1999.

Friend, Theodore. *Between Two Empires: The Ordeal of the Philippines, 1929–1946.* New Haven, CT, and London: Yale University Press, 1968.

Ginn, John L. *Sugamo Prison, Toyko.* Jefferson, NC: McFarland & Co, 1992.

Gleeck, Lewis. E., Jr. *The Manila Americans 1901–1964.* Manila, PI: Carmelo & Bauerman, Inc., 1977.

Halsema, James. "The Liberation of the Los Baños Internment Camp." *Bulletin of the American Historical Collection,* July/Sept. 1987.

Hanayama, Shinsho. *The Way of Deliverance: Three Years with the Condemned Japanese War Criminals.* New York: Charles Scribner's Sons, 1950.

Harclerode, Peter. *Wings of War: Airborne Warfare 1918–1945.* London: Weidenfeld & Nicolson, 2005.

Hartendorp, A. V. H. *The Santo Tomás Story.* New York: McGraw-Hill, 1965.

Holland, Robert B. *100 Miles to Freedom: The Epic Story of the Rescue of Santo Tomás and the Liberation of Manila: 1943–1945.* New York: Turner Publishing, 2011.

Holmes, Linda Goetz. *Unjust Enrichment: How Japan's Companies Built Postwar Fortunes Using American POWs.* Mechanicsburg, PA: Stackpole Books, 2001.

Horn, Dorothy John. The Cage: A Memoir and Diary of a Young Girl's Internment in World War II. Unpublished manuscript.

Hunt, Ray C., and Bernard Norling. *Behind Japanese Lines: An American Guerrilla in the Philippines.* Lexington, KY: University Press of Kentucky, 1986.

Huston, James A. *Out of the Blue: U.S. Army Airborne Operations in World War II.* West Lafayette, IN: Purdue University Press, 1999.

Ingles, Gustavo C. *Memoirs of Pain.* Manila, PI. Mauban Heritage Foundation, 1992.

Johnson, Judith. "Laura Cobb: A Kansas Nurse in a Japanese Prisoner of War Camp." *Navy Medicine,* Jan./Feb. 2003.

Kreuger, Walter. *From Down Under to Nippon: The Story of the Sixth Army in World War II.* Combat Forces Press, 1952.

Lahti, Edward H. *Memoirs of an Angel.* Herndon, VA: Ed. Lahti, 1994.

Lee, Phil. *11th Airborne Division.* Paducah, KY: Turner Publishing, 1993.

Lernoux, Penny. *Hearts on Fire: The Story of the Maryknoll Sisters.* Maryknoll, NY: Orbis Books, 1993.

Lucas, Celia. *Prisoners of Santo Tomás.* London: Leo Cooper, Ltd., 1975.

Macapinlac, Marcelino M. "The Historical Geography of Los Baños During the Japanese Occupation." *Journal of History,* Jan./Dec. 2013. The Philippine National Historical Society, 2013.

MacArthur, General Douglas. "Reports of General MacArthur." *Japanese Operations in the Southeast Pacific Area, Vol. II*, Part II. U.S. Government Printing Office, 1966.

Manchester, William. *American Caesar: Douglas MacArthur 1880–1964*. New York: Little, Brown and Co., 1978.

Marchetti, Donna. *Saving Grace: A True Story of Courage, Love and Hope During World War II*. Unpublished, 2002.

McCall, James E. *Santo Tomás Internment Camp: STIC in Verse and Reverse*. Lincoln, NE: Woodruff Printing Co., 1945.

McRaven, William H. *Spec Ops: Case Studies in Special Operations Warfare*. New York: Presidio Press, 1996.

Mojica, Proculo L. *Terry's Hunters: The True Story of the Hunters ROTC Guerrillas*. Manila, PI: Benipayo, 1965.

Monahan, Evelyn M., and Rosemary Neidel-Greenlee. *All This Hell: U.S. Nurses Imprisoned by the Japanese*. Lexington, KY: University Press of Kentucky, 2000.

Montesa, John. Boxcars on a Narrow Gauge Railway. Unpublished, 2009.

Mora, George. My Los Baños Diary. Unpublished.

Morrison, Samuel Eliot. *History of the United States Naval Operations in World War II, Vol. 12. Leyte, June 1944–January 1945*. Boston: Little Brown & Co., 1959.

———. *History of the United States Naval Operations in World War II, Vol. 13, The Liberation of the Philippines: Luzon, Mindanao, the Visayans, 1944–1945*. Boston: Little Brown & Co., 1959.

Muller, Henry J., Jr. Listen as You Have Never Listened Before. Unpublished.

———. You're a Young Paratrooper. Unpublished.

Nash, Grace C. *That We Might Live*. Tallahassee, FL: Nash Publications, 1984.

———. "The Gallant Buccaneer of Los Baños." *Reader's Digest*, Feb. 1959.

Nuval, Leonardo Q. *Remember Them Kindly*. Quezon City, PI: Claretian Publications, 1996.

Onorato, Michael P. *Japan's Imprisonment of American Civilians in the Philippines, 1942–45: An Oral History*. Westport, CN: Meckler, 1990.

Picciagallo, Philip R. *The Japanese on Trial: Allied War Crimes Operations in the East, 1945–1951*. Austin, TX: University of Texas Press, 1979.

Quesada, Frank B. Freedom at Dawn. Unpublished.

Reel, A. Frank. *The Case of General Yamashita*. Chicago: University of Chicago Press, 1949.

Reyes, Jose G. *Terrorism and Redemption: Japanese Atrocities in the Philippines*. Manila, P.I., 1947.

Rivers, William R. Los Baños Recollections. Unpublished.

Robbins, David L. *Broken Jewel*. New York: Simon and Schuster, 2009.

Rottman, Gordon L. *The Los Baños Prison Camp Raid*. Oxford, UK: Osprey Publishing, 2010.

Rubens, Doris. *Bread and Rice.* Foreword by Carlos Romulo. New York: Thurston Macauley Associates, 1947.

Rutter, David. *Olga's War: The Memoir of Olga Zervoulakes Owens.* Indianapolis, IN: Dog Ear Publishing, 2010.

Salazar, Generoso P., Fernando R. Reyes, and Leonardo Q. Nuval. *World War II in the Philippines: Manila, Bicolandia and the Tagalog Provinces.* Manila, PI: Veterans Federation of the Philippines, 1995.

Salecker, Gene Eric. *Blossoming Silk Against the Rising Sun: U.S. and Japanese Paratroopers at War in the Pacific in WWII.* Mechanicsburg, PA: Stockpole Books, 2010.

Sams, G. R. Andersonville NHS Oral History #452, 1995.

Sams, Margaret. *Forbidden Family: A Wartime Memoir of the Philippines.* Madison, WI: University of Wisconsin Press, 1989.

Sass, Charles. The Story of Me and My Times. Unpublished, 2008.

———. I Jumped at Los Baños. Unpublished.

Setsuho, Ikehata, and Richardo Trota Jose. *The Philippines Under Japan.* Manila, PI: Ateneo De Manila University Press, 1999.

Shiels, Margo Tonkin. *Bends in the Road.* Queensland, Australia: Margo Shields, 1999.

Smith, Donald P. *We Survived War's Crucible.* Bloomington, IN: AuthorHouse, 2007.

Smith, Robert Ross. *Triumph in the Philippines: The War in the Pacific.* Honolulu, HI: University Press of Hawaii, 2005.

Sperry, Ansie Lee. *Running with the Tiger.* CreateSpace Independent Publishing, 2009.

Squires, Margaret Whitaker. Land of the Morning. Unpublished.

Squires, Martin. Andersonville NHS Oral History #465, 1995.

Stevens, Frederic. *Santo Tomás Internment Camp: 1942–1945.* New Jersey: Stratford House, Inc., 1946.

Sullivan, Gordon R. "Leyte." U.S. Army Center of Military History: CMH Pub. 72-27.

Suppa, Dominic. What I Remember About Los Baños. Unpublished.

Talbot, Carol Terry, and Virginia J. Muir. *Escape at Dawn.* Wheaton, IL: Tyndale House Publishers, 1988.

Thompson, Paul W., and Harold Doud. *How the Jap Army Fights.* New York: Penguin Books, 1942.

Todd, C. Edwina. "Nursing Under Fire," *Military Surgeon,* April 1947.

Vanderpool, Jay D. Senior Officers Oral History Program, Carlisle Barracks, PA, 1983.

Vaughan, Elizabeth. *The Ordeal of Elizabeth Vaughan.* Athens, GA: University of Georgia Press, 1985.

Wade, Betsy. *Forward Positions: The War Correspondence of Homer Bigart.* Fayetteville, AR: University of Arkansas Press, 1992.

Walker, Gerald. *My Most Memorable Christmas.* New York: Pocket Books, 1963.

Watty, Lewis T. A Prisoner of the Japanese. Unpublished, 2000.

Whitney, Courtney. *MacArthur: His Rendezvous with History.* New York: Alfred A. Knopf, 1956.

Wilbanks, Bob. *Last Man Out: Glenn McDole, USMC, Survivor of the Palawan Massacre in World War II*. Jefferson, NC: McFarland & Co., 2004.

Wilkinson, Rupert. *Surviving a Japanese Internment Camp*. Jefferson, NC: McFarland & Co., 2014.

Yarborough, Henry. Andersonville NHS Oral History #843, 1999.

Zaide, Gregorio R. *Documentary Sources of Philippine History*. Manila, PI: National Book Stores, Inc., 1990.

Zedric, Lance Q. *Silent Warriors of World War II*. Ventura, CA: Pathfinder Publishing of California, 1995.

# Index

# W

# Y

# Z

## About the Author

BRUCE HENDERSON is the author or coauthor of more than twenty nonfiction books, including the #1 *New York Times* bestseller *And the Sea Will Tell* and the national bestseller *Hero Found: The Greatest POW Escape of the Vietnam War.* An award-winning journalist and writer, he has published work in *Esquire, Playboy, Reader's Digest,* and other periodicals. Henderson has taught writing and reporting at USC School of Journalism and Stanford University. He lives in Menlo Park, California.